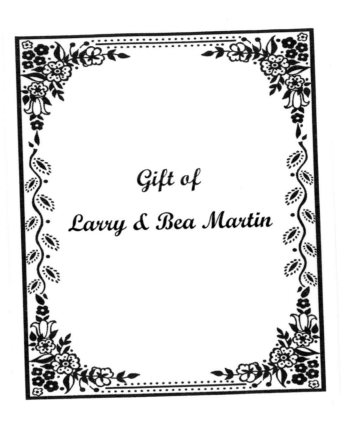

Gift of

Larry & Bea Martin

CHASING JUSTICE

CHASING JUSTICE

My Story of Freeing Myself

After Two Decades on Death Row

for a Crime I Didn't Commit

KERRY MAX COOK

wm

WILLIAM MORROW
An Imprint of HarperCollins*Publishers*

HarperCollins books may be purchased for educational, business, or
sales promotional use. For information please write: Special Markets
Department, HarperCollins Publishers, 10 East 53rd Street, New
York, NY 10022.

Designed by Laura Kaeppel

Library of Congress Cataloging-in-Publication Data

Cook, Kerry Max, 1956–
     Chasing justice : my story of freeing myself after two decades
on death row for a crime I didn't commit / Kerry Max Cook. —
1st ed.
          p.   cm.
     ISBN: 978-0-06-057464-2
     ISBN-10: 0-06-057464-X
     1. Cook, Kerry Max, 1956– —Trials, litigation, etc.   2. Trials
(Rape)—Texas—Tyler.   3. Trials (Murder)—Texas—Tyler.
4. Judicial error—Texas.   5. Death row inmates—Texas—
Biography.   I. Title.

     KF224.C66C66 2007
     345.764'22502523—dc22   2006049172

07 08 09 10 11 WBC/RRD 10 9 8 7 6 5 4 3 2

For Scott, Jim, Paul, Cheryl, and David Hanners.
But for you I would have languished in prison
until finally put to death, innocent,
as simply "Cook, execution number 600."

To my best friend, Sandra, and our son, Kerry Justice:
You gave me the courage to return to that haunted
house, confront all those evil spirits, and tell my story.

Never share the truth
with those who don't deserve it.

CONTENTS

PROLOGUE: 1977

On August 5, 1977, I was a twenty-year-old bartender at the Holiday Club in Port Arthur, Texas. I'd worked there since June, and like so much of East Texas, it was conservative—a suit-and-tie haunt where businessmen drank to such soft tunes as Lionel Richie's "Easy" playing on the nearby jukebox. Usually the Holiday was very busy and a second bartender, named Wayne, and I were both behind the bar; but it was a slow weeknight, so I was working the bar alone. I was mixing drinks and making small talk with a customer when two men in suits—one wearing gold-rimmed glasses and with blond hair that touched his shoulders, and the other with shorter brown hair—sauntered in and took stools beside each other at the bar. They looked at me and smiled. I finished cleaning out an ashtray, wiped my hands on a bar towel, and walked over to greet them.

"Hi. What are you guys having tonight?"

The lanky blond man smiled again and said, "Two draft beers. Budweiser." His partner went over to the jukebox and selected Charlie Rich's "Rollin' with the Flow."

As I set two full glasses on the counter, Pam, one of the waitresses, called out from the "Employees Only" entrance to the bar. "Hey, Kerry! Cy wants to see you in the kitchen for a second."

Cy Kubler was the manager, and we had gotten along well ever since he hired me on the spot two months earlier. I didn't want to leave the bar unattended for long, so I darted through the door to the kitchen. It was pitch-black. I stopped almost immediately—usually the kitchen was fully lit with bright fluorescent lights. Thinking someone had accidentally turned them off on their way out, I fumbled for the switch, all the while calling out, "Cy?"

The second the lights came on a pair of silver handcuffs were slapped and locked on my wrists. My startled eyes narrowed on the Smith & Wesson logo engraved at the base of the shiny restraints. Then two pairs of hands, each pushing me in a different direction, seized my arms from behind. I tried to look around but only saw a flash of blond hair. Apparently, as soon as I'd left the bar, the two men followed me into the kitchen. They were undercover vice officers with the Port Arthur Police Department.

The man who had slammed on the handcuffs said in a loud voice, "My name is Detective Eddie Clark. I am from Tyler, Texas. Kerry Max Cook, you're under arrest for the rape and murder of Linda Jo Edwards."

Everything inside me halted after I heard those words. I looked into the eyes of Detective Clark. This was not the first time I'd been arrested, but I'd never been charged with anything as serious as rape or murder. I'd had a few skirmishes, such as running away from home as a juvenile and taking cars with the keys left in them so my friends and I could get from one place to the other.

Suddenly the back door to the kitchen opened, and the furnace blast of August heat pressed against my body. There were more policemen standing outside. While I was being shoved through the doorway, Detective Clark barked into my left ear, "Kerry Max Cook, you have the right to remain silent. If you give up these rights, anything you say can and will be used against you in a court of law. . . ." The last I saw of the inside of the club was the big round clock on the kitchen wall that read 10:30 P.M.

My body was pulled and pushed toward the sedan that was quietly running, and the top of my head was used to press me into the backseat. One of the vice detectives I served a beer to got behind the wheel and Detective Clark climbed in the passenger side. Cherokee County Sheriff Danny Stallings, who presided over the adjoining county where my parents lived, slipped into the backseat with me. He said he'd persuaded my parents to tell the authorities where I was, and that he was there as a friend of the family to protect me from being harmed.

Detective Clark reached for the police-band microphone mounted on the dash. He depressed the toggle and recited the call letters of the Tyler Police Department. There was a response I couldn't understand. Then I heard Detective Clark say, "We got him. No. There were no problems."

Fred Hollis, owner of the Holiday Club, suddenly appeared out of the darkness. Beads of sweat glistened on the top of his head as the moonlight hit it. He leaned into the driver's side of the car. "If you need anything else," he said while avoiding all eye contact, "you know where to find me." The detective thanked him for his cooperation and the four of us pulled away from the club.

We drove in silence for several minutes until we pulled up to the curb of my apartment on Fifth Street in Port Arthur. A lot of other cars were there—some with identifiable police markings and a couple like the one I was in. I had lived there for little more than a month with a friend named Amber Norris, whom I'd met at a club in Houston the month before. Detective Clark turned his head toward me in the backseat. "We want to search your apartment. Will you consent to this search?"

"Yes, sir. This is some kind of mistake. I'll do whatever you—"

Detective Clark pushed a paper form to the backseat. "Good, sign here." I scrawled my name as best I could, given the handcuffs.

Inside our small one-bedroom apartment, Amber was sitting in her nightgown on the edge of the bed, with a look of profound confusion screaming out of her face. During the thirty minutes or so that police ransacked the small apartment, I was instructed not to talk unless spoken to. I watched as the officers rummaged through the refrigerator, ripping the tops off TV dinners and opening up plastic containers.

Finally Detective Clark walked up to me, exasperated. "What did you do with the body parts, Cook?"

Stunned, I didn't trust what I'd heard. "Did you really say body parts?" I shouted. "That's crazy! What are you talking about?"

After that, I seemed to lose all sense of time. They took me to the Port Arthur City Police Department where Detective Clark pushed me into a small room with a mirror along the far wall. I knew instantly that we were being watched on the other side of the glass.

"We know you raped and killed her, Cook. I just want to know why you did it and how. That's all. Tell me about Robert Hoehn."

"I don't know what you're talking about. What about Robert Hoehn? I don't know anything about any rape or anyone getting killed. Whatever's going on, you've got the wrong person!" I pleaded.

"I oughta stomp a mud-hole in you. We found your pubic hair on her body. Your semen. If you didn't kill her, then explain that, you lying son of a bitch!"

"That's a lie! That's not possible!" I screamed. "I don't know what you're talking about! You're insane. I want to talk to a lawyer!" What I really wanted was my mama, my daddy, and my brother, Doyle Wayne.

"So this is the way you want to do it, huh? We'll play hardball, Cook."

Detective Clark opened the door and told me to follow him into the hallway. I suppose that fear had been working as an anesthetic on my body and mind, and it had kept me even from feeling my bladder.

I looked at one of the detectives I had served a beer to however many hours before and said, "Can I *please* use the bathroom?"

He and Clark escorted me there, and as soon as I tried to make my way to an old, dingy-looking stall, a hand grabbed me by the shoulder. "You're one sick bastard, Cook" was screamed in my ear. It was the blond-haired cop. "We have your fingerprints, your pubic hair, and semen from her vagina, so stop giving us that 'I'm innocent' shit." Using my body as a battering ram, he hurled me against the closed bathroom stall door, shattering the flimsy mechanism that had held it shut.

The brown-haired detective started shouting, "Tell me how you raped and killed the girl! Help me help you, Cook. I'll get him off of you, just tell me." Together they were unrelenting.

"I don't know what you're talking about. I haven't raped or killed anyone!" I screamed. Their response was to plunge my head into the toilet bowl, flushing it over and over. As I gasped for air, I kept repeating, "You've got the wrong guy!" They continued to hold my head in the toilet bowl and screamed, "Tell me about the murder!"

My final words, before the tiny black dots filling my head became united as one, were, "I can't breathe." My last memory was of warm urine running down my leg.

I REGAINED CONSCIOUSNESS in a cell. Before I could piece anything together, the metal door was opening. "Let's go, Cook,"

Detective Clark said. "We're flying back to Tyler tonight." My hands throbbed from the overtightened handcuffs.

Sheriff Danny Stallings accompanied Clark's arrest team, but he must have been waiting somewhere else because I hadn't seen him until we all got into a car to make our way to a private airstrip. When we arrived, we boarded a small prop plane owned by a friend of Sheriff Stallings.

Clark looked over at me. "I hope you're afraid of heights." I don't recall exactly what more he said, but it was clear to me he was implying that I might not be on the plane when it landed in Tyler.

I was seated in the back, along with Detective Clark. Sheriff Stallings got in the passenger side of the plane. As the engine revved up, jokes were bandied about regarding the smell of urine and that the pilot needed to hurry up. The cool night air rushed through the window, pushing its chill into my damp lap, and I shivered amid the loud hum of the single-engine plane. My thoughts were of Mama, Daddy, and Doyle Wayne—and what it would feel like to fall ten thousand feet while wearing handcuffs.

AT DAYBREAK THE plane landed at Pounds Field in Tyler. Sheriff Stallings went in one car and Detective Clark guided me into the backseat of another. As soon as we reached the Tyler City Police Department, Detective Sergeant Doug Collard escorted me into a room and fingerprinted me. He asked if I would consent to the taking of hair samples for analysis. I volunteered both pubic and head hair.

Then he took me to a second office, where I was ordered to sit down in a single chair opposite a large desk, where another detective was sitting. I was exhausted, both mentally and emotionally. I didn't know what time it was, just that it was sometime early the next day. I wanted to sleep, but the fear of how it might anger them forced me to stay awake. The detective asked me about a man I had known briefly in Tyler, named Robert "Bob" Hoehn.

"I don't really know him well at all," I said.

"Do you have a sister?" he asked. "What if that was your sister lying on that floor, all chopped up? Tell me about Hoehn."

Worn-out and fighting to keep my eyes open, I said, "I don't know what you're talking about. Please let me close my eyes and sleep. Please."

"I don't believe you're capable of doing what was done to that girl, Cook, but if you don't cooperate and help us nail the bastard who did, you're just as guilty as he is. Tell me about Robert Hoehn. Help us. There is no sense in embarrassing your family. We know you're homosexual and Hoehn is your lover. Talk to me."

"What? Look, I don't know what you're talking about. I don't know anything about Robert Hoehn or the murder of anyone. Please, just let me sleep now." Somewhere far away I could hear ringing in my ears, as if the plane was still flying around and around in my head.

Captain Bob Bond motioned to Sergeant Collard, who led me through another doorway within the maze of the Tyler City Jail. I was placed in an empty cell with nothing in it but a metal toilet and four steel bunks bolted to the cinder-block walls. There were no mattresses. Bars separated me from the doorway and created a small corridor; the walls were painted a peachlike color. "I need your clothes," the sergeant demanded, "everything down to your birthday suit." When Collard left, I was nude. An air-conditioning duct mounted in the ceiling blasted down an ice-cold wind. A camera attached to the upper-right corner panned back and forth.

Despite the cold—despite everything that had just happened—my body caved in to sleep. But soon another detective, Lieutenant Ron Scott, roughly shook me awake, though I begged him to, please, let me sleep. He said I could sleep for eternity for all he cared, if first I told him about the rape and murder of Linda Jo Edwards. Lieutenant Scott kept leaving and coming back; he clearly was monitoring the camera, because he returned again and again just as I would drift off. There was no clock, no window, and no way of telling if it was day or night.

"You can sleep when you tell me about you and Robert Hoehn and the murder," he said.

I WAS CURLED on one of the steel bunks, trying to keep myself warm with both arms tucked between my legs, when I heard one of the three voices I loved and trusted most in the world.

"Kerry?" my mama weakly asked.

At first I thought it was a dream, or a cruel hoax, and I began to close my eyes and float back to sleep. But then my daddy called out, "Kerry, come over here!"

I jumped up and ran to the bars. "Daddy!" I yelled in my excitement. I reached through the bars and pulled what part of him I could into my cell with me. "Please get me out of here! Mama— they won't leave me alone!" My parents tried to motion casually in the direction of the surveillance camera. They knew the police could see and hear everything we said. Tears poured down my mother's face, and she could not talk.

My daddy pressed his face between two of the bars and whispered, "Did you know the girl who was killed, Kerry?"

I looked cautiously up at the camera and leaned forward to the point where our noses almost touched. "Yes. I did know her. I met her at the pool when I lived with James Taylor at the Embarcadero Apartments in Tyler. I think it was early June. She invited me to go back to her apartment and—"

Hurriedly, my daddy whispered back, "Kerry, listen to me. If you've never listened to me before, listen to me now. Don't tell *anyone* you were ever inside that apartment or that you even *knew* her. Son, if they ever put you inside that apartment, they're going to pin that murder on you. Please, son. Promise me you will keep your mouth shut."

I smelled the cigarette smoke on his breath. I couldn't believe

I would not be going home with them. "I promise, Daddy. I promise."

"Just keep your mouth shut. We're gonna go back home and get you an attorney and make them come up to see you. Just hold on. Just hold on, son."

Lieutenant Scott came to the door and told my mama and daddy it was time to go. Scott had to physically pull my mother away to get her to let go of my hand. I heard her sobbing all the way down the hall. I was petrified. I trusted my mama, daddy, and brother more than anyone in the world. They were my whole world, and given my experience with law enforcement up to that point, I knew there was nobody else I could trust—so I vowed to follow my father's advice.

My eyes followed my parents through the door. I didn't know what to fear more: being charged with rape and murder or being left there all alone. I put my back to the camera and cried. "Please help me, God," I said through tears that burned my face like lava. The weight of all that had happened consumed me. My knees slammed into the cold concrete floor. I willed my brother's face to mind—he is the only person who had really been there for me my whole life. "Help me, Doyle Wayne."

Finally, the blackness came. This time, not even Lieutenant Ron Scott could penetrate it.

2

MY FAMILY

I was born and raised on United States government property. Just after midnight on April 5, 1956, an army doctor introduced me to the surroundings of the Fifth General Hospital in Stuttgart, Germany. I was named after my daddy's favorite comic strip, the crime drama *Kerry Drake*.

My father, Earnest Doyle Cook, was born on the eve of the Great Depression in Jacksonville, Texas. I would share his olive complexion, black hair, and dark eyes—the influence of Cherokee Indian. He was brought up in Tecula, a township in East Texas that is still so small you literally *can* throw a rock from one end to the other. He and his younger sister, Joyce Faye, were born into a poor family. Their parents divorced when Daddy was nine years old, and while Aunt Joyce went to live with their paternal grandmother, Daddy was raised by Mama Moore, his maternal grandmother, who nicknamed him Li'l Dobbin. He made straight A's in school, and when he graduated from Jacksonville High School, he traded in the white shirts that had been his favorite for green and joined the United States Army, which promptly sent him off to Stuttgart, Germany.

On leave in 1952, Daddy returned home to Jacksonville. There, at the Realto Theater, while eating popcorn and watching John Wayne in *The Quiet Man*, he fell in love with a sixteen-year-old Jacksonville girl named Evelyn Joy Green. They were married that September.

While Daddy was stationed at Pattonville Army Base in Stuttgart, my mama lived in Pasadena, Texas—a suburb of Houston—with her father, who worked for an elevator service company. My brother, Doyle Wayne, was born there on April 15, 1954. Six months later they sailed across the Atlantic on the USS *William Darby* and joined Daddy in Germany for the first time. The new family lived on the base at 1102 Colmar Drive, where I was born two years later.

We never stayed in one place for long. Next, we lived on a military post in western Kaiserslautern, eighty miles southwest of Frankfurt, Germany. I attended Vogelweh Elementary School as an eight-year-old; Doyle Wayne was ten. This was when my "mind's camcorder" began to record its greatest memories of my life with Doyle Wayne.

MY DADDY SAT under a soft light in his favorite chair, hard at work with a familiar can of Brasso, shining the buckle on his army belt. Clutching a small, worn T-shirt I retrieved from underneath my mattress, I crouched down by Daddy's chair and smiled up at him. I emptied out the contents of the T-shirt onto the floor.

"Daddy, let me polish your boots. I promise I'll do a good job again."

He looked down at me with a long smile drawn across his face.

"I know you will, son. You always do." He resumed polishing the buckle.

I took my can of Kiwi polish, tweaked the butterfly knob on its side, and opened it. Filling one side of the tin with water from a small bottle, I twisted a small portion of the shirt around my right index finger and dipped the cloth into the water, then rolled it around in the black cream and began to apply it to my father's boot. My heart was swelling because my daddy trusted me with this important task and because I was getting to spend time with him.

"This time will be the best ever, Daddy! Just wait and see!"

With that I started the tedious mission of shining. My father wasn't one to offer hugs or kisses, but I knew this was his way of saying that he cared for me. When I was finished, I looked into the toe of a boot and saw my face smiling back at me. I held the boots by the top and carried them to the bathroom where Daddy was washing the remaining shaving cream lather from his face.

"All done, Daddy! Look. Is this the best ever? Look!"

My daddy put the towel down, looked toward me in the doorway, and in a voice feigning amazement, said, "You're right! This is the best ever, son."

"Daddy, when can I go to the motor pool with you? Please, Daddy, I want to go. Can I go today?" I'd asked this same question so many times, today I wanted the question to sound different, more sincere, if possible.

"You're still too little, Kerry. You will, though. You will. I promise." He tousled my hair. "Now go get back in bed, son."

He opened and then passed through the door, disappearing into the gray predawn of Kaiserslautern, Germany, to begin his day as Sergeant Doyle Cook, head of the Motor Pool Division, Delta Battery, United States Army. As he walked to his car, all that remained was the trailing scent of Aqua Velva, which would be long gone by the time he returned two weeks later—or longer.

My father was a career soldier and was often away on military maneuvers at installations scattered across Europe. Sometimes when he came home he gave my brother and me souvenirs left over from the war games. We particularly cherished the soldiers' C rations. We holed up on our bunk beds and eagerly tore into the boxes, using the P-180 aluminum can opener that accompanied the olive drab cans, and went through the corned beef hash, the chicken and dumplings, and the stale old cookies that were made by a bunch of army cooks who weren't going to win any Betty Crocker bake-offs. They tasted like cardboard and we loved them. The trick was to find the can not just with the cookies, but with the stale piece of black chocolate, too.

"Doyle Wayne, it's my turn! I get the chocolate this time!"

"It's whoever finds it first!" With an impish grin, he increased the intensity of his search.

ON THE WEEKENDS my daddy was home we did everything as a family. When he returned from the fields, our family-oriented activities automatically resumed as if they had never been interrupted. I relished the time my daddy was home.

"Daddy! Daddy! It's Sunday. We want to see the *Pink Panther* movie again!" "Doyle, you know how much I love Omar Sharif," my mama said. "His new movie *Doctor Zhivago* is out." Doyle Wayne and I knew that Inspector Clouseau didn't stand a chance against ol' Omar. When it came to my daddy, Mama always got her way. Always.

"Kerry, soon you'll be ten years old," Daddy said. "This movie is based on the Russian Revolution, and you're getting old enough to learn about history." My daddy was a voracious reader. He would hole up for hours reading enormous books—one hardback book, *The Rise and Fall of the Third Reich*, was so thick I couldn't carry it. Still, any movie was a treat. My mama and daddy got their buttered popcorn. Doyle Wayne chomped his Jujyfruits and Milk Duds, while I devoured my Chuckles and a black cherry

Charms sucker, which always outlasted my tongue and usually was surrendered to the theater floor.

Wherever we moved in Europe, we would visit all the places a city or country was known for, whether it was a famous monument, a cathedral, or a memorial, or occasionally even a zoo, which was always my favorite. We toured the museum ships in Hamburg and walked through the old Elbe Tunnel. Doyle Wayne and I played tag as we ran down the Champs-Élysées, visited the famous Louvre museum, climbed to the top of the Eiffel Tower, and ate in curbside cafés in Luxembourg, skipped rocks in the Donau River, and played in bombed-out old abandoned bunkers in western Germany.

Once we visited the Nazi concentration camps at Dachau, roughly twelve miles north of Munich, where my father was stationed when I was maybe seven or eight years old. As we made our way through the gates, I looked all around.

"Daddy, how come we couldn't park in here? They sure didn't have small cars back then," I said, pointing to what looked like an open parking lot. All around were rows of oblong concrete blocks, each painted white and about three feet long.

"Son, those were not for cars. Those were for people. They're called 'standing blocks.' The Nazis would force the prisoners to stand in front of one for hours—sometimes days—at a time."

"Wow," I exclaimed, remembering the week before when Mrs. Davis made me stand in the corner for thirty minutes for talking in class.

We walked inside a wooden shed. There were three brick ovens, side by side, each looking the same. I walked up to the cast-iron door. Imprinted upon it were the letters *TOPF.*

Daddy looked at us both. "This is the crematorium. This is where they burned the prisoners' bodies—sometimes while they were still alive. With them they burned any reminder of their humanity."

My mind instantly went back to a summer when we were visiting Stella Green, my grandma's house in Jacksonville. My mama's brothers had just ripped out the old linoleum tile from inside the house. They stacked it in the backyard and poured some gas on top of it. I was very young and while they were all talking in the house, I picked up the gas can and walked to the burning pile. I began to pour the liquid onto the pile, and I was instantly ignited and fell into the flames. I screamed and can remember Uncle Jerry tackling me, then rolling me up in a blanket to snuff out the flames. "Why did they do this to people? Burning hurts so bad!" I said.

My daddy pulled me outside by my shirt. "They were full of hate, Kerry. Hate toward anyone who was different from them."

Daddy led the way, and in the distance was a long brick building. We stopped at a steel door with BRAUSEBAD etched above. My daddy translated, "That means *shower bath*. Here they made the prisoners think they were showering, when in fact they would gas innocent people to death."

In the gallery there were hundreds of black-and-white pictures behind glass. Doyle Wayne and I noticed how old and thin everyone looked. They were bald and naked. And dead—they were mostly all dead. I stared at the pictures, while my daddy was reading the description on the wall. I was only listening halfheartedly until I heard the word *injection*—as in shot. My stomach instantly recoiled into a tightly fisted knot. I was afraid of shots. Each and every time we went overseas I had to have a battery of injections: typhoid, measles, mumps, smallpox, or whatever pox. I begged the doctors to let me drink the fluid instead of having the needle stuck into my body. Always they said no and tried to distract me with a sucker.

"Remember when we talked about hate earlier, Kerry," my daddy said. "This is what that hate led to." I thought about all we had seen today, including the ovens, the gas chambers, and these shower stalls. Hate was an awful thing, if it could do all of this, I concluded.

I was so happy when it was finally time to go.

———

AS I MENTIONED, we moved around a lot while Daddy was serving. Just as we made friends in one place, we were off to another base. From Kaiserslautern we went to Brussels, and then my daddy received new orders and Doyle Wayne and I found ourselves in Mainz, Germany. It seemed that as soon as we were beginning to discover how we might fit in in one place, we were catapulted into another. Luckily Mainz turned out to be where Doyle Wayne and I met the best friends we had ever had—Daryl and Allan Hawkeye.

At this point, I was twelve years old and Doyle Wayne was fourteen. Daryl Hawkeye was Doyle Wayne's age, and Allan was a year or two older than them. Doyle Wayne and Daryl were always talking Mama into letting us do all kinds of stuff. I say "us" because no matter what, Doyle Wayne lobbied to take me along—it was both of us or nothing. That's the way it was with Doyle Wayne.

The German countryside was full of opportunities for adventure, and once we set out on a long hike. It wasn't until the end of the day that Doyle Wayne and the Hawkeyes finally decided that we'd better head back because we were a long way from home—and losing daylight fast. On the way back, at first we were walking along as a group, but before too long, Doyle Wayne and Daryl pulled ahead, leaving Allan and me behind. Allan was a rough-and-tumble kind of teenager, but as physically tough as he was, even he was winded and tired from walking all day. And I, who was three years younger, was completely exhausted and began falling farther behind.

In time it was completely dark and getting very cold. We seemed to be surrounded by the darkness, as on either side of the road were vast, empty fields; the scent of the plowed earth filled the cool air and clung to our bodies. Allan was pulling ahead of me, and slowly but surely I was being left behind. I sucked in the cold air and screamed for him to wait, but he replied angrily

"Come on!" and ignored my pleas for him to slow down and wait for me to catch up. The darkness slowly took him.

There is something about the German countryside at night that makes a twelve-year-old think of the scariest movie he's ever seen. When I would hear the rustling of the wind, I heard goblins who were whispering my name.

Crying and screaming out to Allan, I begged him to come back—"Please don't leave me, Allan!" The darkness was cruel: It stole my words without a reply. Even the trees turned sinister— their limbs and branches reached out for me. I heard strange animal noises ahead and behind. I kept going, but I felt like I was being followed.

"Doyle Wayne, Doyle Wayne," I mumbled through my tears. I was crying and every few feet or so, I screamed out, "Doyle Wayne! Doyle Wayne, help me!" After a while I thought I heard something in the distance. Then I heard it behind me. I just knew it was a gremlin, or something worse, trailing me, so I ran even harder, calling out Doyle Wayne's name in a shrill voice.

Finally he appeared out of the darkness. He'd come back for me. He hugged me and repeated over and over again that it was all right now. "I'm here, Kerry. I'm here." He put me on his back and piggybacked me all the way home.

We didn't tell my mama what had happened because we didn't want her to stop me from going out with them again. The next day Doyle Wayne nearly beat Allan Hawkeye within an inch of his life—and Allan was pretty much thought of as the toughest kid on base. The four of us went on more trips after that, but Allan never left me behind again.

Soon new orders came for the Hawkeye family and they moved to another military base. Doyle Wayne and I were devastated; these were the best friends we had ever had. It was the only time we had been able to really share the adventures of Europe with friends. Each of us swore allegiance that no matter what or where, we would never forget one another.

A few months later, my daddy was given new orders and we said good-bye to Mainz forever. Our new home was on the military post of Wiley Barracks in Neu-Ulm, Germany, the birthplace of Albert Einstein. We arrived at our assigned quarters late at night. Our new home was a two-bedroom, first-floor apartment in a six-floor building. Exhausted, my mama simply made up our beds and we crawled into them. It was warm, so my mama opened the window as she kissed us good night and left our room.

Early the next morning Doyle Wayne and I were talking into the space between our twin beds when we heard outside our window the distinct and all-too-familiar voices of two people walking along the sidewalk. We looked over at each other with our mouths forming perfect O's, thinking *This simply cannot be.* Seconds later we heard a knock on the door. We ran to the front door just as my mama opened it. There stood Daryl and Allan Hawkeye! It was a great surprise and it meant our friendship and good times could continue awhile longer.

WE STAYED IN Neu-Ulm for a year, but my daddy's glory days in the military were winding down. The Hawkeyes had already gone stateside because their dad was retiring to their home in Lawton, Oklahoma. In December 1969, the motor pool threw Daddy and Mama a bon voyage party in our apartment. My daddy was very popular with the soldiers assigned to the motor pool. They called him "Sarge." And the motor pool seemed to be my daddy's home away from home. Doyle Wayne and I went outside and lay down on the cold German ground, staring straight up into the night sky. Through the window behind us, Freda Payne blared on Mama's phonograph, lamenting the Vietnam War and telling Nixon that it was time to "Bring the Boys Home." Looking up, Doyle Wayne traced out the Big Dipper for me because I could never find it myself. Silently I thought about what life would be like without Europe and the military. I wondered what my daddy's thoughts were. Twenty-three years in the army is a long time. What now?

We moved back to the United States in the summer of 1970 to await Daddy's retirement papers. His last assignment as Sergeant Earnest Doyle Cook was to Fort Hood in Killeen, Texas, and we settled in a suburb called Harker Heights, where Mama and Daddy found a three-bedroom house. I had my very own room for the first time, and I enrolled in Manor Junior High, which was opening for its first year. Doyle Wayne was bused to Killeen High School, the proud home of the tenacious Killeen Kangaroos football team.

The Independent School System of Killeen was a world away from the military and the quaint European towns with which we were familiar. Instead of lighting cigarettes stolen on the sly from their parents, the kids were smoking cigarettes they had purchased from a vending machine. In the restrooms of school you could smell marijuana smoke wafting above the stalls. Students sold "Orange Sunshine" and "Windowpane," the acid of the 1960s. Other hallucinogens like peyote teemed through the hallways.

A few months after the school year began, Daddy's retirement papers came through. I remember vividly the way my mama, Doyle Wayne, and I decorated the inside of the house to surprise him. Doyle Wayne and I made a banner that read CONGRATULATIONS! There were balloons, streamers, and confetti. When Daddy walked in wearing his olive-green military fatigues for the last time, we showered him with hugs and kisses. It was practically the first time in his adult life that he had come home a civilian.

My mama and daddy wanted to move back to Jacksonville, where they'd both been born and reared. Jacksonville was a small township nestled deep in East Texas, approximately 190 miles northeast from the state capital of Austin. Once known as "the tomato capital of the world," it had a population of roughly nine thousand at the time we made our move—the last in our international traveling career—to an old, yellow three-bedroom house. Daddy had already arranged for a job working for the Pepsi-Cola bottling plant in Tyler. I enrolled in the tenth grade at Jacksonville High School.

IN JACKSONVILLE, DOYLE Wayne did what he could to curb my initiation into the delinquent side of the tracks. But my brother and I were both alienated from the small-town environment, and we clung to each other because our social group was still undefined. We didn't fit an East Texas small-town template. We had traveled the globe as army brats, and we were square pegs in the round holes of Jacksonville's hometown country folk. We missed the friends we'd made in Killeen, so in early 1973 my brother and I took our daddy's dilapidated 1964 Ford Fairlane 500 and drove back to see our only friends. Doyle Wayne's complicity was motivated by a desire to see a girlfriend he had left behind; I just wanted to get away from the suffocating small town of Jacksonville.

Not too long after this, I met a boy named Larry Taylor at school, and together we plotted to run away. We skipped school one morning and went in search of a car with the keys left in the ignition. Somehow we navigated our way to Fort Hood in Killeen. We stalled at a red light, and an MP put on the blue flashing light on top of his jeep and pulled us over. The car was discovered to be stolen. We were detained at the local military police station on the post, and our parents were called to pick us up. A short time later, Larry and I took off again and found an old Chevrolet Impala and drove away, this time to no place in particular.

Upon being returned to Jacksonville by authorities, I was expelled from school. The sudden notoriety attracted similarly disenfranchised youths to gravitate toward me, and oddly, my popularity in Jacksonville grew. So did my reputation with Cherokee County law enforcement.

I kept running away, finding new accomplices and new vehicles until, finally, I ran myself into a corner. The Cherokee County district attorney, Larue Dixon, certified me as an adult at seventeen and sent me to the Ferguson Farm in the Texas Department of Corrections, home of first offenders. I restarted life when I was released April 5, 1974, my eighteenth birthday. I should have kept on running, but I didn't. I returned to Jacksonville.

ONCE YOU GET in the crosshairs of the state and national law enforcement computer, you never get out—especially in a small town. When I returned to Jacksonville from the "Farm," I became a favorite target of local area law enforcement. An armed robbery arrest here, a burglary there—I was a "usual suspect" even though the charges always proved to be bogus. In the worst case, I was held in the Cherokee County Jail for the armed robbery of a local business before I was finally cleared of all charges when an investigator obtained a time card from my place of employment—Discount City in Jacksonville—that revealed it was impossible for me to have been the robber. Stupidly and in retaliation, upon my release I kicked out the front window of the store I had been accused of robbing. Because of the extenuating circumstances of having been wrongly jailed, the charge of "burglary of a building" was thrown out and reduced to a charge of "malicious mischief." I was ordered to pay restitution, and put on five years' probation. After that, Cherokee County officials would show up at my various places of employment wanting to talk to me about local crimes. During this period I ended up at Rusk State Hospital twice to be treated for depression. It wasn't until spring of 1977 that I finally got off probation and was clear of Cherokee County—for practically the first time since moving from Germany, I was free.

3

PRETRIAL, 1977 AND 1978

The quality of a nation's civilization can be
measured by the methods its police use in
the enforcement of criminal laws.

—WINSTON CHURCHILL

My name is Detective Nelson Downing. Put these on," the
plainclothes detective said as he walked into my cell and
handed me the white terry-cloth shirt and black suede
pants I had been ordered to surrender many days before.

"We're taking a ride." The right side of my body ached and was
numb from the cold steel bunk. I willed myself to do what he said;
I quickly put on my clothes, enjoying their warmth. Handcuffed
and shackled at the feet, I was pulled and prodded down a corridor
and into the basement and placed into the back of a blue unmarked
police vehicle. The soft yellow artificial light in the garage seemed
to create stars as it reflected off the hood of the car.

How many days and nights have I been here? I thought to myself. *Had it been weeks?* In my cinder-block tomb with the peach-colored walls, the only signs of life had been the single lightbulb that never slept; the surveillance camera; and the ugly metal vents that never stopped pummeling my naked body with air-conditioned blasts while I lay on the steel bunk. And how long had it been since Daddy had come to the Tyler City Jail and sent Jacksonville attorneys John Ament and Larue Dixon to talk with me? At first, the name Dixon evoked memories of the dark-suited former Cherokee County prosecutor standing before District Judge J. W. Summers and asking that I be sent to prison.

"Daddy, is this the same Larue Dixon that prosecuted and sent me to prison for the car theft in October of 1973?" The last time I'd run away from home as a juvenile, Mr. Dixon sent me to the first offender's prison farm in Huntsville for car theft. I turned seventeen years old while in the Cherokee County Jail and he certified me as an adult. Then he gave me a two-year prison sentence.

"Yes," Daddy said. "He's in private practice now. He's formed a law practice with another local attorney named John Ament."

My head snapped back as Detective Downing pressed the gas pedal. We raced up an incline toward a steel garage door that was opening to reveal the free world. The car drove into the early-morning Texas sun. My eyes squinted to adjust to the piercing sunlight.

We were in downtown Tyler. I peered into the cars as we pulled alongside them at the red light. Some people looked into the backseat, and I looked back at them briefly, fantasizing that our roles were reversed. A few minutes later we descended into another cellar. Detective Downing called it a "sally port" as he talked into a microphone to request access. Slowly the mouth of the metal door screeched like fingernails on a blackboard as it opened.

Waiting below as we came to rest in front of a freshly painted yellow line was a frenzy of microphones, lights, and cameras. Like angry piranhas, the Texas media swarmed the car. Downing opened the door and pulled me out, and like a mime, he motioned and pulled me through the crowd to a white solid steel door. A camera that was following too close bumped me in the back of the head. Downing pushed a button and the door released, activated by someone inside the citadel.

"Can I call my parents? Can you please tell me why I'm here?" I asked as we stepped through.

The detective merely grunted.

Somewhere in the maze of hallways he tugged my arm and we made a right turn into a small, sparse office. Behind a wooden desk sat a lady with white hair. The name tag on her desk said JUSTICE OF THE PEACE LEON HICKS. Detective Downing handed her a set of papers.

Just as quickly as she took the papers, she looked up at me and barked: "You are charged with the rape and murder of Linda Jo Edwards. This is an offense punishable by death," she said. Then with steely professionalism, she announced, "Bail will be denied."

I was pushed along into another room and told to stand behind a two-foot strip of black tape. My hair went every which way, and I looked haggard. I had not slept for days nor had I showered. I looked much older than my twenty years.

"Step up to the line. Stand still. Look into the camera," a sheriff's deputy commanded as he placed a small gray metal chain around my neck that was attached to about an 8½-by-11-inch mugshot marquee. He clipped it closed. I felt the cold of the metal on the back of my neck. Small white letters were pressed into the hard black plastic, spelling out POLICE DEPT. TYLER, TEXAS 19178 08-08-77. The last six numbers told me I had been in the Tyler City Jail for just three days. There was a brilliant flash as the bulb flared. Everywhere I tried to look I saw first the jagged image of the bulb.

I was fingerprinted and then escorted back along the same corridor I had walked through upon entering the building. To my right was a little shoeshine booth where an old black man was attending to the boots of a deputy who was seated on the raised dais. Their conversation stopped abruptly as they led me past. We came to a halt at the double doors of the "jail service elevator" and stepped in. The door closed and Detective Downing turned a key and all the other floors were bypassed. The old contraption creaked and groaned as it lifted our weight to the higher levels. At the sixth floor we came to a rough stop and the doors swung open, revealing two jailers—one was so big I could not see much of the hallway behind him.

"I'm Chief Gene Carlson," the obese man announced. "You are in *my* goddamned jail. You're breathin' my air. Nelson, you want to get your hardware off this *thing*?" Even though he was speaking to the detective, he stared at me hatefully.

Detective Downing removed the handcuffs and the steel chains from around my legs. My ankles tingled as the circulation resumed. Without a word my transport left.

Chief Carlson immediately ushered me around a corner, and, choosing a key from the large collection that was attached by a leather strap at his side, he opened another solid steel door. A small corridor loomed ahead. Along the wall were four metal doors—solitary confinement.

"Cook, let me hear a peep out of you and you'll go in here," the large man said, pointing one of his thick fingers toward the first room, a padded cell approximately five by nine feet with nothing in it but a hole in the center of the floor.

My new home was the second door down. A large key was inserted into the mechanism and it swung open. Stale air rushed out. The smell of suffering and unwashed human bodies was baked into the steel walls.

"Strip," the big man said. "I don't want you killin' yourself in my jail."

Why would I do a thing like that! I thought. But I complied, of course, and was pushed naked into the metal tomb. The door slammed shut and the steel on steel rang through the cell with jarring effect.

"No one is to open this door without permission. No trusty is allowed in my catwalk without a jailer. Except to feed him, I don't want anyone talking to him or coming back here without me knowing about it," the chief bellowed. The thick vaulted door had a little window cut into it that took a key to unlock—it was left shut.

I heard their footsteps as they left the corridor, and then the heavy outer door slammed and locked. Eventually the jingle of the leather strap full of keys faded, leaving only the sound of my breathing.

I stretched out my arms and touched both ends of the cell. I began to pace, two steps forward, turn, and one and a half back. The isolation fed my panic. Above was a square of transparent Plexiglas covering a large bulb. I don't remember how long I slept when I eventually lay down from exhaustion, but the light was on, and it was on when I awoke. The light was never turned out.

Days later, I heard the sound of the leather strap with the big brass key's *jingle jangle*. Instead of the food slot opening, it was the portal in the door that swung open, and there was my daddy's face.

"Daddy!" I exclaimed as I ran up to the door. "I'm so glad to see you!" My daddy wrapped his thick callused hand around one of my fingers as I clutched the bars on the window that separated us.

"Where is Mama? She's not with you?"

"No, son. Your mama can't stand to see you like this. She can't stand to see you in jail like this." I nodded in understanding. "Son, you smell. Are you not bathing?" my daddy asked.

"No, Daddy. There is no shower. I keep asking each time someone comes by. The only time I hear a human voice is during the split second it takes for them to push a brown bag into my food slot. And by 'lunch' or 'dinner' I mean a peanut butter sandwich or one with green bologna. I am trying to eat it, but it's hard sometimes. It's the same thing each and every day. And the water from my sink tastes like metal. I stay so hungry."

My daddy reached down with one hand and I heard him fumbling with something I couldn't see. He pushed a five-dollar bill into the window. "Take this in case you are able to buy some candy or something.

"I can only imagine how depressing this place must be, but your lawyers have talked with us and they said it is important that you not trust or talk to *anyone* but them or us. Do this and all of this will be over soon. You have a hearing coming up on the nineteenth. That's this Monday. Just hold on, son. Hold on," my daddy said as he clutched my finger tighter.

The jailer walked up. "Mr. Cook, the visit is up. Time for you to go."

My daddy looked back at him. "But it has only been a few minutes. I haven't been here long."

"You're only allowed a ten-minute visit once a week. These are the rules," he said curtly and slammed the slot over the window.

My daddy called out to me as he left, "I will be back next week, son. Say your prayers."

I got other visits, but they weren't always from my daddy: the Tyler detectives continued to try to question me. "I want to help you. Tell me about Robert Hoehn," Detective Bobby Vanness said, while peering into my cell with a Snickers candy bar in one hand and a writing pad in the other. These repeated interrogations incensed Ament and Dixon because they were in direct violation of my legal right to have counsel present during any and all attempts to question me.

EXAMINING TRIAL

The uneaten, cold, and soured sandwiches by the door had become my only marker of time.

One morning I heard the now familiar jingle of the big brass keys heading down the hall toward me. I actually had begun to cherish the sound of the keys—it meant that a human face would appear, perhaps that of my father.

"You got to go to court this morning, Cook. Get dressed," the jailer said, as my door swung open, letting in the stale air of the rest of the jail.

This was the first time I would get to leave my tomb since arriving. My clothes were the only tangible possession from my former life as a free person. I stepped out into the catwalk, took a left past the padded cell, then turned toward the jail service elevator. No handcuffs, only the jailer and me. He pushed the button for the second floor.

The moment the doors opened, the media lights exploded into a brilliant, blinding light. I held my hand up to shield my eyes to lessen the stabbing pain. The reporters were shouting at me to be heard over the din of one another. The jailer and I passed a cluster of reporters and photographers circled around a man in a dark suit named A. D. Clark III, Smith County's district attorney. Clark had been appointed by Texas governor Dolph Briscoe to fill the unexpired term of Curtis Owen, who had resigned in March 1976 to run for a district judge position. Clark himself was running in the November election to keep the district attorney position. And he had just found the perfect case to raise his profile.

As we walked past, I heard him declare to the media, "I will personally try this case, and I intend to prove Kerry Max Cook raped and killed Linda Jo Edwards on a murderous rampage."

The courtroom was full of more opinionated faces whom I felt staring at me as I walked down the center aisle heading toward the defense table. My two attorneys were waiting for me. To the left, so, too, was Clark's somber team of prosecutors. The smell of the courtroom was just the same as in those I had been in before—carpet cleaner, wood, and the cologne and perfume of more than one hundred Texans.

"Sit down, sit down, Kerry," Larue Dixon said. The last time I'd seen Dixon in a courtroom was in October 1973 when he was sending me to prison on a two-year sentence for grand theft auto. He was wearing the same dark suit he'd worn then—and I could only hope that he had the same success this time. Dixon's partner, John Ament, reached for my hand; he had been my lawyer when I went up against Dixon on the car theft charge.

"Kerry, just don't speak," Dixon said. "No matter what is said, you don't open your mouth. Understand?"

"Yes, sir. I understand. Will I be able to go home today? I am in solitary at the jail and—"

Dixon smiled weakly. "Soon, yes, but not today. The case is way too hot. Your arrest has been the subject of every newspaper, every local television news broadcast around here since June 10. It's been reported that you have been the subject 'of the most intensive manhunt in East Texas law enforcement history.' It's a circus. The media, the police—everyone. Just sit tight and be quiet."

"But, Mr. Dixon, the police keep coming up to the jail trying to interrogate me. They keep asking me about Robert Hoehn—and homosexuality! They won't stop. I can't sleep. One of the prisoners warned me that the detectives have talked to all the trusties at the jail in an effort to get them to try and get me to talk. This is all so scary. Can you just make it stop?" I said, the words flooding out.

Just then the door to the jury room opened and the judge walked through it and took his seat on the bench. His hair was combed straight back, and he wore glasses. He adjusted his glasses, looked down, and read, " 'Let the record reflect both the state and the defendant and his counsel of record are present. It is Friday, August 19, 1977. We will call case number 33,368-A, the *State of Texas v. Kerry Max Cook*.' Is the state ready?"

I quickly calculated: I had been in the "side cell" for eleven days.

"Yes, Your Honor," Clark's authoritative voice loudly replied.

Dixon looked behind him and scanned the faces of those attending the hearing. He turned to Ament. "John, is that Jerry Landrum back there? What's he doing here?"

Ament looked behind him and made eye contact with Landrum. "Damn, Larue—I don't know. That's strange. What would he be doing at this hearing?"

"What says the defense? Are you prepared to begin?" the judge said as he peered down from where he was perched. The American flag hung behind his big leather chair, and to his right was a large plaque with the seal of the great state of Texas mounted on the wall.

Ament cleared his throat and stood up. "Your Honor, if it pleases the court, we would like to be furnished with a copy of the charging instrument."

Clark immediately interrupted. "You don't have a copy of the arrest warrant? The justice of the peace will have it."

How on earth could my attorneys not have the arrest warrant? I wondered with a puzzled look on my face.

"I requested it from her and she won't give me a copy of it," Ament answered.

Clark turned to one of his assistants and told him to get a copy for Dixon.

Ament then added, "How about any physical evidence that will be offered by the state?"

His words were met with silence from the district attorney. Then the judge interjected, "Call your first witness, Mr. Clark."

"Your Honor, at this time we call our chief witness, Paula Willadene Vied Rudolph," Clark shouted with theatrical effect.

Ament positioned a single sheet of white paper in front of him. It was the sworn statement Paula Rudolph had given Detective Downing the morning she discovered her roommate's body beaten and bludgeoned to death. I shifted my body closer so I could see the parts John Ament had highlighted.

Before me, the undersigned authority, on this 10 day of June, A.D. 1977, personally appeared PAULA V. RUDOLPH, who after being by me duly sworn, deposes and says: I arrived back at the apartment at around 12:30 A.M., June 10, 1977. I reached for the doorknob and found the front door to be closed, but not locked. I pushed the door open and stepped in and noticed a figure jump behind the door in Linda's room. I remember the figure had silver hair cut in a medium touching-the-ears fashion that men wear. The body was that of a Caucasian with a tan wearing white shorts of some fashion. The figure was sleek and slender and he moved quickly behind the door in Linda's room and closed it. I knew that Linda had been seeing my boss, Jim Mayfield. My first impression on seeing the figure was that it was he, even though I did not see the facial features nor hear him speak. I felt the best thing for me to do was to go to my room and exercise discretion. I called out, "Don't worry. It's only me." I went straight into my room. After getting to my room in just a few moments, less than five minutes I'm sure, I heard the patio doors open and close. I started to go into the kitchen to get me a cup of coffee and unplug the pot, but decided not to since Linda might be in the living room or on the patio with the person I assumed to be Jim Mayfield. I got into bed approximately 12:45 A.M. I got up a few minutes later to set the alarm and it was 12:50 A.M. I awoke at 6:30 A.M. this morning but did not get up until 7:00 A.M.

To the side, written in red, were Ament's notes: "Took and passed polygraph on June 14, 1977, administered by Detective Nelson Downing. Results 'non-deceptive' regarding 6/10/77 sworn statement and description of the assailant."

My concentration broke when a petite woman with short blond hair entered the courtroom. She had a pinched face and looked to be about thirty-five years old. When she took her seat in the witness box, Clark flashed her a smile, which she returned warmly.

"Would you please state your name for the record?"

"Paula Willadene Vied Rudolph."

My attorneys were busy taking notes. I had never seen this

person before in my life, and I stretched over to glance at the notes Dixon was taking. I saw her name written with a black felt-tipped pen and then underlined—"EYE-WITNESS." As I was trying to read the rest, he transferred his concentration to the witness box. I did the same. The courtroom was so quiet that the mere creaking of a chair brought the watchful eye of the judge. Clark first questioned Rudolph about the figure she saw when she returned home on the night of the murder. Rudolph answered: "I could definitely tell it was a man. . . . I recognized, or thought I recognized, this figure. I spoke. I said, 'Don't worry, it's only me.'"

Confidently, Clark grinned. "Pass the witness."

The judge adjusted his glasses. "Does the defense wish to cross-examine this witness?"

"Yes, Your Honor," Ament said. Mrs. Rudolph's smile abruptly evaporated and was replaced with a serious face as she turned to look at my lawyer. "Ms. Rudolph, when you saw a figure in the apartment on the night in question, did you think that you recognized this figure?"

"Yes. At the time I did."

"And was it someone with white hair, or silver hair, or what was the deal on that?"

"I don't know." She shifted her weight and slightly turned to look over and meet Clark's face.

"No. Wait a minute. Listen to my question real close here. Did you think you saw someone with white hair or silver hair?" Ament pressed her and held up her sworn statement made the morning she discovered Linda Jo Edwards's body.

Rudolph pressed her lips tightly together. Instead of verbally responding, she nodded in the affirmative.

"I have nothing further for this witness at this time, Your Honor," Ament concluded.

"I have nothing further, Judge," Clark said. The judge excused her.

"Mr. Clark, call your next witness," the judge said.

"The state calls Sergeant Doug Collard," Clark announced, as he turned to search for his witness in the back of the courtroom. A tall, lanky Caucasian man with a mustache came forward and climbed into the witness box. He was sworn in and gave his name and rank with the Tyler City Police Department.

"Sergeant Collard, did you have an occasion to go to the crime scene at the Embarcadero apartment complex on the early-morning hours of June 10, 1977, for the purposes of dusting the premises for latent fingerprints?"

"Yes, sir. I did. I processed the crime scene."

"What, if anything, did you find in terms of fingerprints?"

"I dusted the patio door leading into the apartment. I managed to lift thirteen fingerprints from the apartment. Three off the sliding patio door frame," Collard said.

"Can you tell us who those fingerprints off the patio door frame belong to?"

"They belong to the defendant, Kerry Max Cook. He's seated between the two attorneys at that table right here," he said as he pointed his finger directly at me.

Clark looked first at the judge and then turned as if searching for someone in the audience.

"Sergeant, were you able to determine, based on your experience and your expertise, how long those fingerprints had been present on her door frame?"

"Yes, sir," Collard said without any hesitancy. "I would estimate they were approximately between six and twelve hours old."

"Pass the witness, Your Honor," Clark said.

For the next ten minutes, I listened intently as Ament engaged Collard in a highly technical discussion about fingerprints. From time to time I would look behind me to find the faces of my mama and daddy who'd been there the moment court first began. My eyes ran the gauntlet of the angry courtroom spectators until I finally found them in the sea of faces. I smiled and turned back around.

Clark introduced, and asked that the court mark as state's

exhibit number 3 clinical pathologist Dr. Virgil V. Gonzalez's autopsy report. With that, Clark triumphantly announced, "Nothing further from the state and we now close our case."

Dixon stood and addressed the court. "Your Honor, we would like to move for an immediate release of the defendant based on the evidence heard here this afternoon. The only admissible and competent testimony that's been introduced here this afternoon has been from Rudolph. That is, only admissible as to substance. She cannot identify who was in the apartment on the night of June 10, 1977. She cannot say it is the defendant on trial. As a matter of fact, on the night in question, the person certainly did not have the same kind of hair color as the defendant, Kerry Max Cook. She's never seen him before. The defense rests, Your Honor."

Oh, God. Thank God, it's over, I thought to myself. I wanted to get as far away from this courtroom as possible. I didn't want to see that little cell or live another second of this nightmare.

Judge William "Bill" Coats looked to Clark and asked whether or not he opposed Dixon's motion.

Clark squared off, "Paula Rudolph puts the intruder in the apartment between 12:30 and 12:45 A.M. The pathologist report gives the time of the examination at 11:30 A.M. In the doctor's opinion, the length of time the deceased had been dead when he conducted his examination was ten to twelve hours. Doing mental arithmetic that means Dr. Gonzalez stated that the time of death was between 11:30 P.M. and 1:30 A.M. The prints placed there by Kerry Max Cook were six to twelve hours old at 9:00 A.M. on June 10, which means they had been placed there between 9:00 P.M. and midnight." He paused for emphasis. "The state has established what it feels is more than a *prima facie* case."

"Mr. Dixon?" the judge said.

I pulled on Larue Dixon's sleeve. "Mr. Dixon, Mr. Clark just told the judge that she got home at 12:45. Ms. Rudolph didn't say that."

"Shush!" Ament growled.

"Your Honor, at the conclusion of the examination hearing, the court has a choice, under the evidence, of either remanding this defendant immediately back to the jail, discharging him, or admitting him to bail. The only evidence before the court is that of Ms. Rudolph who testified that she saw someone with white or silver hair. The defendant does not have white or silver hair. There is no probable cause for arrest.

"In a capital case there must be 'proof evident' under section 1903 that the defendant committed the offense as charged in the complaint. He is being charged with 'rape, burglary, and a multitude of other offenses.' There is no 'proof evident' of this complaint."

I tugged again on Dixon's coat sleeve and whispered, "Mr. Dixon, tell the judge my hair was to my shoulders and brown at the time! I am not the person Ms. Rudolph saw! Tell the judge."

"Sit there and don't talk! I told you not to talk to me in court. It's too distracting!" Dixon said.

Judge Coats asked, "Anything else from either side?"

"Nothing from the state."

"Nothing from the defense, Your Honor," Dixon replied.

Frantically I whispered, "Mr. Ament, why didn't you tell the judge, according to this Rudolph woman's police statement, she saw some guy named James Mayfield that night she came into the apartment. From the police department's notes I saw in your file, she even took and passed a polygraph test to show she was telling the truth. Tell them!"

"The results of that test mean nothing in a court of law. Polygraphs are inadmissible as evidence," Ament whispered back.

Judge Coats scooted up closer to the bench. "Bond will be denied. And the defendant turned over to the sheriff, and the case will be turned over to the Smith County grand jury for further study."

I clutched Dixon's arm. "Wait! I'm not going home?" My heart was pounding against my chest. I was certain the entire room could hear it.

"I told you to sit quiet, Kerry! We're not finished here yet," Larue said as he removed my panic-stricken hand from his arm.

"Now, if there is nothing further, this court will be adjourned," Judge Coats said.

Ament stood up. "Your Honor, in view of the court's ruling, we would like to make one request, since you are seated as a magistrate in this matter. We previously filed a motion with Justice of the Peace Leon Hicks announcing Mr. Cook was exercising his right to counsel and to remain silent; that in invoking this right, he was constitutionally terminating any/all interrogations and interviews by police officers and agents of the prosecution. This order was granted by Justice Hicks on or about August 8. This order has since been overruled and as counsel for the defendant we have not even been notified. And despite the order, agents for the prosecution continue to interrogate our client now up in the Smith County Jail without our presence or permission. Judge Coats, we are asking this court to please enforce by virtue of an order my client's rights under the United States Constitution."

"Said motion will be so ordered," Judge Coats said.

Clark bristled at this and launched into an aggressive legal tirade regarding the state's right to investigate its case.

"I don't think the court's ruling was to investigate the case, but to talk to the defendant without his attorney's consent," the judge stated.

The judge's remarks didn't make a lot of sense, but it was the only sense we were going to get out of this hearing.

Clark was still rambling out arguments when Judge Coats announced, "Court is adjourned," and walked away from the bench.

YOUR ATTORNEY IS here," the tall jailer said. I stepped out into the hallway and was escorted to the diminutive room on the sixth floor of the jail where Larue Dixon sat waiting.

"Mr. Dixon." I exhaled. "I am so glad to see you. They have

me in this tiny steel tomb called the 'side cell.' It's used for disciplinary reasons. It's solitary confinement. Please, can you get me out of that box?" I blurted out all in one breath.

"Kerry, you have to trust me as your attorney when I say this really is the best place for you. This way they can't get to you and concoct any tales for us to deal with at trial. You are just going to have to hang on. Your life depends on it."

Back at the cell that night I strained to hear the old black man named "Curly" who ran a small mobile concession selling candy bars and honey buns. I could always tell when he was on the floor from the sound of his rickety cart. My stomach involuntarily responded with a growl. If luck was with me, a jailer would give Curly access to the side-cell area, so I could buy some candy with the money my daddy left me. Finally a mistake was made and Curly found the door leading to my area open and stepped in to peddle his wares. I bought what remained on the cart. As we exchanged money for goods Curly told me the scuttlebutt he'd gotten from downstairs.

"You get any word on a trial date, boy?" he asked me as he was pushing several Snickers and Milky Ways into my cell.

"Not yet, but I wish it was today because as soon as I can get to a trial I am gonna go free."

Curly laughed. "Boy, they want you pretty bad. You'd better enjoy the days you got left and hope they don't take you to trial anytime soon. In fact, you need to be spending more time praying and giving your soul to the Lord, because your ass belongs to Smith County."

AUGUST ROLLED INTO September. Whereas the Tyler City Jail cell was freezing, it was like living in a furnace there in the Smith County Jail side cell. Sweat beaded my body twenty-four hours a day, at times making me nauseated. After a few weeks, I began to break out in a rash all over my body. The rare times I saw a jailer,

I pleaded for a shower, but I was always given the same absurd reply: "You have to talk to Chief Carlson." It was my daddy who finally asked someone downstairs in the Sheriff's Department if I could have a shower. He was promised that I would get a shower sometime that same day. But the day came and went and no one took me to the shower.

The next morning the guy in the cell next to me, Aura Lee Ray, and I decided that we had to push the envelope. We began yelling and pounding on the metal walls for a shower. This went on for two or three hours. Finally, Gene Carlson yelled, "So you want a shower, do you? Someone will be back to get you in a few minutes." Savoring our victory, Lee Ray and I hooted and howled with glee. In my mind, I could feel the cool water cascading over my face and body.

A jailer came for us about a half hour later. We were walked through the corridor until we reached an open door. We stepped inside and the door slammed behind us. It was dark. My mind instantly told me something was wrong. As I stepped into the darkness and tried to find my footing, a woolen blanket was thrown over my body. I felt the blows pummel my body. White stars flashed in my mind. I was beaten to the concrete floor. Through the fabric I saw a flicker of light. In that brief moment I saw Lee Ray also being kicked and beaten. Voices angrily cried out with each blow, "We don't want no fuckin' homosexual woman-killing faggot in our cellblock, Cook. Do you understand?"

Then there was silence. The prisoners, whoever they were, withdrew to their cells. The main door opened and a jailer stood holding the keys. We hobbled our way out. Out in the brightness of the hallway stood Chief Gene Carlson. Grinning at us as we made our way past him he said, "Let me know when you want another shower." A laugh erupted from his huge body.

The next week Daddy came to visit me. My left eye was still swollen and had a bluish hue, and there were bruises across my body. The blood left his face when he saw me.

"I want to know who did this to you!"

"Daddy, is anyone in the hallway? Can anyone hear me?" I whispered back cautiously.

I told him what had happened the week before. Fearing Carlson's retaliation, I begged my daddy not to say anything. Incensed, he went home, told my mama, and they called the *Tyler Morning Telegraph*. A few days later a jailer came and got me. I was taken into Chief Carlson's office on the sixth floor. There behind the desk sat the rotund chief; to his right sat my daddy on a spacious couch; and in another chair sat a reporter, Brad Bailey, for the *Tyler Morning Telegraph*. I told him what had happened to Aura Lee Ray and me.

"I will get around to that after a while," Bailey said. "Now, you've been charged in the rape and mutilation murder of Linda Jo Edwards. It's your fingerprint on her door frame. Tell me about this." Nothing ever appeared in that newspaper about what had happened to me in the showers that day or that I adamantly asserted my innocence. In fact, when it came to my case, the *Telegraph* would rarely challenge the local authority's version of events.

BOND HEARING

I had another chance to go home on September 20, 1977. Larue Dixon and John Ament filed a petition invoking habeas corpus to try to get me out on bond. Dixon came to the jail late the night before and told me I had a good chance to get a reasonable bond set because the prosecution could not meet the standard of proof that would warrant keeping me incarcerated.

"I don't understand. Please explain it to me." Part of me hoped he would talk forever because the longer he talked, the longer I could be out of that suffocating side cell. I had been in jail for forty-three days.

"Look, you're entitled to bail—even in a capital case—unless the state can establish clear and convincing evidence that the person charged with the offense is guilty."

I was confused. "Larue, if this is the law, then why didn't the judge let me go home at the examining trial? Rudolph admitted I was not the man she saw. Was this same law in effect for that proceeding, too?"

"Yes—but there is a lot of heat on this case. It's not going to be easy to get a judge to take the fall and the political heat for being the one who let you out."

"Mr. Dixon, can you really get me out of here tomorrow?"

"All I can promise is to do my best. I know it is hard, but you have to hang in there. Now, go get as much rest as you can. I will see you in court tomorrow." Larue stood up to leave.

"Mr. Dixon, I don't have any money. I can't pay you and Mr. Ament. I just have the eighty dollars coming from the Holiday Club from my last check as a bartender. I don't know how I will pay."

"Don't worry about any of that. For now let's just focus on trying to get you out of here," Dixon said, smiling back at me.

I know I am going to get out of here. This is my last night in this nasty hole! I thought to myself as I was taken back to the cell.

In the morning I was escorted to a different courtroom. They had just opened up a new court—the 241st Judicial District of Smith County. Glenn S. Phillips was the presiding judge; he would also be the judge if my case went to trial.

"Good morning," I said to both of my lawyers, with guarded hope in my voice.

"Mornin', Kerry," Ament and Dixon said. "Sit there and be quiet. Remember, don't try to talk to me or John during court. It looks bad and it breaks my concentration. Here, read this," Larue continued, as he shoved a sheaf of papers at me. "This is the constitutional law governing an accused's right to bail."

The side door swung open and in walked Judge Phillips.

"The court calls for a hearing at this time, number 77-1387, styled ex parte, Kerry Max Cook, petitioner. What says the petitioner and the state?"

"State is ready," A. D. Clark said. His table was chock-full of his aides.

"We're ready, Your Honor," Ament said. My heart accelerated. I just wanted to go home.

"Mr. Ament, call your first witness, then," the judge said.

"We call Mrs. Evelyn Cook to the stand—Kerry's mother."

My mama made the walk to the witness box and a court official swore her in. She looked over at me and tried to smile. My eyes went wet. She hadn't visited me since I was in the Tyler City Jail—Daddy had told me that it hurt her too much to see me.

"Mrs. Cook, do you know the young man seated to my right?" Ament said as he gently placed his hand on my shoulder.

"Yes. He's my son." Underneath her expression I saw the fear. My mama was nervous and scared. I fought to hold in my emotions.

At that moment I remembered her getting me out of the jails when I had run away from home and stolen cars with friends. We never really cared about the effect of our juvenile delinquency. If I hadn't gotten in all of that trouble, I wouldn't have been here. Still, there I was, dragging my mama through the mud again. All I wanted was one more chance to go home and love her more.

"Mrs. Cook, if the court lets Kerry go home today, can you promise that you will care for him, give him a place to live, and make sure he gets to every single court appearance?"

"Yes, I can. I can promise that," Mama said as she dabbed a tissue to her face.

"The defense next calls to the witness stand the defendant, Kerry Max Cook." Every eyeball in the courtroom immediately focused on me as I got up, looked around, and made my way to the witness box. Mama's perfume hung in the air.

Ament asked me if I would make every court appearance and

seek gainful employment should the court see fit to release me. "Yes, sir. I would, Mr. Ament," I said nervously. Everyone in the courtroom stared at me—I had never felt so much hate. I wanted to scream out how wrong it was for me to be there, but both Dixon and Ament had pleaded with me to answer only the questions asked of me and not volunteer anything else. Seeing I was finished, Phillips instructed me to step down.

Dixon stood up. "I can personally vouch for the court that when I was the district attorney in Cherokee County, he came each and every time. We ask that you set us a sufficient bail that will assure his presence here in court."

"Does the state have anything in opposition?" the judge said.

"Yes," Clark replied.

He called Sergeant Collard, who once again reiterated that the prints found on the patio door frame were six to twelve hours old—and therefore they *had* to be the killer's fingerprints.

Then Clark called Paula Rudolph. I sat, stunned, and my lawyers became increasingly irritated, as Rudolph began to dramatically distance herself from both her first sworn statement and her later sworn testimony. She now identified herself as a seamstress, and as such she speculated that the bright light in the ceiling of Linda Jo Edwards's bedroom caused her to misperceive the assailant's silver hair and the "touching-the-ears" fashion.

Clark then said, "Based on your observation of the figure that night, can you testify to this court who it was?"

"I will not swear under oath who it was. I feel like in my own time—"

Ament, infuriated, leaped to his feet and shouted, "Your Honor, I object!"

The judge ignored the objection and Clark continued.

"Can you testify to this court positively who it was not?"

Rudolph, with steely eyes, said, "I would say it was not James Mayfield." I know I saw that name in her sworn statement to police, but that's all I knew. This was all too confusing to me. I tugged at Ament's arm.

Clark called his next witness. "The state calls Dr. Jerry Landrum."

"Would you please identify yourself to the court?"

Landrum stated he was a psychologist who had recently gone into private practice. He also said he lived at the Embarcadero apartment complex. Upon hearing of the murder, he had offered his services to Clark and drawn up a "psychological profile" of the person who committed the crime. If I had even seen Landrum before, it had to have been when my court-appointed attorney, Mr. McVickers, filed a motion in Cherokee County with Judge J. W. Summers in 1973 to have me taken to Rusk State Hospital to be examined by a psychologist to determine my competency to stand trial. McVickers explained to me that as I was seventeen he was only doing that as a ploy to prevent me from getting a record and conviction for car theft. The second time I went to the hospital was for depression because of law enforcement harassment, and the third and last time was when I admitted myself in 1976 because I had nowhere to go, after my mother had angrily kicked me out of the house for coming home late one night. I don't remember ever seeing this guy Jerry Landrum.

"Would you tell the court what, in your opinion, was the psychological profile of the offender?"

"First, this was probably a homosexual or a bisexual male who had had a recent history of psychiatric treatment for anxiety; a person who had an extensive history of hallucinogenic drug abuse or multiple drug abuse; a person who had a past logical hostility for his mother and/or other females; a person who had psychiatric treatment and who had a problem with sexual performances, which was a significant concern to him."

"Now, Dr. Landrum, did you turn over this profile to the Tyler Police Department?" Clark said.

"Yes, sir. I did verbally."

Now I knew that something was seriously wrong. "Mr. Dixon?" I asked warily, but he told me to keep quiet. I tried to return my concentration to Landrum when I became aware of the court-room's strong reaction to the profile he was drawing. In that part of the country, there was no understanding of homosexuality—it was demonized, pure and simple.

"Under my definition, rape would include the removal of body parts, as indicated by the data I have seen," Landrum said. The courtroom collectively gasped. I felt like a pincushion, as it seemed that the eyes of every single person in the courtroom were poking in my back.

The judge then asked for final arguments for and against bond.

"Your Honor," John Ament said, "the purpose of this hearing is to see if there is 'proof evident' to hold the defendant without bond. I think we have several items in conflict in this case that would require a jury to return a verdict of not guilty. Finding the fingerprint on the apartment patio door is insufficient to convict a person and offer proof that this particular person committed this crime."

Clark stood up and boomed out to the courtroom, "Your Honor, Mr. Ament fails to differentiate circumstantial evidence from insufficient evidence. Direct evidence is as follows: Kerry Max Cook was inside the apartment during the time the girl died—direct evidence from Doug Collard indicates that he had to be in the apartment; second, the nature of the autopsy indicates a time frame; third, Paula Rudolph, within five, ten, fifteen min-utes, can put the time in which a male intruder was in the apart-ment. None of this is circumstantial. Therefore we feel that the state has met its burden of proof in this cause and asks the court not only to find the person be properly held under the indictment in this case, but second, under the discretion best in the court to deny bond."

Dixon rose and addressed the court: "We would like for the court to look at part of the testimony of Doug Collard, who said that there were other prints inside of the apartment that were not identifiable, and at the testimony of Paula Rudolph, where she cannot identify the defendant. It could have been anybody."

Judge Phillips ruled as soon as Dixon was finished. "Based on the testimony and evidence, the court is of the opinion that the proof is evident in this case as required by law. Bond is denied to the defendant. The defendant is to remain in the custody of the sheriff, where he will be held under denial of bond pending the trial of this case. The court in this matter is adjourned."

The deputy reached for my arm to pull me toward him. I followed in stunned silence as I replayed and analyzed the proceedings that had just taken place and the words I had just heard. I was pulled to the jail service elevator, which is operated with a special key that lets it bypass all the other floors and go straight to the fifth and sixth floors of the jail.

As the doors began to close, A. D. Clark raced to the elevator, pulling Paula Rudolph by the arm. "Hold the doors," he yelled out to the jailer. The deputy complied and in walked Clark and Rudolph. She planted her back firmly against the elevator wall and stared intensely at me. Clark was staring intently over at her and the doors shut and we moved up. Finally the number four lit up and the doors swung open on the fourth floor. After they stepped off, the doors closed and we were lifted to the sixth-floor jail.

I immediately asked the jailer if I could use the phone to call my attorneys. I was certain that Clark had intentionally brought Rudolph into the elevator to "help" her memory. I needed to tell Ament and Dixon, but the jailer said no, he would let them know if he saw them downstairs. Later I heard the jingle of the keys. I jumped to my feet eagerly, hoping it was one of my lawyers.

Instead, it was a deputy who opened the slot of my side cell, pushed a folded document through, and then slammed it and left without a word. It read:

> The State of Texas versus Kerry Max Cook. Charge: Capital Murder.

I had been indicted by a Smith County grand jury.

The next day my attorneys came by to tell me that Clark had filed notice with the court to seek the death penalty. I showed them the indictment I'd gotten. Dixon chuckled when he saw who was the foreman of the grand jury. "Everett Evans is a Tyler businessman who was just sworn in as a member of Sheriff J. B. Smith's 'reserve deputies,'" he said. "Unfortunately, because this is Smith County, they probably won't see it as a conflict that Evans is serving as a reserve deputy sheriff while serving as foreman of the county's grand jury." In other words, the "good-old-boy network" was alive and well in Smith County.

"COOK, YOU HANGIN' in there, pardna'?"

One of the few prisoners I had contact with was a black man named Bud Dean. He was allowed back in the side-cell area to sweep and mop the corridor. My window had been left open earlier in the day after my daddy visited.

"I'd be a lot better if I could get outta this oven," I replied, anxious to hear a human voice.

Bud inched closer to my window, looked behind him to make sure he was not being watched, and said, "Watch what you and Ray say to each other when you are talking. They be listenin' in, if you know what I mean. And, Cook, watch that nigga' Shyster Jackson. He be workin' for the man."

I nodded. "Thanks."

He looked behind him as he mopped in the direction of an

imaginary spot by my door. "Don't talk to any of the other inmates—no matter what. Before they brought you here from the city jail, two detectives from the Tyler City Police Department were here. They got us all together in the chief's office and asked us to try to get whatever information we could out of you since your attorneys made such a big stink about them trying to sneak around and talk to you. Man, they be laying for you, dude."

"COOK, YOUR LAWYER is here," a jailer announced as he opened my vault door. I had not seen either Ament or Dixon since the bond hearing. I made the short walk to the designated conference room in bare feet and boxer shorts.

"Yesterday I filed for a 'fast and speedy trial,'" Dixon said. "This means that constitutionally they now have only 120 days to take you to trial. If they fail to comply with this, no matter what happens, an appeals court will automatically overturn it and set you free. It's the law. We're in good shape. Just sit tight."

"What was yesterday? I don't know one day from the next in that steel tomb," I said as Dixon got up to leave. He told me it was October 24—over a month since the bond hearing.

MY DOOR OPENED and two sheriff's deputies were standing there. I never had any idea what time it was, let alone what day of the week.

"Cook, here. Put these on. Get dressed. We're going to take a little ride to Dallas."

"Dallas?" I said incredulously as the light from the doorway stabbed me between the eyes.

"All we know is that A. D. Clark has arranged for you to be taken to the Dallas County Jail so you can be interviewed by a psychiatrist named James P. Grigson, for the purposes of determining your competency to stand trial," the deputy answered.

The other officer kneeled down and shackled my legs. The leg irons cut into the back of my Achilles tendon. I had to take baby steps as they escorted me through the prison to their cruiser.

The Doobie Brothers sang on the radio as we traveled along Interstate 20 heading west toward Dallas. On the way the deputies stopped and bought me a hamburger and chocolate malt. One of them arranged the handcuffs in front of me so I could eat. I inhaled the burger—it is still one of the most memorable meals of my life. I pressed my face against the glass. What was green the night of my arrest had changed to a dull brown. Still, it was beautiful out in the free world—albeit handcuffed and shackled in the backseat of a police car.

A few hours later the deputies took me up to the Hospital Division of the Dallas County Jail. We stopped outside a glass office. Inside a thin man with glasses motioned for them to bring me in, though he was on the phone.

The doctor finished up his call. "Okay. I will ask him that. Yes. Okay. I will talk to you after I am done. Very good . . . Good-bye."

"You can leave the handcuffs on, but wait outside," he instructed, and the deputies left me in the room.

"My name is Dr. Grigson. I am a psychiatrist. Do you know why you are here?"

"Yes, sir. They told me the district attorney, Mr. A. D. Clark, arranged for you to interview me to determine competency to stand trial."

"Tell me about the rape and murder you committed. That's why you are here and in handcuffs. Let's talk about your fingerprint and your relationship with Robert Hoehn," Grigson asked.

"I haven't raped—or killed—anyone! I don't know this Robert Hoehn guy well at all!" Dr. Grigson stared at me, with his narrow face, then asked me a series of questions, such as what the date was and who the president and vice president of the United States were. He showed me some inkblots and asked me what certain pictures resembled, and I cooperated. The test was soon over and he motioned for the deputies to retrieve me.

I returned to my side cell and life of solitary confinement late that evening. The next time I was able to see Ament and Dixon I told them what had happened. "Mr. Dixon, you said they weren't allowed to keep pulling me out of my cell to interrogate me. That judge's order said they had to stop. That order isn't worth the paper it's written on because they are still doing it!"

"Kerry, let me do my job. We're having a hearing in the morning on exactly that. Read our motion," he said as he handed me a set of papers.

I read the motion while eating a candy bar Dixon had smuggled inside his briefcase: ". . . This order was later rescinded by the Honorable Mrs. Leon Hicks, promoted and instigated by A. D. Clark, personally, with no notice whatsoever to the attorneys of record for Kerry Max Cook. Immediately thereafter, law enforcement officers resumed the interrogation of Kerry Max Cook, with no defense counsel present."

"But, Mr. Dixon, what about them taking me to Dallas to be interviewed by that doctor to determine my competency?"

"Just read the motion before asking me any more questions," Dixon said. I dropped my head and read on. "[Neither] the attorneys of record for the defendant, nor A. D. Clark, nor Honorable Glenn Phillips have raised any questions whatsoever as to the defendant's competency to stand trial or the defense of insanity at the time of the alleged crime. Nonetheless, A. D. Clark, for whatever ridiculous reasons he may have, with no motion or court order whatsoever, ordered Sheriff J. B. Smith to transport the defendant to Dallas to be examined." The motion ended by asking the court to find Clark in contempt of court for violating my constitutional rights and to impose a stiff fine or imprisonment.

There was a hearing on the motion the next morning. Clark and Assistant District Attorney Tom Dunn whispered at their table. Dunn nodded and then stood up and addressed the court.

He began to make the case that Clark and the rest of the police and District Attorney's Office had never really understood the order of the court. Dunn asked that our motion not even be entertained and that instead the court dismiss it out of hand.

When all was said and done, Judge Phillips dismissed my attorneys' motion to hold the prosecution in contempt. He had decided to look the other way. A sheriff's deputy rapidly came up to take me back to my cell, but Dixon asked her to give us a minute.

"Kerry, I want you to listen to me more carefully than you have ever listened to anyone in your life, because your life depends on it. I know you didn't want to go back to your cell, but for your safety and for the safety of our case, it's best this way. I don't want you talking to *anyone* other than your family. They don't have a case against you—don't let them create one. We are working as hard and as fast as we can to get this thing to trial. The sooner we can get this to trial, the sooner we can get you out."

Dixon occasionally came up to the jail to visit me. Sometime later he told me what I already knew—the "fast and speedy trial" motion was being ignored. Though the thought of spending any more time in the side cell than I had to was chilling, he was of the opinion that this would lead to a guaranteed dismissal—and freedom. I believed him. I had to; he and Ament were my only hope.

MY NEIGHBOR, AURA Lee Ray, began to fall to pieces under the strain and the excruciating heat. He never received visits. Our conversations were relegated to shouting at the top of our lungs through the metal walls. He said he couldn't handle it anymore. Early one morning he yelled over to me that he was finally getting out.

"Did you make bail or something, Aura?" I yelled back.

"Heck, no," he said. "I sent off a letter to the president of the United States threatening to assassinate him when I did get out. That'll get me out of this coffin," he said, the pride in his voice evident.

Any hell was better than the one he was in, the way he saw it. It was a desperate ploy. He had no intention of murdering the president—he didn't even know *who* the president was.

"You're insane, Aura," I yelled back.

He laughed and said, "I'll be 'insane,' you be 'miserable' sittin' in the side cell. Call me anything you want, but I'll betcha before long you'll be callin' me long distance 'cause I'm gettin' out of here, dude." I told him that it was a crazy stunt, one that no one in the White House would take seriously.

But I was wrong. One week later the FBI came and got Aura Lee Ray from his side cell. I stuck my ear against my cell door and listened as he walked by. I heard the belly chains, the ankle cuffs, but above all that, I heard Aura Lee Ray ranting and raving about what all he was going to do to "that bastard Nixon," as he was being led away.

He was taken to a psychiatric facility in Missouri to adjudge his competency. I received a letter from him several weeks later. He said, "I'm sorry to leave you, man, but I just couldn't handle that shit anymore. Good luck on your case." I never heard from him again.

AMENT AND DIXON filed a motion with Judge Phillips to depose James Mayfield, Linda Edwards's ex-boyfriend, with whom she worked at Texas Eastern University. On January 24, 1978, their motion was granted.

A week later James Mayfield entered court represented by Tyler attorney F. R. "Buck" Files Jr. Interestingly enough, a few months earlier, Mr. Mayfield was represented by A. D. Clark's father in his petition to divorce his wife, Elfriede. A. D. Clark Jr. had also represented Linda Jo Edwards in her divorce against Bobby Lester. Edwards was living with Mayfield at the time the divorce was initiated.

Mayfield stated he knew Linda for a year and a half before her death. He met her at Texas Eastern University when she was employed as a library clerk under Paula Rudolph. Mayfield was the director of the library until early June 1977 when he was asked to resign from the university, effective September 1, 1977.

"And for the purpose of the record, would you state the color of your hair, Mr. Mayfield?"

"Gray."

Ament continued, "Again for the purpose of the record, your hair is moderately short, comes down a little over the top of the ears?"

"Yes."

"Mr. Mayfield, how long have you been married to Elfriede?"

"We were married in September of 1954," Mayfield said. He told Ament that for four days, in May 1977, he separated from his wife of twenty-three years, filed for divorce, and moved into apartment number 287 at the Embarcadero apartment complex with Linda Jo Edwards. He returned to his wife on May 16. He then helped Linda move into Paula Rudolph's apartment, number 169, over Memorial Day weekend.

Asked how long he had known Paula Rudolph, Mayfield said, "I've known Paula for several years, since we were both librarians and attended the same conferences." He went on to say that she was a friend and that he, his wife, and Paula had had dinner at one another's homes on several occasions. He confirmed that Linda Edwards had lived with him, his wife, and their sixteen-year-old daughter, Luella, for six months.

"What set of circumstances prompted her to move in with your family?" Ament asked.

"Her husband threw her out of the apartment one night."

"What was the nature of your relationship with her at this time?" Ament pressed.

At that Clark jumped to his feet. "I object to the question on the grounds that it is irrelevant to the subject matter before the court."

Thankfully, Judge Phillips said, "Overruled. You may answer the question, Mr. Mayfield."

Mayfield looked at Buck Files and when Files nodded affirmatively, Mayfield grudgingly admitted that he and Edwards were lovers in May 1977 and had been for several months. Because of the sexual allegations involved in the trial—including rape and anal intercourse—Ament delved into the sexual nature of Mayfield's relationship with the victim. Ament was able to determine that sex occurred between Mayfield and Linda during the six months she lived with him and his family on Sybil Lane. Sex with Linda Edwards involved various positions, oral and anal, with the exchange being mutual. They also viewed the pornographic movie *Deep Throat* while engaging in sexual acts. Then my attorney finally got to the crux of the matter.

"Had you been to visit Miss Edwards at the Embarcadero apartment before her death?"

"I had. The day before, on June 8, I was in the apartment at noon that day because it was my birthday, and she had asked me to come there to give me a painting that she had painted for me."

"How long did you stay on the eighth?"

"Approximately, an hour, an hour and a half," Mayfield replied.

"Would you describe the activities that transpired at that time?"

Mayfield hesitated. "I'm trying to recall exactly. She gave me— we had a Coke and she gave me several presents that she had bought for me and we necked."

"Did you have intercourse with her?"

"No," Mayfield answered.

Ament then stated, "Was this after you and she had broken off your relationship?"

"Yes."

Ament continued, "Could you tell me the nature of your relationship on June 8?"

"Well, I guess I can put it that I loved her as part of my family. I do not know whether it makes any sense to you or not. I told her I loved her as a daughter," Mayfield replied stoically.

The last time Mayfield claimed he saw Linda alive was at 7:45 the night she was murdered. She came by his house on Cumberland Ridge on her way to the home of friends who lived down the road.

The state declined to cross-examine James Mayfield—the man Paula Rudolph first identified as the killer.

ON VALENTINE'S DAY I was brought a copy of Ament and Dixon's motion seeking a change of venue. It made several arguments for moving the trial out of Smith County, the strongest of which was the claim that Clark's office had conducted a smear campaign to bias residents—and potential members of the jury—through the local media. I sat cross-legged on my bunk and read by the bright lamp.

> On or about the 31st day of January 1978, District Attorney A. D. Clark held a news conference in his office in the Smith County Courthouse broadcast through Channel 7, KLTV. The substance of such news conference was to inform the population that the defendant, Kerry Max Cook, was to be examined by a psychiatrist in Dallas, Texas, for the purpose of testimony upon the punishment phase of the trial. The clear import of such statement was to inform the population of Smith County that there would be a punishment phase in the trial of Kerry Max Cook, which presupposed the defendant is guilty. At the conclusion of the press conference held by A. D. Clark, KLTV anchorman Frank Simpson stated, in effect, the defendant, Kerry Max Cook, is to be taken to Dallas to be examined by a psychiatrist "to determine whether or not he will kill again."

The press conference was taped and aired on both the 7:00 and 11:00 evening news. My heart pounded against my chest like a jackhammer. Reading what had been going on beyond my sealed door was unsettling. By court decree, as well as Sheriff J. B. Smith's jail policy, I was not allowed to talk to the media at all—much less convey my innocence. Meanwhile, Clark was waging a media campaign that threatened the ability to select impartial jurors from the community.

Yet as with the bond hearing, Phillips swiftly denied our request for a change of venue. He ruled that a fair and impartial jury still could be had by the good people of Smith County.

ON APRIL 3, 1978, I had been in custody for almost eight months, but there was still no trial date. Ament and Dixon filed a second "fast and speedy trial" motion. The state had never acted on the first such motion, filed the previous October.

"Kerry," Dixon told me at the jail after he filed the second motion, "no matter what happens now—if it gets to a conviction—the appeals court will throw it out because of the violation of the Speedy Trial Act. We filed it not once but *twice* now. Just try to relax. We really are in good shape. You'll get out of here one way or the other now."

Two days later, I celebrated my twenty-second birthday for five minutes while Daddy visited. He looked worn down, so I held his hand tightly and told him, "Soon, Daddy, all of this will be over, and everyone will know I was innocent."

"I know, son—keep your chin up and hold on to that thought. Remember, you are not alone in this cell," he said, making reference to God.

"I love you, Daddy. Give Mama hugs and kisses. And tell Doyle Wayne I miss him and I will see him soon."

At that, my portal was slammed shut. The scent of my daddy lingered in my cell for a few moments longer. I sat down on the bunk and spelled out Doyle Wayne's name on my dirty legs as tears fell on my lap.

God, please let this end soon.

Not long after, Phillips set jury selection to begin on June 5. I always thought trials were for guilty people, but I had come to understand that a trial was going to be the only way to get to the truth and get out of this nightmare. Unlike most people, I suspect, I looked to the trial date with great optimism.

4

1978 TRIAL

JURY SELECTION

District Attorney A. D. Clark III entered through the court-room's heavy wooden doors, paused, and softly caught the door behind him before taking a seat in the very back of the court-room. Clark had been the driving force behind Smith County's prosecution of my case, and so it was eerie to see him lurking in the shadows on the first day of jury selection. But with his election bid looming on the November ballot, Clark had passed on the case he vowed "personally to try" to a newly hired assistant, Michael Thompson.

I was wearing a new pair of tan slacks and a white button-up shirt Mama bought for me at the JCPenney store in Jacksonville. She also borrowed a burgundy suit coat from her brother. It didn't matter that it was several sizes too big; Ament and Dixon said it was important that I have on a coat. My hair was shoulder length, so Dixon also got permission for a local barber to come give me a more clean-cut look before the jury.

Dixon stood up and had a brief conversation with Judge Phillips, who cleared the courtroom of all prospective jurors. Dixon then was allowed to file a motion arguing that the prosecution had interfered with his preparation of the case. He complained that he had met with nothing but stiff resistance when he made attempts to interview witnesses. Their addresses were listed only as "in care of Tyler Police Detective Sgt. Eddie Clark," so my attorneys did not know where to interview them. But despite Dixon's spirited argument, it was the same stoic reaction from the judge: "Overruled." My mind was about to wander elsewhere, when I was shocked to attention by Dixon's next words:

"The District Attorney's Office has refused to give us details on the name or whereabouts of the alleged inmate whom they say our client confessed the murder of Linda Jo Edwards to."

Michael Thompson leaped to his feet and announced, "Judge, the defense could have learned the name and whereabouts of the jailhouse witness from their client, Kerry Max Cook."

What are they talking about! How would I know his name? And how could I have confessed to any inmate? I had been in the same solitary confinement cell since the first day I was put in Smith County Jail, and the only prisoner I ever saw back in the solitary confinement area was Bud Dean, who was allowed only to stay long enough to mop and sweep the corridor.

Yet Thompson's reasoning held up. Then in rapid succession, six other motions filed by Dixon were similarly denied—the trial seemed to be off to a bad start.

The next morning Thompson asked Judge Phillips for a thirty-minute recess to "confer with the defense." Leaving me at the table, my attorneys whispered with Thompson, then walked through a door marked JURY DELIBERATION ROOM. After what seemed like an eternity, a deputy came to the table and ordered me to follow her. She led me into the room, where my attorneys were seated at the head of an oblong oak table. Thompson was not in the room— he must have exited through a second door on the opposite side of the room. The deputy handcuffed me to one of the twelve chairs and then left.

After the door closed, Dixon leaned toward me. "No matter what Thompson says—and I *do* mean no matter *what*—don't utter a peep. Just sit there and do not open your mouth. Do you understand?" I nodded, rubbing the well-worn edges of one of the chairs where a juror would sit and, I imagined, free me from this nightmare.

Thompson suddenly entered through the second door and took a seat. "At this time the State of Texas is prepared to offer Kerry Max Cook a non-capital-murder life sentence in exchange for his cooperation and testimony against the unindicted co-conspirator Robert Hoehn. The State of Texas will not interfere with parole. I will give you a moment to confer."

As he pushed his chair out and began to rise, the prosecutor froze in midair, still holding the side rails of the chair. Dixon was wasting no time. "All you have is the fingerprint on the outside of the patio door. You have nothing else. There's no way you can get a conviction and you know it."

"Very well. It [the same deal] will be offered to Mr. Hoehn, whose attorney, Mr. Duane Stephens, is outside now." Thompson made his way around the table to leave.

"I don't know anything about Robert Hoehn! I am—" Dixon cut me off, telling me to just sit in the chair and keep my mouth shut. Then, a thick silence hovered above the room.

Thompson stared at me, then at Dixon and Ament. "Very well, the offer is withdrawn," he said and smiled.

A few days later, the selection of twelve jurors was completed. Eight men and four women were sworn in and informed that they would be sequestered for the duration of the trial at the Red Carpet

Inn in Tyler. The twelve were ordered not to read or watch any of the considerable local news coverage.

DAY 1

Judge Phillips hurriedly entered the courtroom, his black robe flapping behind him as he assumed his place on the bench. His words filled the small East Texas courtroom.

"The court now calls for trial case number 1-77-179, the State of Texas versus Kerry Max Cook on the charge of capital murder."

It was Thursday, June 22, 1978. The courtroom was packed. Its benches creaked with the shifting weight of the patrons, many of whom had waited a full year to see what was daily being reported as the most sensational murder trial in East Texas history. Smith County had not had a capital murder conviction and execution since Jon B. Willis was found guilty of rape and electrocuted in 1935.

Thompson barely filled out his chocolate-brown suit with gold pinstripes as he stood up to address the court. Measuring five feet seven inches, he looked like a man made of sticks. He presented the judge with a motion to dismiss one of the five counts of the indictment—"murder with the intent to commit aggravated sexual abuse." He explained that the count was an improper allegation in a capital murder case. Delineating graphic sexual exchanges, the count's purpose was strictly inflammatory, designed by the prosecutors to emotionally sway the jury. My attorneys had asked the judge to dismiss this charge many months before, based on identical legal arguments.

"The state's oral motion to dismiss this count of the indictment is hereby granted," Judge Phillips said. "Is there anything further from the state?"

Thompson immediately requested that the judge instruct my attorneys and our witnesses never to refer to "Edward Scott Jackson," their jailhouse witness to whom I had allegedly confessed, by his acquired nickname of "Shyster."

I quickly recognized that name. The Smith County Jail supervisor, Ron Fite, had come to my solitary cell one morning and informed me of a jail trusty named "Shyster" Jackson who had been working for them. Fite said they had caught him stealing all of the prisoners' money from the book-in office. That was all I knew about this inmate: I had never seen him before in my life. Nevertheless it seemed that "Shyster" had earned his name. The judge instructed my attorneys that, at all times, they were prohibited from addressing him by anything other than his surname.

But Thompson's team was not done yet. Last, they wanted to bar any mention before the jury of Shyster's past criminal history. Dixon immediately interrupted and demanded that Edward Scott Jackson's criminal record be turned over to him and Ament for cross-examination purposes, because it went to the heart of Jackson's credibility. Unbelievably, however, Thompson claimed to have no documentation of their inmate's criminal history to give to the defense. My attorneys argued that the only way for them to secure this information was through the state's database, to which they did not have access.

The judge added to the insanity of the moment. "The court's ruling is as follows on the state's motion: As I recall, I ruled previously that the state was not required to deliver to the defendant any criminal records of any proposed witness unless and until that person was called as a witness. Only at that time would you be entitled to it in order to cross-examine the witnesses."

I didn't need the documents to tell me that "Shyster" Jackson was a career criminal who knew how to work the system—why else was he making up a story about how I "confessed" the murder to him? He had nothing to lose.

Ament responded, "With respect to the state's first motion, we

understand Mr. Jackson will testify that the defendant purportedly confessed to him during a jailhouse conversation. We have
subpoenaed two prisoners who have shared the same tank with
Mr. Jackson on the fifth floor of the Smith County Jail and who
will contradict his testimony based on the things Mr. Jackson admitted to them; but we have been run out of the jail and are not
allowed to talk to them. Therefore, we have no way of getting to
our witnesses to inform them to not—under any circumstances—
refer to the man they know only as 'Shyster Jackson' by his Christian surname, should they be called to testify."

Michael Thompson immediately flew to his feet and blasted
back, "Your Honor, if the defense wants to take up this matter on
a collateral motion, the State of Texas has evidence that a material
violation of the Canon of Ethics has occurred. This is why they
have been excluded from being allowed to go into the jail and interview their two jail inmate witnesses." Phillips glared at my lawyers and questioned Thompson about the violation. "Well, Your
Honor, they are not representing those men. For this reason they
should not be permitted to interview them or talk to them for any
reason."

Ament rose up, his hands pressed on the edge of the table
from his seat, exasperation etched all over his face. Dixon gently
tapped his elbow. "Let it go, John. Just let it go."

"MR. COOK, STAND up and come around and face the bench.
The state will now read the charges against you," Phillips announced after the bailiff brought in the jury.

Thompson cleared his throat, faced the jury, and in a loud,
clear voice began to read the indictment:

> "Kerry Max Cook did then and there intentionally and
> knowingly cause the death of an individual, to-wit: Linda Jo
> Edwards, by striking the face and head of Linda Jo Edwards

with a statue and by stabbing Linda Jo Edwards in the back
with a vegetable knife and by stabbing Linda Jo Edwards in
the throat with scissors and the said Kerry Max Cook did
then and there intentionally cause the death of the said Linda
Jo Edwards in the course of committing the felony offense of
Aggravated Rape, to-wit: did then and there intentionally
and knowingly have sexual intercourse with Linda Jo Edwards, the said Kerry Max Cook knowing that the said Linda
Jo Edwards was unconscious and physically unable to resist,
caused death to Linda Jo Edwards while in the course of
committing the felony offense of Burglary of a Habitation,
with intent then and there to have sexual intercourse with
Linda Jo Edwards, that; with intent to commit the felony offense of Aggravated Sexual Abuse, to-wit; with intent to then
and there arouse and gratify the sexual desire of the said
Kerry Max Cook . . . engaged in deviate sexual intercourse
by placing his mouth in contact with the genitals of the said
Linda Jo Edwards and by placing his genitals in contact with
the mouth of the said Linda Jo Edwards, and the said Kerry
Max Cook knowing that the said Linda Jo Edwards was unconscious and physically unable to resist. . . ."

The rest of Thompson's words faded. I poked Dixon's arm to
get his attention. "That's the inflammatory count of the indictment that the judge, not twenty minutes ago, dismissed at *their*
request! So they get to read it, but they don't have to prove it?"
Almost like a ventriloquist talking from the side of his mouth,
Dixon told me, "Wait until court is over before you try to talk to
me. This is the last time I am going to tell you." Meanwhile, the
reading of the indictment continued.

"And did then and there commit theft, to-wit; did then and
there unlawfully appropriate property, to-wit; a stocking,
from Linda Jo Edwards, and with intent to deprive the said

owner of said property, with intent to commit Aggravated Assault, to-wit; did then and there cause serious bodily injury to Linda Jo Edwards by striking Linda Jo Edwards in the face and head with a statue and by stabbing Linda Jo Edwards."

Finished, Thompson looked up from the indictment, turned from the jury, and looked directly at me. "To which indictment, how do you plead, Kerry Max Cook, guilty or not guilty?"

Flushed, I turned and looked at the jury. "Not guilty," I said nervously.

Opening Statements

I was the reason all of these people had converged; yet, strangely, no one seemed to acknowledge my presence. The process muted me. So did the "legalese" that I heard batted back and forth by the attorneys. It was like a foreign language to me, and the court system did not provide translators.

"Good morning, ladies and gentlemen of the jury," Thompson began his opening remarks. "The people of Smith County will show in the case before the jury today a lust for perversion and blood in the mind of the defendant. The evidence will clearly show a lust for blood and perversion, which he exercised through the very inhumane murder of a young woman, a twenty-two-year-old woman, who was but a complete stranger to the defendant."

I turned around in my chair to find the faces of my mama and daddy. They were holding hands tightly.

Thompson pounded the jury with the evidence he promised to prove and that he said would lead them to but one verdict: guilty of capital murder. "The state will call as its first witness Lieutenant Doug Collard, an expert in the area of fingerprint technology. He will testify that he responded to the crime scene called in this case. He will narrow the time of the leaving of those fingerprints—"

"Objection, Your Honor. May we approach the bench?" Dixon said.

Phillips instructed the sheriff to remove the jury. After the door had closed and the last juror was out of earshot, Dixon proceeded, "Your Honor, the defense would strenuously object to any allusion to the timing of the prints that were left on the door. The prosecution's opening statement is highly prejudicial. It places in the minds of the jurors that the defendant was there at that particular time of the murder."

"Is that all you have?" Judge Phillips said.

"Yes, Your Honor."

"Your motion is overruled. Be seated, Counsel. Sheriff, bring the jury back in. Proceed with your opening statement, Mr. Thompson," the judge said.

"The fingerprints," Thompson continued before the jury, "would have had to have been made between 10:00 o'clock that night and 8:00 o'clock the next morning, which is the relevant time frame for the murder in question.

"Next the state will call young thirteen-year-old Rodney Dykes, and his eighteen-year-old brother Randy." Thompson stated that both Dykes brothers would testify that a few days before the victim was found raped and murdered I had told them that while I was walking to the apartment complex's swimming pool I had gone up to Linda Edwards's bedroom window and watched her undress.

That's a lie! I didn't go out of my way to "peep" in her bedroom window to "watch her undress." The first time I saw Linda, I was making my way to the swimming pool one evening and she was standing nude in front of a lighted window, which overlooked the sidewalk, with the curtains pulled back—in short, she was exhibiting herself in plain sight, for any passerby to see. I wanted to scream this to the jury so I could correct Thompson's subtle manipulation. *I couldn't have been the only one that witnessed these events,* I said to myself.

Meanwhile, Thompson restarted, as the jury looked on, captivated. "The State of Texas will call Robert Hoehn." My mind was immediately transported to the plea bargain Thompson had offered me in exchange for information against Hoehn. Since I had met Hoehn only a few times, I felt I didn't have anything to offer. Thompson said Robert Hoehn would testify he arrived at the apartment around 10:00 P.M. on June 9 and that we drank beer together and watched a movie, *The Sailor Who Fell from Grace with the Sea.*

By way of this movie, Thompson introduced a bizarre theory that became the linchpin of the prosecution's case. He stated that Hoehn and I watched a portion of this movie in which a boy peeps into his mother's bedroom as she sits nude in front of a vanity, caressing herself sexually, and later, the boy sneaks into her bedroom and steals one of her stockings—just like, Thompson claims, I peeped into the bedroom window of Linda Jo Edwards, later sneaking into her apartment, murdering and raping her, and stealing her stocking, stuffing it with body parts, and disappearing into the night. When that scene in the movie came on, Thompson told the jury, that is when I immediately suggested Hoehn and I walk to the swimming pool. Thompson said Hoehn would tell them that along the way, I tried to get him to look in Linda Jo Edwards's bedroom window and he refused. All this happened not thirty minutes before she was murdered. Thompson said Hoehn and I watched the remainder of the movie and engaged in lascivious homosexual acts. When a scene depicting the sexual mutilation of a cat aired, I got down on all fours facing the television set and masturbated.

My attorneys stood up and shouted, "Objection, Your Honor! May we approach the bench?"

The judge nodded.

"Your Honor," my attorney pleaded, "we strongly object on the grounds, number one, that it [the defendant's alleged homosexuality] has nothing to do with the allegations in the indictment. Secondly, the defendant has not taken the stand in this case to raise any motive on his behalf. Thirdly, that such homosexual conduct between two people is a criminal offense against the laws of the state of Texas. This makes it an extraneous offense. The prosecution has already interjected that in the minds of the jurors. It is not admissible for any purpose whatsoever, and we would ask first of all that the court instruct the jurors that they cannot consider that for any purpose."

"May the state be heard?" Thompson said.

Needing no more argument to make his ruling, the judge said, "Mr. Dixon, your motion is overruled."

"Then we would next request an instruction to the jury that they cannot consider—"

"That will be also overruled."

Back in the presence of the jury, Thompson resumed hammering the state's case. "The people will further show by the testimony of Robert Hoehn that as a mutilation of a cat was portrayed on television the sexual interest of the defendant was greatly aroused, and that they engaged in their homosexual act that watching this mutilation . . ."

Alarms rang in my head.

"And that, eventually, on television there was portrayed a young man who was about to be sexually mutilated also by the participants in the mutilation of the cat. And about the point and time that the sexual mutilation of a young man was to occur, the defendant completed his sexual act with orgasm; that when he had completed his sexual act, that he went into the kitchen and came out of the kitchen with a butcher knife in his hand . . ."

With each word, my mind retreated further to keep the lies from finding me. It was all cleverly twisted. Though I didn't know Hoehn well at all, it was difficult to believe he was going to put his hand on a Bible and say these lies. I fought against the paralyzing humiliation and turned to find my parents. Mama was tightly clutching a white Kleenex and tears were streaming down her face. Daddy's face was ashen. I lowered my head and inched closer to Dixon's chair.

Thompson neared the end of his attack by informing the jury of the forthcoming testimony of Edward Scott Jackson and Paula Rudolph, who would identify the assailant she saw in the victim's bedroom the night of the murder.

Finished, the prosecutor finally exhaled. I looked in the direction of my attorneys, waiting for them to refute Thompson's statements.

But Dixon and Ament opted not to make an opening statement. Sensing my nervousness, Ament gently squeezed my arm underneath the table and whispered for me to just sit quietly and deadpan as much as possible. "Try to be expressionless, Kerry."

The judge instructed Thompson to call his first witness, Lieutenant Doug Collard.

Lieutenant Collard

At Thompson's command, the courtroom's lights were extinguished and an overhead projector was turned on. Lieutenant Collard's testimony took the jurors on a photographic journey inside the victim's apartment on the morning of June 10, 1977, beginning first with him dusting the glass patio door with a black powder for fingerprints, and later, ending up inside Linda Jo Edwards's small but neatly arranged bedroom. The dust particles that were illuminated by the projector turned red as the seminude body of Linda Edwards was shown sprawled, spread-eagled, in the center of the carpeted floor with blood pools outlining her lifeless form. One ankle stocking was still on her left leg, and the other leg was bare. Her eyes were wide open, and a small plaster of paris statue lay broken in bits and pieces on the floor beside her. A pair of women's panties and blue jeans were in a crumpled pile by her feet. The television was on, as was the iron sitting atop the ironing board.

On the carpet was a pair of scissors, with orange handle grips. A close-up of Ms. Edwards's head showed that a lock of hair had apparently been snipped from her head. Hair lay beside her head in the photo. There were no defensive wounds, and according to Collard, this indicated that the victim knew her assailant. Nor were there signs of forced entry or evidence of a struggle.

Collard testified that three weapons were used in the attack: the plaster statue, which was taken from the living room and used to render her unconscious; the pair of scissors, which Collard theorized were used to cut a portion of her hair and maybe even stab her in the throat and face, perhaps even to snip away at the inside of her vagina; and a large knife taken from a kitchen drawer, used to stab her in the back and perhaps in the vagina. Seventy-three photographs were projected onto the courtroom wall, showing injuries to Edwards's head, neck, face and mouth, breast, hip, upper thigh, and vaginal area. One picture showed three stab wounds to her back and buttocks. By her head, hair could be seen.

I had seen more than enough and I wanted to look away, but my attorneys had warned me beforehand, no matter how gruesome, not to look away; it would send the wrong message to the jury, they said. I was told to sit at the table with a countenance that showed nothing. In the face of tragedy, these were hard instructions to follow.

The gory slide show took all morning. Ament objected nineteen times, arguing that many of the photos were repetitious and highly inflammatory. Phillips overruled him nineteen times.

The rest of the afternoon was spent hearing Collard describe the "tented-arch" fingerprint he found on the sliding glass patio door. He testified as an expert witness that it just "jumped out" at him and was only six to twelve hours old, at most. In other words, the print had to be the murderer's calling card—and it belonged to none other than Kerry Max Cook.

This can't be right! I was not there at any time Thursday or Friday, June 9 or 10. I wanted to scream. Thompson and Collard had just converted what should have been an innocuous set of fingerprints into the crime scene fingerprints of the murderer!

The rest of the afternoon was a blur.

I was taken back to my steel tomb, and I added yet another untouched brown paper bag to the growing pile in the corner. No matter how hard I wanted it, sleep never found me, I wasn't sure sleep would ever find me the way it once had.

DAY TWO

The next day Larue Dixon began his attempt to poke holes in the credibility of the prosecution's expert witness. It turned out not to be very difficult. In his cross-examination of Lieutenant Collard, who was a sergeant at the time of the murder investigation, Dixon questioned the officer about his police work at the crime scene. When asked about the analysis of the blood found at the crime scene—including a drop found near the patio door—Collard testified that the blood was never submitted to a crime lab for analysis to determine its type.

"Why not?" Dixon incredulously asked the man in charge of the crime scene.

Collard paused, cleared his throat, and, in an unsure voice, explained that the blood was all the "same general color" and, further, that he just assumed it was the victim's.

Most important, Dixon also questioned Collard's analysis of the fingerprints found at the apartment. To begin, the lieutenant revealed that he had only gained his accreditation through a six-month correspondence course—a fact that Dixon suggested ought to cast doubt on Collard's expertise. I, of course, knew nothing about fingerprinting and tried to follow the conversation as best I could.

I learned that there were four basic categories of fingerprints.

I have what is called the "tented-arch" variety. Only 5 percent of the population has this pattern. However, on exhibit number 84, the scissors—one of the three murder weapons—there was an unidentified fingerprint on the handle that was categorized as a "whorl" pattern. Dixon pointed out that 65 percent of the world has this pattern. Collard squirmed, but he explained away this print as possibly belonging to the victim, who also had a whorl pattern, though there were insufficient points to make a positive ID. One thing was certain: the print was not mine. This was the *first* victory since my arrest. My heart burst with excitement as I looked over at Dixon.

The Dykes Brothers

Following Collard, Thompson called Rodney Dykes, who walked nervously into the courtroom and stepped into the witness box. The nephew of James Taylor, my former roommate, Rodney was wafer-thin and small for a thirteen-year-old, but he seemed to be reveling in the attention focused on him.

"He said he seen a naked woman and she was playing with herself," Rodney said, delivering the words with a lisp. Thompson asked him to step down and point out the apartment on a diagram of the Embarcadero complex. Rodney pointed to Linda Jo Edwards's apartment.

My attorneys had no questions for him and the judge excused him.

Thompson called Rodney's older brother, Randy Dykes, to the stand. Randy's testimony mirrored his brother's, until he told the court that I said I had gone up to Edwards's window to "watch her undress" instead of simply noticing that she was nude as I walked past along the sidewalk. I had never seen anything like this before, and I had told the Dykes brothers about it. Though Randy didn't mention it, he and I laughed carelessly about it, with Randy humorously punching my arm and telling me how lucky I was. Also, he said he came to his uncle's apartment that Friday around 10:00 A.M. (the morning Rudolph discovered her roommate's body) to take me job searching. While driving through Tyler, a news flash came on his truck radio about the death of Linda Jo Edwards and the search for a suspect. Upon hearing this "news flash," Randy stated that I looked "somewhat shocked" and then immediately asked him to drive me to my family's home in Jacksonville. Before we left Tyler, we stopped back by the Embarcadero Apartments, and I picked up a grocery bag. Randy said that he never saw me again. My eyes chased after his, but he would not look at me.

I HAD NOTHING but time in solitary confinement to retrace my every step since coming to Tyler and Rodney and Randy's uncle's apartment. On the morning of Friday, June 10, I woke up to the sound of pounding on the front door. I was wearing the same clothes I had had on the night before, feeling lousy from the alcohol the night before. I opened the door. Randy and Rodney were excitedly pointing to a part of the apartment complex that I saw had been cordoned off with yellow police tape.

"Did you hear?" Randy almost yelled out breathlessly. "Some girl was found over there beaten or something!"

I wiped the sleep from my eyes and cupped my right hand above my eyes to shield them from the sun. I could see people milling about—some dressed in police uniforms, others dressed in their pajamas.

"No, I dunno what is going on over there. I just woke up!" I said.

After a while, the conversation moved from someone being found beaten to their original reason for visiting. Randy said they dropped by to ask me if I could help him deliver his mom's TV to a repair shop—it was too heavy for them. I said okay, but added, "After I help you with your mom's television set, do you mind doing a few errands for me?" Finally, since it was Friday and I always spent my weekends, when I could, with Doyle Wayne, I asked if he would still take me to my brother's house as he had agreed to do days before. After I had taken a shower and dressed, we left.

Immediately after starting his pickup truck, Randy put on the radio hoping to catch any details about the focus of all of the police activity. He didn't have long to wait. Tyler station KTYL's breaking news was that a girl had been found severely beaten in a South Tyler apartment and the authorities were in hot pursuit trying to develop a suspect.

We looked at each other and said, *"Wow!"*

After we delivered his mother's television set, Randy then took me to the Department of Public Safety office in Tyler, where I had to get a replacement driver's license. I gave James Taylor's address at the Embarcadero as the permanent address to which the state should mail my license.

As we got in Randy's truck I asked if he could run by his uncle's apartment so I could pick up a change of clothing and an eight-track tape I wanted my brother to hear. I stuffed the change of clothes in a brown grocery bag, grabbed the tape and threw it on top, and rolled the bag shut. Randy drove me to Jacksonville, where I stayed until that Sunday, when Doyle Wayne drove me back to Taylor's empty apartment.

Paula Rudolph

A conservatively attired woman entered through the double doors. Paula Rudolph, the state's fourth witness, greeted Thompson and the rest of his team with a warm smile. She never looked in my direction or at the defense table. Her testimony began by stating that the victim had lived with her for two weeks prior to the murder.

Thompson then took her through the discovery of her roommate's body to the arrival of the police that morning. She said she woke up at 7:30 that morning, got up and made coffee, and noticed the patio gate open. She couldn't find her cat, so she called out to her roommate, Linda—there was no response. She went to Linda's room, pushed open the door, and saw her bloody arm outstretched on the floor. Thinking Linda had been beaten, she ran to the kitchen and called the police. She poured herself some coffee and then as an afterthought returned to see if Linda needed help. As she entered the room, she saw the full carnage.

After calling the police, she went outside and sat on the front porch steps to await them.

Thompson questioned her about the previous evening. Rudolph testified that an old acquaintance, John Adams, called and she went to meet him for drinks at the Roadway Inn at 10:30 P.M. Meanwhile, at the very moment Rudolph was meeting her friend, I opened the door and let Robert Hoehn into James Taylor's apartment.

"About what time did you return back to your apartment?" Thompson asked her.

"Well, as near as I can determine, because, of course, I couldn't actually look at my watch, but it was, I would say, about 12:35 to 12:45. It is perhaps possible that it was 12:30, but I really doubt it, because I may drive a little fast but I don't speed that much, that would be a little bit too much, but it was 12:35 or 12:45."

I was worried. In previous testimony and even in her police statement Rudolph said that she arrived home at 12:30 A.M. I remembered this time clearly, because 12:30 A.M. was the time that Robert Hoehn dropped me in front of the Embarcadero complex parking lot after we drove to get cigarettes.

Rudolph also introduced new testimony about the room given to Linda, explaining that it was actually a sewing room equipped with a bright light in the ceiling. A year after her initial testimony, Rudolph now claimed that these "bright lights" caused her to "perceive" the person she saw standing over her roommate's dead body to have been tan, wearing white shorts, and as having "silver hair in a medium, touching-the-ears fashion." She said she only saw the person for a split second and that she did not see any facial features or other distinguishing marks—just a "broad flat face" and a "silhouette" of the person's body.

Thompson zeroed in. "This person who you saw in Linda Jo Edwards's bedroom on the night in question, is he present in the courtroom today?"

"Yes," Rudolph said, emphatically and without hesitation. She turned and pointed straight at me. "Him!"

"She's lying!" I shouted out loud. Rudolph stared, the judge scowled, and my attorneys smothered me. Phillips threatened to gag me and chain me to the chair if my lips even looked like they were trying to form another word.

"Pass the witness," Thompson stated, his eyes never leaving Rudolph.

Ament quizzed Rudolph about the discrepancies between the sworn statement she'd given Detective Nelson Downing and her new testimony. Ament extracted an angry outburst from the prosecution table when he questioned how her memory could have improved after a year.

Flustered, he tried a different tack. "Have you ever identified this person seated to my right under oath?" Ament asked.

Rudolph bitterly stated, "I have never identified him, no," even though she had testified twice before and given a sworn statement. Rudolph conceded that her description of the person she saw—the silver, medium-length hair and other physical characteristics such as "fit and tan," height, and the broad face, broad shoulders—all described James Mayfield to a tee.

Phillips recessed the court.

DAY THREE

The next morning, Saturday, June 24, Ament had Rudolph return to the description of the person she saw. She said the person was approximately five feet, five inches—the same approximate height as that of James Mayfield. She acknowledged the person had on some sort of white shorts—"definitely not underwear." They were like tennis shorts. The person was bare-chested, with a "golden tan" and a trim physique. I learned James Mayfield was an avid tennis player and wore the type of white tennis apparel she described—and had done so on the day of the murder. I am five feet, eleven inches, and my face is narrow. Mayfield had, according to Rudolph, a broad face, and was broad-shouldered, and as an avid tennis player he frequently wore white tennis shorts. I had wavy dark brown hair that was shoulder length in June 1977.

A knowing smile appeared on Ament's face. I looked over at the papers lying in front of him and saw that it was an official transcript from the September 20, 1977, habeas corpus hearing. Ament had underlined the portion where A. D. Clark III was pressing Rudolph to make an in-court identification of the assailant she saw the night of the murder. Rudolph had said instead, "I will not swear under oath who it was."

Ament directed Rudolph to the transcript but was stopped cold by Thompson's loud outburst. Thompson filled the courtroom with his words as he pummeled the judge with an objection, arguing that the official transcript was not admissible because the judge's court reporter hadn't signed it. Phillips granted Thompson's tirade and disallowed any portion of the crucial transcript to be used by the defense in cross-examining Rudolph. *This was absurd!* I screamed out in my head. *How else can we show this new identification of me is a lie?*

Ament implored the judge to take notice that this was the official record of that transcript transcribed by the court reporter. The judge was adamant, however, and refused to reverse his ruling. That was a mortal blow.

With no transcript to force her honesty, Rudolph continued to smile and state, "No. I don't recall," when Ament asked her about her previous statements.

Defeated, Ament whispered, "I believe we will pass the witness, Your Honor."

On redirect, Thompson asked again, "Would you look at this jury and tell them whether or not you are positive that it was the defendant, Kerry Max Cook, that you saw?"

"Yes."

"I have no further questions," Thompson said as he sat down triumphantly. Without having her contradictory testimony presented to the jury, Rudolph's new identification stood.

I remembered A. D. Clark dragging Rudolph to the jail service elevator months earlier and knew the scary truth: The prosecution had worked with Rudolph to produce this chilling courtroom identification. *How could they do this? How can this really be happening?* The judge didn't appear to be a neutral arbiter. I knew enough to know the judge was not supposed to work in tandem with a witness and the prosecution like this. It was bizarre—and frightening, because not only was I powerless to do anything about it, but now so were my legal representatives. I couldn't help feeling that Murphy's law was in effect: Everything that could go wrong was going wrong.

Robert Hoehn

After a recess, the jury returned, and a moment later the pasty-white, overweight figure of Robert Lee Hoehn ascended to the witness stand. The prosecution had given forty-nine-year-old Hoehn blanket immunity from prosecution for his testimony.

Why does he need immunity? Questions—and concern—filled my thoughts.

The courtroom lights went out as if it was a Saturday-morning matinee. *The Sailor Who Fell from Grace with the Sea* played on the wall, where the victim's body had been plastered two days earlier. Thompson showed the scene with actress Sarah Miles masturbating while sitting at her vanity, her son looking on through a hole in the bedroom wall. It was the first time I had seen the movie.

"Mr. Hoehn, after you sat in the company of Kerry Max Cook and watched the scene that you have just seen portrayed on the wall, what, if anything, occurred?"

"He suggested that we go to the swimming pool." I had suggested we go to the swimming pool because, from the moment he arrived at Taylor's apartment, Robert Hoehn was coming on to me. That's the only reason I wanted out of the apartment!

Thompson took out a large diagram of the Embarcadero Apartments and mounted it on a tripod for the jury to see. Hoehn then traced the route we took on the way to the pool, stopping to look toward a window. "That is the apartment that Kerry Max wanted me to look into. He said something to the effect, and I cannot give the exact words, 'Come look in this window. There is a good-looking chick or girl here.'" The window, Thompson told the jury, was the window of Linda Jo Edwards. And the implication was that the peeping scene in the movie had inspired me to suggest we walk past Edwards's apartment.

Hoehn, like Randy and Rodney Dykes, wasn't telling the whole story of what I had *really* told them: One day on my way to the swimming pool, from the sidewalk I saw Linda nude and fondling herself by an open window; I later met her at the pool, and she invited me back to her apartment and we made out. I told them her name was "Linda," and I showed them the passion marks she gave me on my neck.

Hoehn said we went on to the pool and, after a while, returned to the apartment to watch the rest of the movie. The lights went back out and the projector spun out another scene. My concern grew—*Why is Thompson placing so much significance on this movie?*

"Tell the jury, if you will, what you did then," Thompson instructed.

"During the course of time and during the course of this movie there was a lot of it missed because we had sexual relations between the two of us." Hoehn said I was watching the TV and rubbing my penis.

That's crazy! That never happened!

Thompson wanted to know what part of the movie was playing while I was supposedly doing this.

"I've gone blank," Hoehn said, saying he could not remember. He said he was too preoccupied performing oral sex.

He's gone blank because he never saw the movie until the police and prosecutors showed it to him, that's why, I thought—*because we didn't watch it!*

"Was this during the cat mutilation scene?" It had already been established that we were out at the swimming pool when that portion of the movie aired on the Z channel that day, so the judge ruled the jury would not be permitted to watch it or hear about it. The ruling seemed to matter little to Thompson.

Ament objected to Thompson putting things before the jury that were not in evidence. The judge sustained Ament's objection.

Thompson, relentless, pushed past Ament and the judge. "Did the children have their knives out at that point and—"

Ament objected and the judge again ordered Thompson to refrain from interjecting issues not in evidence before the jury.

"Mr. Hoehn, did the children at that point in time, did they have the knives out? Were they preparing for the cat?" Thompson said.

Ament shouted his objection.

Tired of fighting with Thompson, the judge instead instructed Hoehn to go ahead and answer Thompson.

"I do not believe it was," Hoehn said.

"What portion of Kerry Max's body were you playing with?" Thompson asked.

"His anus," Hoehn told the jury without flinching, adding that he also performed oral sex on my anus and then had intercourse with me.

A gasp came from the audience—me included. Four of the jurors were staring at me with disdain dripping from their faces.

What did Thompson want? Why was Hoehn working with Thompson and providing this salacious sexual narrative? What does any of this have to do with a rape and murder of Linda Jo Edwards? I thought to myself.

Hoehn said he tried to get me to perform anal sexual intercourse with him, but that I was unable to get an erection. Thompson asked Hoehn to describe for the jury his anal intercourse with me. Hoehn complied, detailing graphically how he lubricated my anus first and then slid inside me and climaxed. Everyone in the courtroom glared at me.

MY BODY MAY have been at the defense table, but by now my mind had sought shelter far away. Before ending up at James Taylor's apartment in April of 1977, I had been working as a bartender at a gay bar in Dallas called the Old Plantation. Robert Lee Hoehn was James Taylor's friend and I had met him at a barbecue at his house. He was nice, but I was not sexually attracted to him, no more than I was to his best friend, James Taylor. The night of June 9 was the third time Hoehn and I had met.

That night Hoehn had a few beers, as did I, and he became relentless in trying to have sex. That was the *real* reason I played musical chairs, switching from sofa to love seat, trying to avoid his unwanted advances, finally suggesting we go to the swimming pool. Once we got back, he was still not taking no for an answer, and I did get cornered and let him take off my clothes. He went down on me, but that didn't work. I couldn't get it up because, quite frankly, I was not turned on. I didn't want to hurt his feelings and tell him that outright—I never was good with that part.

"WHAT DID KERRY Max put on that night? Did he put on any underwear?" Thompson continued. Hoehn said I put on a pair of red and blue Everlast swimming trunks, then pulled on a pair of blue jeans. He said we left the apartment to find a store that would be open at that hour to buy me a pack of cigarettes. After I declined to go home with him, he dropped me off in front of the apartment complex and went home.

On cross-examination, Ament took Hoehn back through the sequence of events to establish a time line. The movie ended at 11:45 P.M. We left the apartment for the pack of cigarettes at roughly 12:05 A.M. We went to Williams Grocery—it was closed—and finally found a Kroger's open, eight miles away. He drove the forty-five-mile speed limit back to the Embarcadero complex and then went home.

"Do you know what time it was when you let Kerry out?" Ament asked.

"I would say around 12:30 A.M.," Hoehn replied.

"Could it have been 12:20 A.M.?" Ament pushed.

"No. It [the trip for cigarettes] couldn't have been done in fifteen minutes."

Ament finished by taking a bag marked DEFENDANT'S EXHIBIT #9 off the table—the pair of Everlast blue and red swimming trunks I had on the night of June 9.

"Did he have on any white clothes?"

"No," Hoehn said.

Just in case it wasn't clear, Thompson wanted another round with Hoehn, revisiting all the homosexual acts and eliciting Hoehn to confirm that he had been an avowed homosexual for thirty years.

THE PROSECUTION'S STRATAGEM had become clear: Their case was that Linda Jo Edwards was a complete stranger to me, and the only time I had ever seen her before was in Peeping Tom episodes in which I snuck up to her bedroom window in hopes of catching a glimpse of her undressing. Though the judge had to rule that most of the movie could not be shown to the jury because Hoehn did not testify we saw it, Thompson argued that the movie provided the motive for the brutal rape and murder of Linda Jo Edwards; for just as I had suggested that Hoehn and I peep on Edwards, so, too, did I reenact the movie's final scene, a murder in which a group of young boys surround the main character and, it is assumed, though not depicted, stab him to death. Thompson also took my inability to get an erection with Hoehn as evidence of impotence. My alleged sexual frustration—and homosexuality, which at the time was thought of as an indisputable sign of deviance in East Texas—caused me to go out to rape and kill a complete stranger. How someone suffering from impotence could commit rape was not addressed.

Hoehn's testimony had caused serious damage. But hidden amid the salacious details and Thompson's wild speculation was the most important point: Hoehn had dropped me off in front of the Embarcadero apartment buildings at 12:30 A.M. This fact made it impossible for me to be the person Paula Rudolph saw at 12:30 A.M. and moments later heard exit through the patio door.

DAY FOUR

Shyster Jackson

"The State calls Edward Scott Jackson," Thompson said. Ament and Dixon objected, aware of what the prosecution's intentions were in calling this witness—to testify to a bogus "jailhouse confession." The jury was removed for the hearing.

My lawyers were soundly convinced Shyster's tale would never get to the jury's ears for two reasons: one, Jackson claimed the so-called confession story took place on or before August 19, 1977, and two—not that we would need it—he would get the records from the jail and establish that I was assigned to solitary confinement and never in a cell with this Shyster.

Dixon sat down, patted my leg. "Don't worry, Kerry. Calm down. This guy's story isn't coming in as evidence. The law is clearly on our side and we'll be able to keep it out. Here," Dixon said, as he opened up a green book that was the Texas Penal Code to an earmarked page, and then pointed to a section highlighted in yellow:

"Ordinarily, statements by one in custody about a crime for which he is being held are not admissible as evidence," I read with relief.

Edward Scott Jackson, a tall, young black male with designer eyewear, took the stand. He had resided in the Smith County Jail for the last nineteen months under an indictment for murder.

"Are you acquainted with the defendant, Kerry Max Cook?" Thompson began.

Jackson replied that he was. "The first time that I saw him was when they brought him in in late August and they put him in the side cell. I started bringing him cigarettes and we became acquainted. They wouldn't let him take showers, so I was a trusty at the time and fairly influential with the head jailer [Chief Gene Carlson] up there, so I went to Carlson and asked him if he could come in my tank and take a shower. Eventually he agreed, and I went on to ask him if he would move him out of the side cell if I promised to protect him," Jackson said.

"Why did you ask for him to move out of the side cell?"

"Because I have a heart. The man had bumps all over him, heat bumps and rashes."

"Did you have occasion after Kerry Max Cook had been moved into the Felony Holding Tank in which you were held, did you have occasion to talk with Kerry Max Cook regarding this case?"

"We were looking through some *Hustler* magazines and *Playboys* and he came upon a dark-haired woman, and he said some pretty vulgar things." Prodded by Thompson, Jackson went on to say that if there was a nude picture of a blond female or a red-headed girl, I would say, "Now, they are fine."

"I asked him again if he had in fact done the crime he was accused of. He told me, 'Edward, promise me you won't say anything to anybody. I trust you and I believe you are my friend.' I told him that I wouldn't and that he could trust me. He told me he had stabbed her in several places on her body. He said he cut along the hairline of her vagina and that he had come down and cut a 'V' shape between her legs and that he gouged her several times in her vagina [with a butcher knife]."

"Did he tell you any of the facts about the case?" Thompson pushed.

"He said that he had cut some hair from her head and that he had taken her vagina, and the hair with him."

"Did he say anything else about the case?"

"He said he thought he had been seen in the apartment by some lady."

When asked about the circumstances in which he contacted the police, Jackson answered, "Well, they contacted me, to be honest. I was offered no deal but they wanted to speak with anyone who had been in the same tank with Kerry."

"Has the State of Texas offered you any deal, made you any promise of leniency in an effort to obtain your testimony in this proceeding?"

"No, sir," Shyster Jackson said as if offended by the question. After a few other assurances from Jackson that there has been no deal or promise for leniency in exchange for his testimony, Thompson surrendered his star witness.

Ament tried for the jugular: "Let me call your attention to the second and third paragraphs of your October signed statement to police. Kerry Cook told you his killing of the lady prior to the time that he had to go to the examining trial. Isn't that correct?"

"Yes, sir," Jackson replied.

Ament looked at the judge and said that was all we had to ask of the witness for the purpose of the hearing.

I took a deep breath.

"Your Honor, based upon the witness testimony, the State of Texas would offer the testimony of this witness on the case in chief before the jury," Michael Thompson argued.

"Mr. Ament?" the judge said.

"Article 38.22 of the Texas Code of Criminal Procedure clearly states that such in-custody statements are inadmissible as evidence." Ament's words soothed my racing heart. Ament was citing a law that was in effect until September 1, 1977. A new law had been passed to allow such in-custody confessions, but it hadn't gone into effect until two weeks after Jackson allegedly heard me confess, nor was it retroactive. Though it was a technicality of sorts and the real issue remained that the confession never took place to begin with, nevertheless it was sufficient to bar the introduction of Jackson's story.

Incredibly, Thompson continued to press for the admissibility of Jackson's testimony, making the suggestion that my conversation with Jackson might have taken place in September after all.

"I don't think you can change the testimony of this witness," Phillips told Thompson.

Thompson kept hammering at the judge, asserting the importance of Jackson's testimony and the need for the jury to hear it. Ament fought to make certain the judge wasn't swayed by Thompson's maneuvering. He interrupted Thompson's tirade and told the judge that the defense wanted to issue a subpoena immediately for the Smith County chief jailer, Gene Carlson, to bring down the jail records, for these records would clearly show that I was never in a cell with Jackson. The court took a brief recess.

Thirty minutes later the judge returned. "The bailiff told me during recess Chief Jailer Gene Carlson is on vacation in Arkansas."

The chief jailer just went on an unscheduled vacation in the middle of the day? I had seen him this morning when they came to get me for court.

Dixon grimaced. He asked for Sheriff J. B. Smith to secure the records and bring them into court. Regrettably, we were told that the sheriff was in Nacogdoches. Dixon then asked for the sheriff's chief deputy who was just seen out walking the halls. But now he, too, was nowhere to be found. Finally, Ament called Brad Burger, administrative assistant to the sheriff, to the stand.

"The time period that you are relating to is not available," Burger answered. It was not that prisoners' cell assignments weren't kept, he said, but just that the month of August 1977 was inexplicably gone from the master files, as were September and October.

Having reached a dead end, the judge's next move was swift and decisive. "The court is going to rule any statements, any conversations had between Kerry Max Cook and Edward Scott Jackson are voluntarily made and the testimony will be admitted before the jury. Mr. Elliott, have the sheriff in charge bring the jury back in." Acting Sheriff Chief Deputy Jim Collins suddenly reappeared and escorted the jury back into the courtroom.

With the jury now looking on, Shyster Jackson told the same story but embellished.

When Thompson asked what he was doing in jail, Jackson answered he was in jail on the indicted offense of "defensive murder." There is no such criminal code. Thompson asked how I was reacting while I was commenting on the nude pictures of the dark-haired nude females. "Like a hyped-up nut," Jackson said, "crazed" and "wild." At one point I supposedly threw the magazine with the nude dark-haired girl down to the floor and stomped on it, in a rage. I allegedly became calm when the page was turned to a shot of a blond woman.

I pushed my nails into the wood of the chair, wrestling to control myself, but the dam of emotion was collapsing.

"What in particular did Kerry Max Cook say about these dark-haired women?"

"He would make a comment like 'I would like to fuck her hard' or 'this bitch needs her ass kicked—'"

The dam finally broke.

"Liar!" I screamed with all of my might as I spoke from the table for the second time.

Thompson moved forward. "Would you testify as to the physical description of the women you saw in that magazine that Kerry Max Cook saw in that *Hustler* magazine?"

"They were well-built women of basically big frame and had dark-colored hair." Jackson had just described Linda Jo Edwards. Most of the jurors were staring hard at me.

"Pass the witness, Your Honor," Thompson said loudly.

Dixon did what he could.

"Did you make a statement on the elevator last week that you were getting out of here, that your case was going to be dropped to involuntary manslaughter, and you were going to be given credit for time served if you testified in this case?" Dixon said.

"No, sir."

"Have you ever been convicted of a felony crime?"

Thompson objected to this line of questioning as "immaterial and irrelevant."

The judge agreed and prohibited Shyster Jackson from having to answer the question.

Wait! I fought the urge to shout. The judge promised he would make the prosecution give us Jackson's criminal history once he took the witness stand. In addition to the murder charge, Jackson had prior convictions for aggravated assault and burglary—certainly enough to call his credibility into question.

Thompson had a few more questions for his star witness.

"Tell the jury what I promised you, Eddie," Thompson shouted to dismiss any inkling of a notion that a deal had been struck to secure Jackson's testimony.

Jackson turned to look at the jury. "You promised that when my case comes before you, you would prosecute it thoroughly, and to the best of your ability."

"What else did I offer you?"

"You said you would ask for a life sentence if I was found guilty." Jackson went on to say, should he (Jackson) want to plea-bargain by pleading guilty, Thompson would recommend only the maximum—a sentence of ninety-nine years or life imprisonment.

Dr. Gonzalez

"The State will call Dr. V. V. Gonzalez," Assistant D. A. Randy Gilbert announced.

On the morning of June 10, Dr. Gonzalez was picked up at Mother Frances Hospital in Tyler and taken to the crime scene, where he conducted a preliminary examination of the body at 9:30 A.M. Neither a forensic pathologist nor a board-certified clinical pathologist, Gonzalez then had the body taken to the Burks-Walker-Tippit funeral home, where he finished his autopsy in the sink.

The lights of the courtroom went out and the body of Linda Edwards reappeared on the wall undressed, suited in blood. Using the graphic autopsy photos blown up almost to the size of the courtroom wall, Gonzalez described each of her wounds. There were multiple penetrating wounds over the right side of the neck and mouth, which to him were cut by a knife or scissors. Plaster of paris was found inside her mouth, as were broken teeth. The right and lower portions of the ear were lacerated. He pointed out wounds to the lower chest and breast area. There were penetrating wounds to the vagina, rectum, pubic, and perineal regions. There were no defensive wounds.

More photographs went up on the wall, and he gave a chronological sequence of how the various wounds occurred. The first wounds were from the plaster statue, to the front of the head. With the victim likely knocked unconscious, her mouth region then was snipped with scissors. Next, the wounds to the neck were made by the knife. Horrible close-ups of the vaginal region were projected to describe the internal wounds. Gonzalez claimed some of the wall of the vaginal canal had been cut off prior to her death and was not found at the scene.

"Dr. Gonzalez, based upon your examination, were you able to determine an approximate time of death?" Gilbert asked.

"Yes, sir. At the scene, there was what you call postmortem rigidity. I concluded she had been dead for approximately ten to twelve hours." Plus, Gonzalez stated that given the use of three different murder weapons, it would have taken some time to perform the awful crime.

Ten to twelve hours from 9:30 A.M. was 9:30–11:30 P.M. the night before—during which time I was with Robert Hoehn, for better or worse. Gonzalez's testimony ought to rule me out as a suspect. I grabbed a pen from the table and began to write this to Dixon. He quickly scribbled back, "We already know. Sit still and be quiet!"

Evidently, the prosecution also caught the discrepancy.

"I believe you testified your examination was made about 11:30?" one of Thompson's assistants asked.

"At 11:30 I started the examination in the funeral home," Gonzalez replied. Gilbert passed the witness.

Ament caught Gonzalez trying to shift the "ten-to-twelve-hour" time frame in which the murder could have occurred. Rather than calculating the time frame beginning at the murder scene that morning—as his official autopsy notes revealed—he referred to a time two hours later when he performed the full autopsy at the funeral home. Gonzalez was tweaking the time of death to coincide with Collard's aging of my fingerprints, and

Rudolph's testimony of entering the apartment and seeing the murderer.

Ament confronted Gonzalez head-on. "I am a little bit confused as to when the ten-to-twelve-hour period you talked about is from. Is it from the 9:30 A.M. examination at the scene?"

Gonzalez blinked but recovered quickly. "From the time I performed the autopsy, which was 11:30."

Ament directed Gonzalez to his own report and asked him to read from it.

Gonzalez adjusted his glasses and studied the document for a moment, "Examination of the body at the Embarcadero Apartments shows rigor mortis of the neck, extremities, chest, and abdomen, which would indicate that she had been dead approximately ten to twelve hours."

Though much of the trial had been like a foreign language, this required no legal education to understand: Gonzalez was lying.

Ament repeated his original question regarding his timing of the death.

I was shocked when he said, "I would say from the autopsy at 11:30 A.M. plus or minus a few hours because of the environment."

The environment? She was in her bedroom, not exposed to the elements. My head throbbed, pounding against the bruised walls of my mind.

"So, this paragraph here in your report would just be a kind of typographical error?" Ament asked incredulously.

"No, sir. I think this is—I should not say the reason why is because I don't like to explain everything here as far as the factors that you have to consider in the hardening of the body," Gonzalez said.

Ament repeated his original question regarding his timing of Edwards's death. Gonzalez stated, "From the autopsy, I would say from the autopsy at 11:30 A.M., plus or minus a few hours because of the environment."

Ament had to move on. Gonzalez said he counted approximately forty-six wounds to the body of Linda Edwards, but he couldn't count the number of stab wounds inflicted in the vaginal bulb. The damage to the vagina alone, Gonzalez stated, took at least "five to ten minutes" to complete. Upon his testimony that her vagina was "cut out and not found at the scene," I looked over and saw the jurors staring at me with undisguised hatred. I was forced to look away.

Gonzalez was dismissed.

Thompson stood up. "Your Honor, the State of Texas would rest its case."

The judge turned to the jury and told them it had been a long day—for once, he recognized the truth. Court was adjourned.

DAY FIVE

My attorneys thought the most damning piece of "evidence" was the Jackson testimony. I had no money to hire an expert to refute Collard's testimony wherein he precisely aged my fingerprint, putting me at the scene of the rape and murder of Linda Jo Edwards.

My defense consisted of three Smith County Jail prisoners—William Fomby, charged with theft; Jimmy Joe Dean Evans, burglary; and Jerry Wayne Sewell, in jail on two charges of delivery of a controlled substance. Like Jackson, they were all prisoners who had criminal charges pending. Unlike Jackson, who was permitted to walk in groomed and well dressed and without an escort or handcuffs, the three prisoners who were brought in to show Jackson was lying were paraded before the jury in chains and leg shackles. The message was clear: They were untrustworthy criminals.

Fomby testified that Jackson told him that the district attorney was going to reduce his charges from murder to involuntary manslaughter and give him time served. Fomby went on to say Jackson confided in him that he was shown slides of how the girl was cut up and where she had been stabbed—details only the real killer could have known. Fomby revealed that when the prosecution found out he was going to testify for the defense, he was brought up to Chief Carlson's office, where he met with Thompson and his staff. Thompson threatened that if he testified for the defense against Jackson, he would file perjury charges and see personally that he got more time on top of what he was going to give him for the theft charge.

Further, unlike Edward Scott Jackson's, the past criminal record of William Fomby became immediately admissible before the jury. He had a prior conviction for the offense of burglary in May 1975, and Thompson made sure the jury knew it. Thompson accused Fomby of lying when he testified that Jackson told him that Chief Carlson had given him Valium before he went to take a polygraph exam.

Next Ament called Jimmy Joe Dean Evans to the stand. A young black male of about twenty-four lumbered to the witness stand, escorted by sheriff's deputies and shackled at the feet and hands. With multiple burglary charges pending, he had the most to lose—in fact, his court-appointed attorney had advised him not to testify in the Kerry Cook matter. Yet Evans told the court that Jackson had told him that he had been offered a deal from the D.A.'s Office whereby, in exchange for his testimony, they would reduce his murder charge to involuntary manslaughter, give him credit for the time he had already served, and release him within a short period of time—maybe two or three days. Jimmy Evans also testified that Jackson admitted his testimony was going to be a lie and that my case was Jackson's meal ticket out of his murder charge, for which he would otherwise be facing life in prison.

Evans stated that upon finding out he would testify for the defense, he, too, was taken up to Carlson's office. It seemed to him as though everyone in the entire D.A.'s Office was there. Thompson threatened him loudly, saying that if he came downstairs and testified against his witness, he was going to file perjury charges against him. If that wasn't enough, he was going to throw the book at him when he took him to trial. Like Fomby, Evans said that Thompson ignored his request to have his attorney present while the D.A.'s staff was interrogating him about his possible testimony.

Jimmy was soft-spoken, polite, and articulate despite his shackles.

Ament called Jerry Wayne Sewell, who currently lived next door to Shyster Jackson. He said Jackson told him he wasn't going to testify at first because A. D. Clark III would not put anything in writing about the deal. Second, and more important, Jackson told Sewell that he couldn't testify because he didn't know anything about my case. *After all, I never confessed anything to him.*

"The defense would rest, Your Honor," Ament announced.

The jury soon was released until the next morning.

DAY SIX

Closing Arguments

The judge explained to the jury that we had reached the point in the trial where the attorneys would address them directly. Each side was allotted forty-five minutes to address the jury and sum up their case, with the state going first. The state would have a second forty-five minutes after the defense rested, which struck me as unfair. Dixon whispered for me to sit quietly, and no matter what Thompson said to the jury, to just remain expressionless. I nervously fidgeted.

Thompson began: "A young woman lies not far from this courtroom in her grave because of this young man's warped lust for blood and perversion. Robert Hoehn had no reason on God's earth to lie to you to suffer the embarrassment and humiliation of thirty years of his perversion in this courtroom. You see, that is what makes this young sexual psychopath tick." I listened with only half of my attention because I was worn down from the battering ram of Thompson's barrage. I only listened now for my attorneys' objections.

Thompson told the jury that the morning after the murder I had fled Tyler "like a bat out of hell" to Jacksonville, never planning on coming back. That was a blatant lie. He reminded jurors that Collard, an expert in the field of fingerprint technology, had testified that the fingerprints on the patio door were just six to twelve hours old.

"The evidence," Thompson said, "was that Kerry Max Cook left his fingerprints between the hours of 10:30 and 8:00 o'clock in the morning." He reiterated the "confession" to Shyster Jackson. He directed the jury to the testimony of the Dykes brothers, who stated I had pointed out the window of a woman I had watched undress. Thompson repeatedly labeled me a "perverted homosexual killer." He ranted and raved that I had mutilated Linda Jo Edwards in the same way the kids had mutilated the cat in the movie. Though the judge had sustained Ament's objections and chastised Thompson for trying to place this inflammatory cat-mutilation scene in the minds of the jury when it was not in evidence—Hoehn had testified we were out of the apartment when that part of the movie aired—here Thompson was rearguing it as fact in his closing jury arguments. Michael Thompson confidently strode back to the prosecution's table.

Larue Dixon slowly rose as if he was still figuring out his approach and walked the short distance to the wooden podium to face the jury. "I don't apologize and I cannot explain why people engage in homosexual activity. I don't know—that's beyond me." Dixon continued, "The doctor told you that the wounds to the vagina alone took five to ten minutes. The defendant was dropped off at 12:30, and at 12:30 Paula Rudolph comes home. Ladies and gentlemen, it doesn't make sense. By the state's *own* testimony, Kerry cannot have had anything to do with this crime. While the murder of Miss Edwards is an injustice, it will be a greater injustice to make a person answer for a murder they didn't commit. The fingerprints don't convict him. Paula Rudolph doesn't convict him. The homosexual testimony of Robert Hoehn doesn't convict him. Edward Scott Jackson's testimony certainly doesn't convict him. All four added up do not meet the burden of proof required to convict. I submit there has to be a doubt that Kerry Cook committed this crime, a substantial doubt based on reason— sound reason. The evidence offered by the state does just the opposite: I think it exonerates Kerry Max Cook. And I trust that you, by your verdict, will say 'not guilty.'" Dixon quietly sat down and ceded the remainder of his time to his partner.

John Ament methodically tackled the time element, using the testimony of Robert Hoehn and Paula Rudolph to demonstrate that I could not have committed the crime. There simply was not enough time from when Robert Hoehn dropped me in front of the Embarcadero apartment complex and the time Paula Rudolph came home and made her identification of the murderer. My attorneys closed with an impassioned plea, reiterating that the prosecution had not met its burden of proof for a finding of guilt beyond a reasonable doubt. An acquittal, they argued, was mandatory.

Thompson was fast to his feet and began to hammer down the nails that my attorneys had loosened. Michael C. Thompson, dressed in that chocolate-brown suit with the gold pinstripes, his thinning blond hair swept to the back of his head, screamed for a conviction, as if the louder he got, the more believable his words would become.

"For the better part of a day you saw the perverted mess on the wall of this courtroom. Kerry Max Cook went on this trip of sex and perversion. Kerry Max watched this scene of a young dark-haired lady masturbating [in the movie]. He said, 'Come on,

Robert, let's go walking down by the swimming pool.' Kerry Max, leading the way, went right by her bedroom window and said, 'Come on up here and look in here and see what I have seen before,'" Thompson belted out.

"He entered her apartment, found the butcher knife in her drawer, and then he started to work on her while she was still alive. You heard the pathologist, Dr. Virgil Victor Gonzalez, tell you those blows to the head didn't kill her; that she was still alive when he started in on her with the scissors, cutting her very mouth from her face, cutting her sexual organs apart so bad the doctor couldn't even identify them. Then when he was through with that, he rolled her over and stabbed her in the back just a few more times for good measure. In his own confession, a confession in a manner that only the man who committed the crime could know, Edward Scott Jackson, a jail inmate, told you how he told him he stabbed her, told him how he cut out her vagina. The defense attorney wants to talk about Edward Scott Jackson and the deals that he had with the State of Texas. That man has got no deal with the State of Texas. I will be yelling for his head right before this rail of justice just like I am on this killer. I don't make deals with killers.

"See, Kerry Max Cook's lust for blood and perversion does not stop with raw homosexual acts depicting knives, cats, and men on television. No, he has to act it out. He went on his final trip and he murdered that young woman in the most brutal and inhumane fashion you could ever hope to see. I would be remiss in my duty if I didn't show you every last grotesque detail of that because the killer sits right before you in this courtroom. It's time for twelve good people from this county to put this man on the scrap heap of humanity where he belongs. He has a warped perversion. He will not reason with you. He does not understand rehabilitation. You people have no right to even submit prison guards to the kind of risk that this man poses. I ask any of you, do you want to give Kerry Max Cook his butcher's knife back? There are no more grotesque electric chairs in Texas. It is a humane process now. It is a simple matter of giving him a shot and then he is gone from among us.

"Now you saw that young woman lying there and she had one of those nylon stockings that goes up her ankle. The other one was missing. That pervert needed something to take her sexual parts, her hair and her lip, out of that apartment on June 10, 1977, while he was ripping and tearing her body up. That was the most convenient thing. I wouldn't be surprised if he didn't eat those body parts—"

One of the female jurors leaned over and struggled to control the urge to retch. Another juror, a male on the far end, squinted his eyes and stared so hard at me I thought he was going to come over the banister at me. It seemed the entire courtroom, including the prosecutor's table, paused to take note of the jury's reaction to Thompson's comments. Dixon objected to inferences and arguments not supported by evidence, but Thompson, as always, won.

"I submit that is a reasonable deduction from the evidence, Your Honor," Thompson yelled defensively.

"Overruled," Phillips responded, allowing him to continue.

"What good and honest person would take them body parts with him? He committed aggravated rape on this young woman's body. He committed aggravated sexual abuse. There is no question that he committed theft; a woman does not wear one stocking around. He took her body parts in that stocking. That is theft. Period.

"Kerry Max Cook has demon cult friends out there," Thompson stated out of nowhere. He knew his audience perfectly. "If they want to play their little perverted games, if they want to engage in their homosexual acts in the process of watching mutilations, then let's take all the freaks and perverts of the world and let them know what we do with them in a court of justice—we take their lives! I got no real interest in chasing homosexuals. They keep me busy prosecuting rapers and robbers down here.

"He needs to die. Do you want to see your little girl's smile cut from her face with a pair of scissors or see her body tore apart?

"I have proved to you that this man is one of the worst perverted killers that this county has ever seen. I hope to God you take his life."

Finally he finished, "Thank you on behalf of that young lady that lies not far from this courtroom in her grave."

The silence was such that all I could hear was the faint humming of the courtroom air conditioner. The district attorney walked around to the state's table, pulled out his chair, and sat down. As the thick cushion of his padded chair deflated under his weight, he seemed to draw the breath of the audience with him in a collective sigh.

The judge then took over the proceedings. He informed the jury that both parties in the trial had concluded the case on the merits. A deputy took me from the defense table and escorted me downstairs to the basement of the courthouse. I was led into the jail kitchen service area and sat down at a long stainless steel table, where Ament and Dixon were waiting. Soon Michael Thompson, Tom Dunn, and other prosecutorial members sat down. Dixon made lighthearted conversation about anything and everything except the case. I never opened my mouth.

An hour later the deputy poked his head in the kitchen. He looked at Thompson first and said that the jury had reached a verdict. The deputy took me back up to the courtroom and left me at the defense table.

Necessity knows no law except to conquer.

The Verdict

"Mr. Foreman, has the jury arrived at a verdict in this cause?" the judge asked. It was 10:00 P.M., Wednesday, June 28. Underneath the defense table I was clenching my knees to distract myself from the mental anguish of not being able to keep my thoughts from racing through the worst-case "what if" scenarios.

"Yes, Your Honor."

"Mr. Foreman, I will read the verdict of the jury.

" 'We, the jury, find the defendant guilty of the offense of capital murder as charged in the indictment.' "

A joyous outburst erupted from the audience, but I was barely aware of it. I had become seized by panic.

Phillips thanked the jury for their diligence and dismissed them until 9:00 the following morning. The jurors silently left. Their eyes were glued to the cheap carpet on the floor. I stared into the sides of their faces, searching for an answer.

There will never be a reply.

The judge remanded me into the custody of the sheriff and ordered him to return me to jail. Minutes later I was back in the steel tomb, alone.

Jerry Sewell yelled out to me, "Kerry, is that you? You back? What happened? You get a verdict? Kerry?"

I couldn't will my mouth to move or speak, and I slowly sank to the coolness of the concrete floor. I awoke the next morning with my jaw pressed into the floor, sore and wet.

DAY SEVEN

Punishment Phase

At 9:00 A.M. the jury was brought back into the courtroom. Thompson had summoned twenty character witnesses, and one after the other, all were asked the same questions: "Are you acquainted with the reputation of the defendant, Kerry Max Cook, in the community where he resides for being a peaceable and law-abiding citizen?" And after a yes response, "Will you tell the court and jury whether that reputation is 'good' or 'bad'?" Texas Ranger Bob Prince, my former Jacksonville high school principal E. G. Osborne, Vice Principal Ray Darby, East Texas oil man Bill Bailey Jr., Cherokee County District Attorney Pete Menefee, among others, all testified that my character was bad.

Lieutenant Doug Collard was called back and introduced before the court and jury what is called a "Pen-Packet"—a record of arrests and convictions. Mine showed that on October 10, 1973, I was convicted of car theft and was sentenced to two years in the Texas Department of Corrections.

Dr. Grigson

Next Thompson called Dallas County Jail psychiatrist Dr. James P. Grigson, who I had illegally been taken to meet in January in order to determine my competency to stand trial.

"Your Honor," my attorneys objected, "we would object to calling Dr. Grigson based on the fact that any interview he may have had with the defendant was in violation of the laws of the State of Texas and a violation of the rights of the defendant on trial."

But the objection was predictably overruled, and Grigson now entered the courtroom and took the stand. He was a tall, thin man in a business suit, with white hair and glasses.

Thompson asked, "Were you able, based on this examination, to arrive at a diagnosis in the case of Kerry Max Cook?"

"Yes, I was," Grigson said. He began by saying that he had diagnosed me with an antisocial personality disorder, which he defined as an illness of an individual who is without a conscience. Individuals with this illness repeatedly break the rules. They know what they are doing, but they simply derive too much pleasure from doing it. They have no regard for other people's lives.

Thompson asked, "Doctor, were you able to form an opinion

as to whether or not there is a probability that Kerry Max Cook will commit continuing acts of violence constituting a continuous threat to society?"

"He certainly will." Grigson told the jury that I posed a severe danger even to fellow prisoners, if given a life sentence. "I feel absolutely 100 percent certain that he is and will continue to be a threat, no matter where he is."

Expert witnesses cost money, and I had no means to pay for a psychologist's time to help counteract Grigson's damning testimony—or that of the witness who followed.

Jerry Landrum

"Have you had an occasion to examine the defendant in your capacity as a psychologist?" Thompson asked Tyler psychologist Jerry Landrum.

Landrum replied, "Yes."

"Based on the facts of your examination, have you been able to arrive at a diagnosis of Kerry Max Cook?"

Landrum stated he found me to have an antisocial or sociopathic personality.

Thompson asked whether there was any treatment available for a psychopath as sick as me. Landrum responded by saying that there was no known cure or help for this disease, and he went on to say I would be a continuing threat to society in the world of prison if I were sentenced to life instead of death. Landrum stated under oath, "Even without any knowledge of conviction of this case I would have said that he would be a threat to society."

Ament asked Landrum where this diagnosis came from. Landrum claimed that he made these evaluations while he was in charge of Rusk State Hospital, where I had been sent when I was seventeen, to determine my competency to stand trial as an adult for car theft.

Ament inquired whether Landrum had any of these notes, evaluations, or reports with him to prove this. Landrum said he didn't have any supporting documentation. Further, he didn't recall any dates, just that it was within the last three years. Without being held to the actual hospital records, Landrum was free to tell the jury I was found to have a dangerous, sociopathic, antisocial personality disorder. I knew that the reason Landrum testified with no records and notes was that no such notations, files, or documentation of what he was telling them existed. If those records were before the jury, they would have shown that Landrum had diagnosed me as no more than a troubled youth, one in need of counseling. Reports from Rusk later obtained by the *Dallas Morning News* would clearly illustrate, contrary to his 1978 testimony before the jury, that while I may have been capable of venting my anger and taking out my frustrations against property—like kicking a store window—venting them against humans was extremely unlikely.

Thompson had the last words and asked Landrum what particular sexual deviation I suffered from. "I would say a pansexuality. In my opinion, there is the presence of a sexual deviation of such extreme that it would quite obviously not be concerned with the rights or feelings of other persons."

Thompson announced that the State of Texas rested its case.

"Who will the defendant have in this case?" the judge said.

I was shocked to hear the words "The defense rests, Your Honor." Ament and Dixon didn't want to open any more doors for the prosecution. I didn't know who or what they could call on my behalf—but I felt that the jury needed to hear from *someone* other than the charlatan doctors Grigson and Landrum.

PHILLIPS ANNOUNCED EACH side would have twenty-five minutes to make their final arguments.

Only twenty-five minutes to convince the jury not to sentence me to death?

Thompson practically begged the jury to kill me. He implored the jury to give justice to the mother and father of Linda Jo Edwards by delivering a verdict of death. Thompson called me "the very personification of evil." He reminded the jury that they had heard from two doctors who told them that I was the most dangerous of the dangerous. He reminded them that "the defense team in this case could have hired other experts to analyze Kerry Max Cook, but there was none."

I dropped my head and a strange resignation enveloped me. Experts were not in the five-hundred-dollar budget Ament and Dixon had to work under. That's all Mama and Daddy could afford to represent me. Through the fog, I sat and watched the familiar scene of Dixon standing to replace Thompson.

My attorney stared into the jury box and began talking with more passion than I had seen throughout the six-day trial. I think he was nearly as shocked as I was to be at this point.

"Go back and review the evidence that was admitted in this case. If there is something at all in your minds that tells you, maybe the pattern on those scissors do not belong to Kerry, or Kerry couldn't have possibly made it from the parking lot to apartment 169, and as the prosecution stated, spent fifteen to twenty minutes killing someone, then I think that is something you should strongly consider. And we didn't have any psychologist testify because they charge sixty-five dollars an hour. Kerry has no money."

The punishment phase was over.

The judge went over three "special issues" that the jury had to consider in their deliberations. How these three questions were answered would determine whether I lived or died. A unanimous yes answer would mean an automatic death sentence.

The three questions developed by the Texas Legislature were:

(1) Whether the conduct of the defendant that caused the death of the deceased was committed deliberately and with

the reasonable expectation that the death of the deceased or another would result;

(2) Whether there is a probability that the Defendant would commit criminal acts of violence that would constitute a continuing threat to society;

(3) If raised by evidence, whether the conduct of the Defendant in killing the deceased was unreasonable in response to the provocation, if any, by the deceased.

The jury was excused for their deliberations, but the court didn't stand in recess for long.

"GENTLEMEN, THE JURY has reached a verdict. Sheriff, if you will, bring the jury in please," Judge Glenn S. Phillips announced. It was standing room only in the small East Texas courtroom.

I searched the face of a female juror, seated on the end, who had unwittingly offered me reassurance at times during the trial by an occasional smile in my direction. She wouldn't look at me now. I turned my head to the back of the courtroom and saw Mama, Doyle Wayne, and Daddy. I saw their fear. I closed my eyes and turned back around.

The judge took control of the courtroom. "Mr. Foreman, has the jury arrived at a verdict through answers to the special issues submitted to you?"

The foreman of the jury, Charles Reasonover, looked directly at the judge.

"Yes, Your Honor. We have."

The judge accepted the slip of paper from the bailiff.

"Mr. Cook, you will rise."

I stood on wobbly legs, obeying the judge's command.

"Kerry Max Cook, the jury composed of twelve good and lawful men and women have on June 28, 1978, unanimously found you guilty of the offense of capital murder. It is now the judgment of this court that you are guilty of the offense of capital murder as charged in the indictment and your punishment is assessed at death to be carried out by lethal injection as provided by the laws of the State of Texas.

"You are hereby remanded to the custody to the Texas Department of Corrections until such time you are put to death. Sheriff, remove the defendant from the courtroom."

The judge's wooden gavel slammed down, its sound ricocheting like a gunshot. Two armed sheriff's deputies immediately claimed me from my defense attorneys, as my Mama, Daddy, and Doyle Wayne tried to reach over the courtroom rail to touch me.

"You belong to the state now, boy," a uniformed voice growled into my right ear. My arms were pulled behind me and handcuffs slammed down on my wrists to confirm it. As the deputies led me through the double wooden doors of the courtroom, I felt someone touch me. Quickly, I looked around—it was the hand of Doyle Wayne. For a split second, I saw him picking me up after I had fallen along a cobblestone road in Germany. But the deputies were quickly carrying me away, and my last memory of the courtroom was of Doyle Wayne's face, smeared with tears.

AS THE COURTROOM doors swung open, I was bathed in the hot lights of the media—television crews, newspaper reporters, and photographers surrounded me and the officers. I could *smell* the heat from the burning lamps.

"Kerry, why did you rape and murder Linda Jo Edwards? Can you tell us now that you have been convicted?" one reporter from a local ABC affiliate shouted. Another yelled as the boom nearly hit me in the head, "Tell us why you did it!" It was a feeding frenzy.

"I am innocent. I have been framed. But one day I'll prove I didn't do it. If it takes me ten years, or twenty years, I'll prove I didn't do it," I said as a deputy whisked me away.

I looked behind me just in time to see my mama coming

through the courtroom doors, shielding her face from the cameras, with a look of shame and mortification. No matter how innocent I was, this was a public disgrace she would never allow me to overcome. In that moment I lost my mama forever.

The deputies pulled me along through the halls until, with a final tug, I was thrown back into my cell.

"Strip, Cook. Need all of your clothes," the deputy barked. "We wouldn't want you trying to hang yourself before you get that needle put in."

The solid steel door slammed shut.

5

WELCOME TO DEATH ROW

On July 18, 1978, the jingle jangle of the brass keys made its way toward that door for the last time. I had left my tomb only once since the jury convicted and sentenced me to death nineteen days earlier—that was to briefly hug and kiss Mama, Daddy, and Doyle Wayne good-bye before they sent me away to death row.

The heat was stifling. Though the air outside my door wasn't much better, at least it circulated and hit me a moment after my door was opened. God, it felt good.

"It's that time, Cook. Time for you to go *home*," one of the two deputies said as I squinted and let the fresh air wash over the sores that speckled my roasted body.

"You can't take your personal belongings. Here, sign this piece of paper. It authorizes us to release them to whoever you want to leave them to."

As I looked at the piece of paper, I was called back to the night I was arrested. It seemed a century ago—in a world I no longer belonged to. My black wallet with my driver's license was listed. The number 8124998 popped into my head—I always had a near-photographic memory. Inside it was a small blue-and-white Social Security card, which I applied for during study hall when I was fourteen years old in Killeen; I had felt so proud of my first adult piece of identification that I got it laminated. There was also the Ford key ring for my apartment on Fifth Street in Port Arthur, and a thick black comb I used to deal with the unruly long brown hair I grew to make up for all of those years my daddy made Doyle Wayne and me wear crew cuts.

I signed it all away to my parents, and I was left with nothing to my name, save a death sentence for a rape and murder that I had not committed.

The officer ordered me to step into the narrow corridor. An assortment of rusty chains and manacles awaited me. As did Shyster Jackson, who had his face pressed against the bars of his cell. I dropped my eyes to my ankles where the deputy was fitting leg irons around my right leg.

"Hey, man. I'm sorry—*I had* to do it. I was gonna get life in prison if I didn't," Shyster Jackson said in the same well-modulated voice he used on the witness stand.

I looked up just as the deputy was turning his Smith & Wesson key inside the last hole. "It's God you need to get right with," I said. Tears burned my face. "I forgive you, Shyster, for what you did to me. Only you, me, God, A. D. Clark, and Thompson know you lied."

Somber and polite without any display of anger, my demeanor rattled him. He replied, "Man, once I get my deal and get out, I'll tell the world what really happened. Just wait, you'll see!"

While the deputies went about their business of fastening all their steel to my body, I mumbled, "Whatever, Shyster." He didn't sound as convincing as he did three weeks earlier.

A wide leather belt went around my waist; in its center was a thick metal loop through which the handcuffs were inserted, pinning my arms against my side. The leg irons were made snug around my ankles. "Let's go, Cook. This way," the lead deputy commanded as he pulled me forward.

As I baby-stepped my way toward the jail service elevator, Shyster yelled to me, "One day I'll tell the truth and you're not gonna believe what they—" Shyster's words were drowned out and then cut off completely by the steel elevator doors. A minute later, the deputy pulled me into the backseat of a police car purring quietly in the basement garage.

THE RADIO PLAYED faintly up front. It took three hours to drive to the prison diagnostics unit just outside of Huntsville. Regular prisoners were sent there before they were assigned to their respective prison "farms," as they were called, within the system. The process normally took four to six weeks. With a death-row prisoner, it took less than an hour.

As I entered the pale green double doors of the diagnostics unit, a melting pot of nude male bodies were awaiting processing. I stared into the eyes of the two deputies who had driven me there. *Please don't leave me,* I pleaded with my eyes as they began to remove the manacles, then turned to leave. I watched as the bright summer sun bathed them as they passed through the doors. Then they were gone.

I was told to remove anything I didn't come into the world with. Then I was marched to a wooden stool, a prisoner shaved my head, then another guard pointed to the green-tiled shower stall. As I stepped in, cold water stung me hard in the face. I picked up a green bar of soap with a Texas State seal stamped into the center.

I had barely begun to apply it to my body when the water was shut off and the guard barked, "Time's up. Get out."

Seconds later a prisoner instructed, "Raise both of your arms

straight up into the air." I was sprayed from a pumped canister—
the same kind used by the Orkin Man. "Lift up your nuts." I
complied and was sprayed there, too. I was given a pair of "mark-
outs," a white prison uniform with someone else's name blackened out that was used for transitioning prisoners. The shirt was
too small and the pants were so big they kept falling down. A
guard dropped a pair of white cloth "slides" at my feet. Everyone
within the prison system knew a convict in those cloth slides was
"a walking dead man." All other prisoners were issued sturdy,
state-made black shoes.

Back in handcuffs, I was escorted upstairs to a little room,
where I was brought to the front of the line and told to strip naked
again. A Texas Department of Corrections (TDC) employee examined every square inch of my body for identifying marks like
scars or tattoos. I do have one tattoo, a cross with the word *Mama*
in the center, at the top of my left arm, a souvenir from my time
in the Cherokee County Jail in 1973.

I was given another prison number—# 600. This meant I was
the six hundredth person in the state of Texas to be sentenced to
death. No one would ever have this number again. It was mine—
and the grave I was to be sealed in—forever.

A WHITE FORD prison van waited for me. Two guards sat up
front; the guard occupying the passenger seat cradled a shotgun.
I heard the faint sound of Debbie Boone singing "You Light Up
My Life" as the vehicle started up and merged on to the highway.
Chained in the back, I watched the outside streak by for perhaps
the last time.

It was almost nine miles to the Ellis Unit. As the van made its
way to a back gate that was topped with hurricane fencing, a
bucket was lowered from a tall guard tower that loomed over the
entire prison. The driver and his partner proceeded to place their

standard-issue .357 Magnum pistols into the bucket along with two shotguns. The bucket was raised and secured in the guard tower, and the chain-link fence topped with razor wire opened like a gigantic mechanical mouth, then closed automatically behind us after we drove through. Another hurricane fence loomed in front.

A tall, lanky man entered through the forward gate. "Let's go," Assistant Warden Lightsey said as the van turned off.

We walked through the second gate and entered a large, open courtyard. The smell of laundry was pervasive. He tapped three times on a green door with a small window and a crisply uniformed black prisoner, a trusty, looked out, saw the warden, and quickly opened the door. It was the bathhouse. Walking past vacant, wet shower stalls, we came to an identical green door, where the warden gave a tap and another face peeked through the window and opened the door to reveal a long hallway. Two brightly painted yellow lines divided the floor into three lanes.

We walked straight down the center of the hallway. The general-population prisoners walked along the two outside lanes. They all seemed to be watching me. I later learned that the center lane was reserved for death row.

I sensed that Warden Lightsey knew something of my case. He had few words for me as we walked down the hall to the farthest wing, J-23. "Keep your mouth shut and your nose clean and you won't have any problems here, despite being so young. Don't accept anything from anyone," the tall warden said.

With that we entered death row.

"D.R., Cook, execution number 600. Add him to the head count," he told the guard inside the wing.

Inside the locked doorway of J-23, to my immediate left, was the enclosed "picket," where the cellblock's doors were opened and closed. It housed a large chrome wheel with a fist-size metal knob that was used to open or close a cell door. A wooden board hung inside, and on it were three columns, with worn white paper tags running diagonally—on them were the name and the execution number of the prisoner occupying the cell.

The guard promptly wrote my last name and number on a piece of yellow cardboard paper, slid it in an empty slot, number 17.

Warden Lightsey ordered me to remove all of my clothes. "Open your mouth, lift up your tongue, raise your arms and bend over, and then lift up the bottom of your feet," he commanded, to make certain I didn't have anything hidden in places the sun couldn't shine—not that the sun would be shining on me anytime soon. Then he walked me down the long row. Eerily, by the first cell was an orange metal chair. *Oh my God—it's the electric chair,* I yelped to myself. As we passed by the other cells, I heard lewd comments and a few whistling catcalls.

"Pretty ass," one phantom voice whispered.

When we got to number 17, Lightsey shouted down the row to the picket—"Roll it." It squeaked slowly open and I stepped in and faced the wall as I was ordered—"Close it!" The door closed and the warden told me to back up to the bars so he could remove the handcuffs. He was gone by the time I turned around.

Three walls made up my five-foot-by-nine-inch living space. There were nothing but dirty yellow concrete steel bars, and a porcelain toilet, tiny sink, and the grubby canvas-covered mattress that looked ancient and smelled strongly of mold. There was no light fixture in the cell. I noticed a grilled vent at the back of the cell. Looking through it, I saw the backside of the grill in the opposite cell. On the other side a body lay sleeping on a metal bunk like mine.

I tapped on the wall to my left and called out, "Excuse me, anyone there? Hello? How do I get sheets and a pillow?"

"Shoo! Go away, I'm busy," a hostile voice shot back.

I sat down on the dirty mattress and assessed my surroundings. The inventory took the better part of four seconds.

"What is it you want? I'm meditating," a voice from the other side of me barked after a few minutes.

"Hi! My name is Kerry. I just got here. How do I get sheets and a pillow? It's pretty nasty."

"This isn't the Holiday Inn, man. See the concierge!" a voice above yelled down.

"Ignore the idiots. The name's Byrd. Jerry Joe Byrd."

Another voice from somewhere above me said, "And I'm Alton Byrd, no relation. I'm in 19 cell just above you."

"God, I am just glad I won't have to be here too long," I replied.

"Oh, yeah? Where you going?" Jerry Joe Byrd said mirthlessly.

"I got railroaded—I'm innocent. I'm gonna be getting out of here soon. They violated the Speedy Trial Act by not trying me in 120 days. Heck, my lawyers had to file a second one, to remind them to act on the first. My lawyers said it's merely a question of filing my brief and getting the ruling from the Texas Court of Criminal Appeals in Austin. Then it's adios, amigos!" I said with confidence.

The wing of fifty or so prisoners erupted in laughter.

Jerry continued, "You're gonna find out the hard way it's not about your guilt or innocence any longer, dude. The whole process from this moment on is about whether you were given a fair trial. The burden of proof is completely on you now—that's the legal standard."

"Then I'm in much better shape than I thought because I know my 'trial' was a sham. It was anything *but* fair."

"Are you deaf?" Jerry said in an almost fatherly way. "I didn't say the burden of knowledge was on you; I said the burden of *proof.* Were you listening to anything I just told you? Knowing in the abstract and proving in the material are two different things. You'll come to learn that."

BEGINNING IN 1928, Texas death row was located in a facility known as Walls in downtown Huntsville. It also was the prison medical facility, and the designated prerelease center for the entire prison system. Family members anxiously waited outside for their newly released loved one to appear, glowing with their freedom and a prison check for one hundred dollars in hand. In 1965 death row was moved down the road ten miles to the newly built Ellis Unit, though the execution chamber was kept at Walls.

Those facing execution remained at the Ellis Unit until the United States Supreme Court declared the death penalty "cruel and unusual punishment" on June 29, 1972. The Court ruled in *Furman v. Georgia,* holding that the determination of who got the death penalty as opposed to life imprisonment was so "capricious" and "freakish" that it was comparable to "winning the lottery" or "being struck by lightning." When the decision was rendered, there were forty-five men on death row in Texas. The newly elected governor, Dolph Briscoe, commuted their sentences to life imprisonment and death row was empty by March 1973.

By January 1974, however, Texas had already amended its penal code to resume capital punishment. John Devries, execution number 507, was the first person sentenced to death under the new statute—he arrived on death row in the winter of 1974, and on July 1, 1974, he hung himself with bedsheets. Texas continued to *sentence* people to death under its new statute but needed another Supreme Court decision before it would be allowed to *execute* them. That revitalizing breath blew down from Washington on July 2, 1976, when the Court in *Gregg v. Georgia* relegalized the use of the death penalty in America by a 7–2 vote.

Gary Gilmore was the first person put to death post-*Gregg*. He dropped his appeal and Utah responded by blindfolding him, pinning a red heart over his own, and shooting him to death by firing squad. The Texas Legislature amended its death penalty statute again in 1977, switching from death by electrocution to killing by asphyxiation, or to use the commonly accepted euphemism, "lethal injection." The electric chair dubbed "Ol' Sparky" was finally retired with 361 deaths to its name.

Although the machinery of the Texas prison system had a model public and political appearance, behind the walls there was nothing smooth about the harsh, archaic, savage world of this penitentiary system. One lifer once called it "a gladiator school" for its sheer brutality.

I entered this theater in 1978, during the most turbulent, volatile era of crime and punishment in Texas.

In fact, in 1980, federal judge William Wayne Justice agreed with the evidence brought forth in a lawsuit by David Ruiz, a TDC inmate who claimed that serving time in the Texas prison system amounted to "cruel and unusual punishment," in violation of the Eighth Amendment. In his historic ruling, Judge Justice found innumerable fundamental violations that were so systematic and pervasive that it was impossible to fully "convey the pernicious conditions and the pain and degradation which ordinary inmates suffer within the TDC prison walls." Despite the passage of new laws aimed at reducing the state's prison population, by the mid-1980s Texas's prisons were again "among the most dangerous in the country, with gang violence and fatal stabbings routine," the Associated Press later reported.

Most dangerous of all was overcrowding and the use of other inmates as "guards," called "building tenders," a practice by which the prison administration handpicked prisoners—sometimes the worst of the worst, including murderers and rapists—and made them supervisors over the rest of the inmates. These inmate guards were given titles like "turnkey" and "trusty." In some instances, these building tenders had more authority than a prison captain. The very people whom society had sent away for being too incorrigible and dangerous to walk the streets became the law in the prison system, armed with knives, shards of glass, chemicals, eating utensils, and, most disastrously of all, power.

Those were the risks of doing time in the Texas prison system and on death row in the summer of 1978. Officials did not oversee the daily operation of the prison system; the inmate guards did. In many ways it was as brutal and primitive as the Turkish prison system portrayed in *Midnight Express,* which horrified audiences the same year.

ON THAT FIRST night on death row, my mind replayed courtroom scenes and the last seconds with my family. Meanwhile, there was noise all around me. Conversations were yelled between cells; televisions blared in the hallway; and the poorly tuned radios that were mounted to the wall of each cell each rang out shrilly as all three radio stations—Magic 102, KLOL, or WPAP, Dallas—blared and combined as one big noise.

Lights went off at 10:00 P.M. No talking was permitted after "rack-up." This rule did not apply to, nor was it enforceable with, the mentally ill. Through the shadows, screams and shouts found me. I heard a crashing noise, and then an unknown voice calling through the darkness, "Goddamn rats." As crippling as my isolation was in the side cell in Smith County Jail, I missed the security it provided. There, hope was easier to come by—Doyle Wayne and my mama and daddy were right down the road in Jacksonville. Now I felt as if I had been taken off to Hades.

I retrieved the image of my mama shielding her face from the media as she exited the courtroom after the verdict. *Oh, Mama. Just wait; everyone is going to know what they did to me—to us—and how they did it. Please don't give up and leave me here,* I cried to myself.

"You fuckin' pussy—shut the fuck up!" a voice screamed out.

Another one followed. "Baby want Mama's tit? You fuckin' punk, I'm gonna get some of that ass tomorrow and make you my bitch."

I grabbed the largest block of courage I could find and plugged the hole my emotions poured from. I held my breath to minimize any sound, to avoid drawing any more attention to myself. *How am I ever going to make it through this? How am I going to be able to show the world that I am innocent while I am in this place?*

At 3:30 A.M., the lights returned. My next-door neighbor, Billy Hughes, pounded on the wall separating our two cells to make sure I was awake for breakfast. "If you aren't up, they pass you by. You snooze you lose," he said in a friendly tone. With what looked like a rolled-up newspaper, an arm reached out and tapped a naked lightbulb in front of his cell.

"Don't worry—I'm awake," I replied as quietly as I could.

A black man in a white uniform like mine pushed a metal tray underneath the door. The biscuits, or "cat heads" as Billy called them, were knocked off, not making the narrow clearance between the floor and the lip of the cell door. Watered-down molasses splashed from my metal tray as I picked them up.

"Here," Billy said, pushing a dark brown plastic cup through his bars. "You can have this. It'll be awhile before you can get your family to put some money on your books so you can make commissary. You'll need something to drink out of until then." Billy explained that I could spend up to thirty dollars every two weeks if my family deposited money in an Inmate Trust Fund in Huntsville.

"I used to love going to the military commissary with my mama and daddy overseas."

"You're not going anywhere here. They drop commissary off in front of your cell."

The breakfast process took about an hour, then the lights went out again and the sounds of sleep returned. Sometime later a guard passed my cell with a flashlight. On his way back I stopped him and asked the time.

"It's 6:00 A.M., shift change. Don't ever stop an officer at count time," he grumbled.

At around 8:00 A.M., a burst of light caught my eye. I pressed my face against the steel bars and saw that a TV mounted to the wall had come on down the row. At 9:45, I heard the creaking wheels of the food cart being pushed back into J-23.

I tapped on Billy's wall. "Billy, is this like a midmorning snack?"

Billy snorted. "Yeah, right. You'd better eat it because you won't see anything else until 3:30 P.M.—this is lunch!"

A voice hollered, "Chow time 23!" The bland food—no salt or pepper, no spice of any kind—was shoved underneath my door a second time. The green beans were so gritty, they tasted like they had sand in them, and the pork chop looked like it still had fur attached. Disgusted, I tossed it back on the tray. The drink, a version of iced tea, stank like rotten eggs.

Like most of the other prison farms, Ellis Unit grew its own food and raised its own livestock. Even the water was treated and run by the prisoners right on the grounds. The smell of sulfur in the water system was gagging. I couldn't get it down, even when holding my nose. I finally got so thirsty I had no other choice.

Staring down at my silver tray of cold food, I heard the clanking of metal on metal as the trusties collected and stacked the trays while the voices of prisoners echoed up and down the halls. Through the fog of noise, a sound caught my attention.

"Cook?"

"Yes? Are you talking to me?"

A harsh voice responded, "Did you really cut out and eat that girl's pussy like they said you did on TV?"

I immediately yelled back, "What the hell are you talking about?"

The voice shouted back, "Yeah, man, it was you. You cut up that girl, raped, and killed her. You're a homo, man—a faggot," a man named Huff told me.

Before I could respond, another voice chimed in. "That's him down there? That's the one that's been in the papers from Tyler?"

Voices began to pour out of the cells. I stood by the bars as the prisoners yelled back and forth to me.

"Who is he? Is that the new guy Huff said got caught with the girl's fingers in his back pocket?"

"The new guy; just got here yesterday—that's him."

"What cell's he in?"

The threats began. "We're gonna get that bitch, man. You're a faggot out there killing women. Now you're gonna be my bitch in here."

Finally, I cracked. Shaking the bars, I screamed, "You're a liar! Huff's a liar! I didn't do any of that! It's all a lie!" At that point, Huff reached my cell. He was picking up breakfast trays, one of his duties as a trusty. He seemed almost pleased as he leaned over to pick up the tray.

He casually shrugged his shoulder. "Hey, Cook, it's just what I read—just what I read."

"Well," I responded, "it's a lie!"

Huff's muscles tightened as he glared at me and yelled, "No, they didn't lie, man. You're a rapin', killin' faggot and you know it. You killed that girl and ate her pussy." He began to laugh.

Blood rushed to my face, and my body trembled with frustration and disbelief. It all seemed like a giant blur until I heard a voice demanding, "What the hell is going on here?" I looked through the bars to see an obese man with a crew cut, whose name tag read Major Steele. The cellblock went quiet and I knew in that moment that Major Steele commanded respect.

I pointed to Huff. "That guy is lying—telling people I was arrested with a girl's vagina in my back pocket and—"

"Get the fuck outta here, Huff!" Steele shouted as he lifted his stubby leg and kicked Huff off in the ass. Huff's face turned beet red for a moment, and then he sauntered down the cellblock, rubbing his backside.

When "Big Jelly" Steele left, the onslaught resumed.

"He's not just a dick-eating faggot, he's a fucking *snitch*!"

Horror-struck, I faced the inside of my cell and stifled a scream.

Dinner came at 3:30 P.M. A tray of food slammed underneath the lip of the door. It was Huff again. He seethed. "Bitch, I'm gonna get you for snitching on me with Big Jelly. You're gonna pay, bitch!" he growled as I backed away from the door.

"Look, just leave me alone. I don't even know you. What is your deal, anyway?"

"I know you're a punk and now that you got to death row you are just trying to 'stud up.' I got a letter from a homeboy in the Smith County Jail and he told me he got some of your pussy." The voices rained down all around me with insults and threats. Huff smiled as he turned and walked off.

Soon *Days of Our Lives* replaced the verbal attacks and I heard Billy, barely audible, whispering something to me. "Just come over here to the bars. I don't want anyone hearing me talking," he said. I smashed my ear against the bars. "I'm not trying to tell you how to run your business, man, but I wouldn't say anything more to Huff. You seem okay—just young. Huff, he's just instigating. You can't win," he whispered.

"Billy, none of what Huff said is true. They accused me of those things, but I am not guilty—"

"Everybody says that in here. That's for you and your lawyer. But now you live by the cardinal rules of prison, however, and if you want respect, then you have to kill Huff or your life in here will be a living hell—*if* you even live long enough to experience that hell. Once you lose your respect, it is a free-for-all. Everyone will take whatever they want, when they want it. You will be forced to keep your asshole greased and your mouth open and live as a punk for protection. And if you snitch for getting punked out, you're dead. You just got here and already you're digging a pretty deep hole. Ignore Huff before it is too late. That's just my advice."

In prison vernacular, once a person is raped, or "turned out," as the phrase goes, that person is forever stripped of his masculine identity. A metamorphosis of enforced feminization and sexual enslavement takes place until the person either kills himself—as some did—or just accepts it and finds ways to live with it, rationalizing that one day he will get out. In the meantime, he is obligated to trade in the prison-issued boxer shorts for a pair of panties, answer to a girl's name, and shave all his body hair off. A punk has absolutely no rights—he is the sole property of his owner. Everything that he is and everything that he owns belongs to his prison "daddy" in exchange for protection. It is a fate worse than death. Just a piece of human meat for everyone to take a bite.

There is only one way to escape: stab—and preferably kill—the person who punked you out. This is a unique and horrific fact of prison life. The moment another person even uses the term "punk" toward you or questions your manhood, the bizarre world of prison justice takes over—you either must attempt to kill him or live as a sexual slave according to the whims of dark and twisted men. The point is to demonstrate to the prison hierarchy that you are prepared to keep your respect at all cost.

I didn't want any part of that world. It was for people who had decided this was the rest of their life. *Me, I am innocent and I am getting out of there*, I thought to myself.

"Don't worry, Billy. I'm not going to be here long enough to deal with all of this crap. He can call me whatever he wants to because before too long, he will be callin' me long distance," I said.

I heard Billy sigh. "In here, Cook, the 'punk' word will get you killed. Do like I do—just ignore all the games and the shit people do in here and just keep to yourself."

"**GET READY FOR** recreation, J-23!" a voice boomed.

The walls of the cell had acted like a vise, gripping and mentally torturing me. Despite the threats and my growing concerns about other prisoners, many of whom I had not even seen yet, I decided to leave my cell. The doors squeaked opened and we all filed one by one into the dayroom. The guard locked a solid steel door behind us. I was alone with the death-row population.

When I turned around, four or five prisoners were facing me. I knew something bad was about to happen. I had never experienced so much fear. "Doyle Wayne," I whispered under my breath. One door led to a small outside recreation cage. It was opened. I turned my eyes and made my way the short distance through it. There were two short, old concrete benches to sit on. Outside, the ground was damp.

A hulking black man walked up to me. The name stenciled onto his left breast pocket read "Demouchette." "Bitch, you a pretty mothafucka just like they said." His hand moved to the fabric in front of his crotch, rubbing in circular motion. His eyes looked determined, like a wolf's. The muscles throughout my body tightened.

"Look, I don't want any problems. Just leave me alone—" He jerked what appeared to be a steel shard wrapped with dirty white tape at the base.

"Take off your clothes." The words hung in the air for a few seconds before my brain made sense of them. I hesitated nervously.

"What it's gonna be, bitch—blood on my knife or shit on my dick?"

I wrestled to remain standing and my legs were trembling. I wondered if they could see that. I needed them not to see that.

"You don't have to hurt me—just please don't—" I said.

"Bitch, I'm not gonna tell you again: Come out of them clothes."

Out of the corner of my eye, I saw two other prisoners looking on. "Yeah. Let's see that pretty ass. C'mon, make her take her clothes off."

I looked around frantically, searching for a single sympathetic face, just one to tell me he would help me. But there was no one. No guards. No windows to leap through. No door to bolt to. I pressed my eyelids together as tight as I could. I unfastened my pants, pulled them down, and tried to displace myself from reality.

"All of it, bitch—get naked," the voice growled.

With my eyes tightly closed, I removed all of my clothes until I stood nude. I wanted to live to be with my brother again. I shut down all other thoughts and brought him to the center of my mind. I would do anything to be with Doyle Wayne again. *Anything.*

The prisoner pushed the jagged blade of the knife against my stomach. "Now, turn around and lean over and spread your legs wide apart."

A lightning bolt of white-hot pain shot to my brain as he forced his penis inside me. His thick arm held me in a bear hold as the pain moved throughout my body. I screamed into his callused hand that hurriedly clasped over my mouth—he pushed harder inside me.

In a raspy voice, dense with nicotine, "Bitch, you know you like it. Now, just be still or the next thing I put in you won't be my dick. . . ." Somewhere in the distance his moaning entered my head and he was done. "You've got some good pussy. You're my bitch now, Cindy. That's what I'll call you. That and 'Good Pussy.' That'll be your name." He used his knife to carve both names into the flanks of my backside. I felt skin tear, but I now was immune to pain. Blood washed over my shaking legs. Afterward he slammed me to the wall. "Bitch, if you snitch on me like you did Huff, I'll kill you."

He made me wash the blood away with dirt.

Even before I could limp back to my cell, the word was out that Huff was right—I was a punk. I had become trapped in one of the world's dark corners. I *had* to find another way out, if I was ever going to see Doyle Wayne, my mama, and my daddy again. Many people know that rape is a routine aspect of prison life, but most men take the position that it couldn't happen to a "real man," or say "I would have made them kill me first." The reality is that when you have two or more prisoners coming at you with a rusty steel shank, these rationalizations go out the window.

This single episode would haunt me all the remaining days of my prison life. I could run but never hide from it. I was desperate to find another way out.

DAYS LATER, THE guard made his usual morning rounds, passing out state-issued razors for mandatory shaving. We were not allowed to have the razor long, five minutes at most, so I had to hurry. Death row was suffocating me. I had to remove myself from it somehow—without snitching.

I swiftly slipped the blade out of the razor, set it back between the bars, and then lay down on the bed and covered up, as if to make it appear I had shaved quickly and then went right back to sleep. I hoped the guard wasn't paying close attention and didn't discover the blade was gone. I heard the clank of the metal razor hitting the bottom of the steel tray as the guard passed my cell. *It worked.*

I took a deep breath, closed my eyes, and forced a picture of Doyle Wayne and my mama and daddy to the front of my head. *On Christmas in 1969 I got the ten-speed bicycle I had so badly wanted, and we were all holding one another by the Christmas tree in Neu-Ulm, Germany.* I put the icy blade to my wrist. Once again, pain splashed throughout my body and fear filled my mind—but I *had* to get out of this environment. I waited endlessly for a guard to make his routine head count.

Finally, a flashlight beam came through my bars. The guard bolted from my cell, yelling as he ran.

The door rolled open and the enormity of Big Jelly's bulk towered over me. He spoke in a gentle voice: "Let me see your arm."

I stuck it out to him.

"Let's go, Cook," Major Steele said flatly.

I was taken across the hallway to the clinic, where a prisoner quickly tended to my wrist.

"What's this about, Cook?" Major Steele asked in a nonthreatening tone.

I shook my head from side to side. "I don't want to talk about it."

WHEN I RETURNED from the clinic, I was moved to the first cell on the row so the wing officer could keep an eye on me. I collapsed on my bed, exhausted. The metal wall speaker spit out "Dreamboat Annie," by Heart.

"Who'd they just put in that first cell down there?" a voice said.

"That fuckin' punk Cook. He cut himself, I think."

Big Jelly placed me on "suicide precaution." And I tried to understand how this had happened. Before entering death row, I would never have considered cutting myself, but the hopelessness in this place and the constant abuse had created a new reality— surreal as it was. The rules and assumptions that govern outside life didn't fit there. Whenever possible I withdrew from the walls of death row and replayed how I got there. Again and again I thought about my farcical trial and fumed about how the justice system had ground me up and spat me out on death row, to die. Somehow, I had to understand how I went from being Kerry Cook to execution number 600.

Around 3:30 the next morning, an old metal cart stopped in front of my cell; its wheels announced its arrival long before it appeared. Two dingy tomes were slid into the bars. There was no light fixture in my cell, just three concrete walls and the dingy steel bars that made up the front of my cell. Twenty feet beyond these bars was a window made of opaque shower glass. But it was broken, a corner of the pane gone, and through the missing shard, soft, yellow moonlight stole into the corner of my cell. I read by this ray of light until it was replaced by sunlight.

My very first request to the Inmate Law Library was simply "A law book, please." I ordered it repeatedly until I had read it from cover to cover. I had no idea what I was looking for, but I knew that I had to start to understand the system that had put me there. I had to show the rest of the world I was there and how I came to be "Cook, Ex: #600." If I didn't, I was going to Joe Byrd's penitentiary cemetery nicknamed "Peckerwood Hill," where they buried executed prisoners. The only thing I would leave behind would be a death certificate that read "Cause of Death: State Homicide."

"COOK, YOU GOT a visit. Let's go," I heard a guard call out in mid-October.

It's my mama and daddy! I just know it. I was so excited I was hobbling all over the floor of my small cell trying to shove a leg in my pants. Each weekday, Monday through Friday, I had hoped and waited for a visit. The months had crept by without any word from my family.

My cell door rolled open. I stepped out and began the journey to the visitation room. I hadn't seen this long hallway since Assistant Warden Lightsey first brought me to J-23. Accustomed to a small cell, my eyes hurt as I took in the length of it. We entered the Ellis Unit Visitation Room, and I walked past a few of the other prisoners until I stopped and saw the eyes of my parents on the other side of the glass. I pressed my hand against the glass to meet my mama's.

"Mama! Daddy! I am so happy you're here!"

As we began to talk Daddy left to buy me a Coke, a bag of chips, and a Snickers bar from the commissary window. With the guard's permission, he passed my goodies through a small trapdoor. I popped open the soda and felt the bubbles tickle my nose and burn my throat. In an instant, a fountain of memories spilled into my head.

My daddy told me that Michael Thompson had committed suicide two days earlier at his sister's house in Tyler. He stepped into her closet, bit down on the barrel of a shotgun, and pulled the trigger. It didn't make sense: Thompson had secured the most sensational murder conviction in East Texas history—mine—and he celebrated by killing himself? I knew there had to be more to the story.

"Time is up, Cook." The guard was poking me in the arm.

My mama began crying and I begged her to stop—I didn't want to go back to my cell with that as my last image. For an instant, as they slipped from sight, I wanted to break through the glass and run after them. But I knew I was in the kind of trouble they couldn't save me from. I was going to have to rescue myself this time.

IN NOVEMBER I got my first visit from Doyle Wayne. We joked and talked about everything except the fact that I was on death row. We talked a lot about the latest music—the rock group Styx, the Cars, and Stevie Wonder's *Songs in the Key of Life*. I wiped tears away when the dreaded tap came.

"Time to go, Cook."

"*Wa go ken san,*" Doyle Wayne said as he placed his hand against the glass. "Promise me you won't ever give up, Kerry. *Swear* that to me."

I remembered the Japanese friend we had in Kaiserslautern, Germany, who used to say that to us when we were exploring the countryside, hot, tired, and exhausted, faced with quitting and having to turn back around. Translated, it meant "Never give up."

"*Wa go ken san,* Doyle Wayne," I said as I met his hand and the guard pulled me away from the glass to go.

———

ONE MORNING AFTER the holidays I was rousted from sleep and told to pack my stuff. I was being moved up to three row three cell. The death row was already a furnace, but the upper levels were unbearable. On top of that I was next door to a leaking shower stall. But there was a fluorescent light overhead in front of my cell. *This could be good.* It beat trying to read by moonlight.

It wasn't until April that my parents came to visit again. They told me that an attorney named Harry R. Heard from Longview, Texas, had contacted them about my case. A reporter named Bob Howie with Longview Newspapers, Inc., had just published a large front-page story entitled "Is the Real Guilty Party Now Awaiting Execution on Death Row?" I had kept and protected the article as much as someone else would care for and protect a Bible. For me, it was. It was the beginning of the proof that I had been railroaded to death row. Heard said he could get the conviction overturned and get me out of this horrible mess. My parents said that Heard wanted to come see me and bring with him another reporter, Donnis Baggett of the *Dallas Morning News*, who was also interested in looking into my case.

Heard told my parents that he could not talk to me as long as I was still represented by Ament and Dixon, but he wanted to come visit me as soon as possible. That night, underneath the bright ceiling light in my new cell, I wrote a letter to Ament and Dixon thanking them for their representation but discharging them as counsel of record. It was time to move on.

Later that month Harry Heard visited me. "Kerry, the 12:30 time frame that Robert Hoehn was certain he dropped you off, Paula Rudolph, this 'Shyster' Jackson thing, the pathologist moving up the time Linda Jo Edwards died to coincide with Collard's aging of your fingerprints and Rudolph's seeing the person—you were *railroaded*. There is absolutely no way in my mind the Texas Court of Criminal Appeals will allow this conviction to stand.

"Kerry, the evidence to throw out this conviction is overwhelming." He was telling me exactly what I wanted to hear. "Judge Phillips erred in viewing Shyster Jackson's 'confession' story as direct evidence of guilt. Phillips should have granted your attorney's motion for an 'instructed verdict of acquittal based on the insufficiency of the evidence.' At the very least, Phillips should have permitted a charge of 'circumstantial evidence' to go before the jury—such a charge raises the state to a much higher burden of proof. Not a single element of that indictment that was used to get you before a jury was ever proven. It was a bunch of unproven allegations—that jury convicted you without a shred of proof. Hell, Kerry, from what I can see, every witness in your case perjured themselves.

"Just hold on, Kerry. I am going to get you out. There is absolutely no way the appeals court is going to allow this conviction to stand. You will not die. Not here, and not by the State of Texas. I promise you that. You have to trust me. All you have to do is hang on," Heard said.

"I will fight as long as there is breath in my body," I told him. *Finally,* someone saw what I saw. The catharsis was total: I rested my head on my folded arms and cried quietly.

"K.C.! K.C.! YOU'RE on the radio, man! You're on the radio!"

I drew a calendar on my wall so I could keep track of the days and weeks. By mid-June 1979 I had been in that cavity for almost a year, yet I still felt like a stranger. One Friday an excited voice shook me from my thoughts. It was Raymond Riles, known to death row as "King Motto." He lived two cells down from me and was the only person I had to talk to, though he seemed crazier than anyone I had ever known.

"Go put your wall box on WBAP, Dallas! You're on the radio! You really are innocent! You be goin' free! Kay-CEE going free-EEEE!" he chanted.

There was something about the urgency in his voice that made my heart begin to pound in both fear and expectation. I rushed to the wall speaker and nervously fumbled with the worn-out black knob. I caught it just in time to hear the closing comments by the radio reporter: "There has been no comment from the Smith County prosecutor's office since Jackson recanted. Now, in other stories . . ."

Oh my God! It was *about me!* Thoughts ricocheted through my head.

"Raymond," I yelled, "what did he say? I didn't hear all of it!" From his excitement one would have thought the news was about him, not me.

"K.C., you going home, man. You going home! The Shyster guy has admitted he lied against you because he had a secret deal! They said that Shyster and the fingerprint was the whole case against you. Kay-Cee goin' free-eee!" he kept shouting.

I waited for the next broadcast. *Jesus, please let it be true. Please let it be true,* I said to myself over and over.

A guard strolled by my cell. "I read about you in yesterday's *Dallas Morning News.* Looks like you might be getting out of here, Cook," he said.

That clinched it. Unable to do anything but needing to feel like I was doing something proactive, I grabbed a pen. "Dear Mama," I wrote. "I am being told about a *Dallas Morning News* investigative article that involves Shyster Jackson admitting he lied at my trial. You've got to send it to me. Please come visit me and bring the article with you. You can hold it up to the glass! Hurry! I am going crazy. Please write back!" Next I wrote Heard, then another quick letter to Doyle Wayne.

Finally after what seemed like an eternity, the newscast came on again and I heard it myself. It was easier this time—the entire cellblock echoed in silence.

The *Dallas Morning News* is reporting in a copyrighted story that ex-inmate Edward Scott "Shyster" Jackson lied when he told Cook's jury that Cook confessed to the brutal rape and mutilation murder of Tyler secretary Linda Jo Edwards in the highly publicized East Texas murder case.

The story went on to say that Jackson admitted his testimony was all part of a secret deal with Smith County prosecutors—a deal prosecutors still denied making—in exchange for his coached testimony. Jackson told two journalists, a Texas Ranger, and a local KTBB television reporter named Mike Edwards that police and prosecutors showed him photographs of the crime scene to prepare him for his testimony. Courthouse insiders told the *News* that Jackson's testimony was crucial in convicting me.

"Yes! Yes! Yes!" I screamed. Beset by emotion, I rushed to my cell door and rattled the bars as hard as I could. "I told you mothafuckers I was innocent! I told you, man! *What?* I can't hear you?"

Somewhere below me a voice mumbled, "Man, that nigga's going home!"

Two days went by, and then finally a white envelope was stuck in my bars at mail call. I tore it open, snatched out a single piece of notebook paper Mama had scribbled on. She wrote, "Kerry, keep your mouth shut. You are going to get out. Jackson told the truth he lied on you. He got his 'deal' and you got death row. He is under investigation for murdering someone else right after he got out in Tyler. A real estate man. More about all of this when I see you on Wednesday. Remember to keep your mouth shut. We're too close now. Love, Mama." There was a P.S.: "Say your prayers."

Attached to her letter was the *News* article, with the headline "Ex-Inmate Says His Lies Put Innocent Man on Death Row."

A former Smith County Jail inmate, whose testimony was crucial in sending a Jacksonville man to death row for a 1977 sex mutilation murder, says he lied on the witness stand so he could get a lighter sentence. A murder charge that had been pending against Jackson for almost two years was reduced to involuntary manslaughter two months after he testified against Cook. He was sentenced to two years in prison but was given credit for the 21 months he served in Smith County Jail awaiting trial. He was sent to the Texas Department of Corrections in Huntsville, processed in and out almost immediately, then set free.

Jackson had revealed this information to a Texas Ranger, Stuart Dowell, and two reporters the previous September. He stated that the police and prosecutors had made it clear that his "legal problems" would be solved if he created the story and told it to the jury. Jackson revealed how he got his intimate knowledge of the murder: He told reporters that he was brought into the District Attorney's Office and found the crime scene photographs were carefully laid out on the desk, in plain view, showing the grisly murder of Linda Edwards. Jackson absorbed the crime scene pictures so he could create his story and testify with details that could only have been known by her murderer. Jackson went on to admit that he fabricated his story about how I had reacted violently when viewing nude pictures of women who resembled the victim. Further, when he failed the first polygraph, Jackson was given Valium so that he could pass the second test.

Jackson's testimony had been devastating in 1978. During the first break after he testified and the jury was retired, Thompson looked over at our table and said to my attorneys, "You have to admit, the boy was *good*. He had the jury eating out of his hands and didn't budge." Now I had to hope that the truth would have a similar effect on the court of criminal appeals in Austin.

Donnis Baggett and Howard Swindle of the *Dallas Morning News* continued to write investigative stories after Jackson's recantation, and on June 18, 1979, a front-page article titled "Death Row Dreams Haunt Condemned 'Mama's Boy'" appeared. The piece focused on my past troubles, including running away from home. Unfortunately, the article also detailed Jerry Landrum's psychological profile of Edwards's killer being a homosexual male as well as the humiliating and damaging testimony of Robert Lee Hoehn, which identified me as a homosexual.

After this article appeared, the rumors and harassment from the other prisoners gathered speed. The need to take a stand grew daily. I had tried to ignore it as much as possible, but that caused the harassment to get worse. Hurting myself was the only way to escape. But it only seemed to be a Band-Aid to get me from cell to cell. I couldn't go to the prison administration for help: I learned my lesson the first time I tried; the guard listened all right, but then he just backed away from my door and yelled, "Leave the girl alone."

MY NEIGHBOR WAS generally quiet, but he began to offer me commissary items with conversation. Any human voice was inviting. One night I relaxed and got too comfortable, thinking perhaps I had finally found a friend other than Raymond Riles. He whispered, "Come to the bars. I want to tell you something. You there? Stick your mirror over here for a second. I want to show you something." I did and there he stood naked with an erection. "Reach over here and touch it," he said quietly.

I never spoke to him again no matter what he said to me. The price for his conversation was more than I would pay.

It didn't take long for erosion to set in and tarnish my new home on three row by the shower with the light to work by at night.

The only person I really had to talk to was an S.S.I. ("Support Service Inmate"—or trusty) who came into J-23 from the general population as a porter, whose responsibilities were to mop all three tiers, pick up the day's dirty laundry, and lay out fresh clothes for the next day. His name was John Hayter and he was assigned to the graveyard shift on J-23. He was about forty-five years old, white, and had a different kind of death sentence—chronic tuberculosis. It was never quiet on death row, but night-time was relatively calm, save the sporadic screaming and yelling from the mentally ill death-row residents.

Hayter would come up to my cell late at night and pass the time talking. As soon as I heard the light shuffle on the staircase after 10:00 P.M., I knew it was Hayter. He brought me little things you just couldn't get on the row—like a steak sandwich smuggled from the guards' kitchen. He seemed okay and I liked him for a time. But he knew the jacket and began pressuring me into either giving him head or reaching between the bars and masturbating him. "Be my ol' lady, I'll take good care of you," he would say. I laughed in return. But he never grinned.

One morning I woke up to laughter and heard a prisoner directly below me shouting down to the dayroom about how he had looked up on the upstairs glass and had seen Hayter having sex with me. I had to take the stares and comments all day and I impatiently awaited Hayter's return so I could get him to straighten this out, tell everyone it was not true.

A career criminal, Hayter was territorial and wanted to mark me as his property, and he was basking in the spotlight the rumors had created and did nothing to set them right. Instead he grinned and said, "Be my ol' lady. I promise to take real good care of you." He cared little to nothing of the dangers they created for me. I'm sure Hayter was hoping it would cause me to run to him for protection and agree to be his "wife."

I wasn't going to stab a human being to death to satisfy a barbaric criterion for manliness. No one would ever believe I was innocent if, even to save my own life, I had to resort to stabbing and killing another prisoner. I did the only thing I knew to do; I requested I be moved to another wing. I had written numerous requests to no avail in which I complained about the heat and my inability to sleep because of the light constantly on and shining in my face. I was stuck with no way out, except the only one that had worked before—I threatened to hang myself if they did not move me. The prison administration answered my I-60 the next morning by stripping me naked and removing all of my personal property from the cell.

I WAS MOVED to J-21, the death-row cellblock behind J-23, and put between Stanley Burkey and James "Small Paul" Burns. Stanley was real quiet, and I learned through our discussions that his father was an ordained minister. Small Paul and I talked a lot about my trial. Because of the recent publicity he nicknamed me "Hollywood" and said if half of what I told him was true, my story was going to be a movie. On J-21, it seemed I had found a little refuge from a ravaging storm so I could concentrate on my case and not always on the immediate mental, physical, and psychological threat of my environment. I even had a lightbulb inside the cell that I could turn on or off.

Upstairs on J-21, a pair of old friends, Edward King and Anthony Pierce, were always playing and joking with each other like brothers. King was extroverted and a prankster. Pierce was very quiet. Their playing and laughing trickled down to me at all hours of the day. They were so close they wrote each other's families and shared commissary. They were a united front against the madness of prison life.

"Don't bring your black ass out of that cell!" the voice of Edward King gruffly said. I almost laughed when I heard it, picturing the tall King looming over the small stature of Pierce. But it didn't take long to see they were not bantering as friends.

"You better go ahead on now. Let that shit alone," Pierce said. King persisted, however.

"I'm gonna fuck you up when the door opens up for recreation," King promised. I thought it was just two close friends blowing off steam. Stanley and I were discussing the upcoming pro-football season when a guard's voice interrupted.

"Get ready for recreation, Group Two."

Then I heard a scuffle, marked by the squeaks and scuffs of rubber shoes. Soon there was a groan, followed by the sound of something heavy but soft falling to the floor. That thud was Edward King falling dead, a chicken bone stuck in his heart.

From that point on, when chicken was on the prison menu—it was boneless.

MY TIME IN J-21 was short-lived. One day I went out to the day-room to pace and exercise for an hour. The hour flew by and before I knew it, I was nearly back to my cell when someone grabbed me from behind and took me to the concrete floor with the strength of an angry bull.

"Bitch, I'll kill you for talking about me," he screamed in my ear, pulling ever so tightly on my neck.

It was Richard Vargas, who for a while now had been kept in the first cell for observation; he had to wear a motorcycle helmet and was strapped down to a metal bunk at night because he had taken the lightbulb in his cell out of the socket, smashed it against his head, and cut all the way into the artery.

Vargas's grip tightened and I struggled for air. But I was lucky—three guards raced in from the hall after hearing the me-lee and pulled Vargas from me and dragged him to his cell, while he yelled obscenities and threatened to kill me if he saw me again. In prison, it didn't matter who started the fight: both participants were guilty and punished the same—unless one of the two snitches and gets the favor of "the man." In this case, poor Vargas got the worst of it: They dug the leather restraints out again and strapped him down naked to the steel bunk, spread-eagled. I saw Vargas as a mental patient pumped full of Thorazine and slide into an oblivion known only to the criminally insane.

As crazy as he was, I needed to watch myself and heed the threat he had made. In his schizophrenia, he was extremely paranoid and had begun thinking everyone was making fun of him. The prison administration must have seen it the same way, because it didn't take long to get the order to pack up my stuff. I was being moved back to J-23.

I WAS PUT in the cell of one of my former tormentors on three row, but I had a piece of mail from my brother waiting for me.

"You know, Kerry," Doyle Wayne wrote, opening a passageway to his soul, "when time passes and passes you wonder how in the hell did all of this get so confused and mixed up with my life? I mean, *my life*.

"But, Kerry, when everything is all said and done, you will see that even in the misfortune they've dealt you, you'll come out the winner. Sometimes I cry for you because I know you're not where you can be. You see, I was used to you. And you'll never know the pain I feel when I get to thinking about where we have gone, the places we've seen. We were always different from the others because we were never scared to say what we felt inside. I love you so much." It was written with a felt pen and I knew he had cried because the ink was smeared.

Hold on for me, Doyle Wayne. I am going to get out. I may be living in the land of the dead, but as long as my heart beats, I am going to fight. You have to hold on—wait for me.

A week or so later, Heard sent me the appellant brief he filed with the Texas Court of Criminal Appeals, detailing why my conviction should be reversed. The court had set the date of February 13, 1980, for him to appear and orally argue the case. *That's today!* I realized. I knew it was one of the most important days of my life. While Heard was in the state capital fighting for my life, I was thumbing through his thirty-five-page legal brief. In Heard's conclusions he told the court that the evidence was insufficient to support a finding of guilt beyond a reasonable doubt. "The statement of Edward Scott Jackson, and his later retraction, *must* give this court food for thought, as it is obvious his statement in open court was, and had to be, instrumental in placing the appellant on Death Row," Heard wrote. As much as I had been afraid to hope, I was convinced I was going home as I read his well-written document.

There was absolutely no way anyone, especially an appeals court judge, could ignore the enormity of proof that Tyler officials had framed me for the murder of Linda Jo Edwards. *Anything else is just impossible*, I thought.

Later that day Heard sat across from me in the visiting room, beaming with confidence, and told me that everything went well. Smith County hadn't even sent an attorney, as required, to oppose his arguments. Instead, Heard said, Smith County rested on their written response. I asked Heard if I could read that.

"Kerry, it will just upset you to no end. It's all bullshit. They're caught. What else can they do but continue to deceive and manipulate the facts?" It didn't make me feel any better. "It's all going to be over soon, Kerry. This I promise," Harry Heard said as he got up to leave. He left me money so I could buy stamps to write him.

Unfortunately, what followed would make legal history. I languished for eight excruciating years waiting for the Texas Court of Criminal(ly-Long) Appeals to rule on Heard's brief. Meanwhile, Texas was gearing up for its first execution by lethal injection.

THROUGH THE KILLING FIELDS

December 1982 was bitterly cold on J-23. Everyone was talking about Charlie Brooks Jr.'s approaching execution date—it would be Texas's first since the death penalty was reinstated. Brooks, or "Sharif" as his fellow Muslim brothers called him, arrived on death row in April 1978. He had been convicted in Tarrant County for the December 1976 murder of a mechanic in Fort Worth. His codefendant, Woody Lourdes, escaped the death penalty by striking a deal with their prosecutors, and his case was reduced to murder with a sentence of forty years. I was on death row with prisoners whose codefendant was the actual triggerman, but because he was the first to contract a deal, the prosecution permitted him to escape the death penalty or sometimes any punishment or accountability at all.

Up to now everyone's execution had been stayed, pending a

review by a higher court. We assumed it was going to be no different this time for Brooks. By 4 A.M. on December 6, the usual night owls were still talking when the sound of the cellblock door keyed and opened. I stepped to the front of my door and peered out in time to see the light by the staircase catching the silver captain bars on the lapel of a shirt. The form was moving quickly and was followed by an officer named Sergeant Langley. They carried all of the steel chains familiar with a bench warrant. The procession stopped at the cell of Charlie Brooks.

"Brooks, it's that time. Time to go," a voice of authority said firmly yet gently.

"I'm ready," Brooks said. For a few minutes there wasn't any noise other than the movement of the metal chains and handcuffs as they were being attached to his body.

Then a loud voice announced, "Roll it!"

As he stepped from his cell, someone yelled out, "Sharif, you'll be back by chow time, bro." His chains became quiet each time he stopped and told a friend good-bye. I listened to him take the baby steps brought on by the ankle irons all the way down the long hallway of the Ellis Unit.

Brooks seemed to be the only one who knew he wasn't coming back.

The next night I had the new radio Doyle Wayne had sent me tuned to the Sam Houston University student program. I listened intently after each song as the college student disc jockey gave updates on Brooks's status. Late into the night the United States Supreme Court rejected all claims and refused to halt the execution.

It wasn't long until I heard, "Texas has completed its first execution since 1964. At 12:09 A.M. tonight, Charlie Brooks was put to death for the 1976 death of a Fort Worth mechanic."

"Goodbye, Charlie," I whispered tentatively—he had been on death row just two months longer than me.

IT HAD BEEN a long time since I had heard from Doyle Wayne. My birthday came and went without a card, then Christmas. This was uncharacteristic of my brother. He had vanished from my life, and it was more frustrating because Mama and Daddy now rarely answered letters. And it had been over *four years* since the court heard my appeal. Harry Heard was equally perplexed and as frustrated. Other analysts reminded me how political and controversial death cases were and theorized that the court was looking for the right time to quietly push me out a side door.

Meanwhile, the Department of Corrections had begun a work program for death-row prisoners, and in April 1984 I was moved to the designated work-capable wing of G-15. I was excited about the prospect of having a way to take my mind off prison or Doyle Wayne and my case. That excitement didn't last long because I shared my new cell with Jerry Hogue, a short man who was long on ego and paranoia. He had been given the name "Boss Hogg" from the television series *The Dukes of Hazzard,* and he hated it. Only those he was truly afraid of could get away with calling him that; otherwise, he promised to kill you.

When I arrived, Hogue leaped off of his bunk and announced, "Cook, I don't fuck around, you need to know that, and you have to find a cell to move to. You can't stay in this cell with me." Jerry was all of five feet tall. I had the top bunk and he the bottom. While I was reading through a few of Doyle Wayne's letters that I received when I first got to death row, Hogue stood up, his head barely grazing the lip of my top bunk, and said, "I mean it. I know all about you, *Cookie.* I don't want you in this cell. I don't fuck with punks."

I stared down at his forehead. "I didn't ask to come into this cell. I will scout around for an empty one tomorrow and see if I can get moved." I thought it was best to use caution because if I got into a fight now, I would be banished to one of the J wings and continue to rot.

The next day I looked on as Joseph Starvaggi and Buddie Marrs played Kenneth Brock and Jim Moreland at handball outside in the small fenced-in recreational yard built adjacent to the G-15 dayroom. I put my name down, and when Brock's partner got called for a visit, Brock asked me to join him.

For the next hour and a half Brock and I went head-to-head with Marrs and Starvaggi. Brock was witty, and he had been there long before I arrived in 1978. "K.B." was liked by all and considered a "stand-up convict," a distinguished prison title that earned the ultimate peer respect. He was white and wore glasses, but he was actually blind in one eye and could barely see out of the other—I don't know how he became so good at handball.

Marrs and Starvaggi were two of the best handball players on death row. But after nearly two hours of intense playing, K.B. explained to me, "Well, we may not have beaten 'em, but we sure scared the hell out of 'em!" We never got a single point. Afterward, K.B. and I were sitting on a green painted bench under the hot sun. He had overheard Jerry Hogue the night before yelling at me to find another cell. "Be careful with that one. He's paranoid. It might be best if you can find the right excuse to get moved to another cell here—maybe one by yourself," K.B. said. The "right excuse" was critical: It was important that it didn't appear as though Jerry had caused me to "catch-out"—prison lingo for an extremely weak prisoner who refused to stand up for himself and instead ran cowardly to "the man" for help.

Surviving prison was all about appearances and respect. Brock had it in spades. With respect you could be left alone, and that was all I ever wanted. It depended on what you were willing to do to get it and keep it.

In the next few weeks K.B. and I began to spend more and more time hanging out and talking. I talked to him about Doyle Wayne and my conviction. Brock was a former marine and fairly conservative, so in the beginning he wasn't convinced that I might have been innocent. He was his own person, straightforward and honest, and he had a strong value system. I had never had a close friend on death row before K.B. But it was a friendship that we both had to fight to keep.

Because of my "punk" jacket, there were always challenges from other prisoners, and especially from Brock's friends. "Bear," a massive black prisoner, said while passing us in the yard, "So you've decided to settle down and become a family man, yeah, Brock?"

Brock straightened his gold-rimmed glasses, never breaking his stride. "Nah. Now, you know me, Bear. I don't mind the one that winks, but I ain't down with the one that stinks," he said with a smile. That smile quickly fell off his face when he turned to look back at me. K.B. understood prison well. He had an image to protect, and I had a rap on me that I could not get rid of. Over time, I told K.B. how frustrating it was to hear Jerry Hogue making me the butt of every joke.

K.B. said the time had come to stand up and be counted. "I like you, Kerry, but this is prison. You keep letting the Jerry Hogues exploit you like this in front of everyone and you might as well go back to lockup and talk to the man about putting you on protective custody. That's the only place you're going to be safe. He's engraving 'doormat' all over your forehead, to go with that good pussy all over your ass. I don't mean to be mean, but that's just the way it is."

"You don't understand. My whole *life* is my fight for innocence. K.B., you have no idea what those people in Tyler did to me. If I get into a fight, they will interpret that as proof of my propensity for violence. I don't care about the world of death row—I just want to get out of this cesspool," I said.

Brock laughed, but the worry lines returned. "I know, but, Kerry, I can't protect you, and I won't always be here. Eventually I will be executed—I deserve it, you don't. And as much as it pisses me off when I hear the things they say about you, it's *you* that has to do something about it. It's time you shut that midget up. Otherwise you're gonna just have to keep taking it up the ass—literally."

"Okay, okay," I said. He made so much sense, but in my gut it still felt childish. I blew out a long breath and stared into the direction where Hogue was playing handball with his cronies.

"I'll watch for the guards so you won't get busted, and will make sure none of his friends jump you from behind. I will be there for you. Just clock that motherfucker once," Brock said. He stood on the step going into the dayroom and before long there was a chain of lookouts all the way to the G-15 entry door wing—Lawrence Buxton, Raymond Landry, Charles Rumbaugh, and Rusty Thompson were all helping out. K.B. signaled "Go," and I made my move.

"You need to stop running your mouth and telling people lies about me," I called out to Hogue. He charged me with everything he had, his short stubby arms swinging widely. I punched him in the face, knocked him down, and when he got back up, I knocked him down again. In between breaths I spoke. "If you instigate against me anymore, we will just do this all over again until finally you either get the message and shut up or we are busted and locked down in the dungeon of J-21. It's up to you." Hogue stared back in disbelief, but he was never a problem after that.

K.B. appeared and we walked away together.

ACROSS THE CINDER-BLOCK wall that separated G-15 from the next cellblock was the general-population wing of H-17. They were double-man cells—twice the size of the single-man cells we were doubled up in on G-15. The administration was turning H-17 into a death-row wing to accommodate the expanding work program. An I.O.C. (Inter-Office Communication) was posted in the dayroom asking us to decide if we wanted to change current cellmates when H-17 was opened to us. K.B. and I joined a large caravan one morning two weeks later, around June 1984, and moved over to H-17. Our new home was on two row, five cell.

It didn't take long for trouble to begin. One day, over Labor Day weekend, the whole wing was placed on lockdown status— which meant no visitors, showers, recreation, or warm meals. Three prisoners on the Ellis Unit had been stabbed and killed— K.B. and I dubbed it the "St. Labor Day Massacre." For the next two weeks we were locked up 24/7 and put on a ration of cold peanut butter and bologna sandwiches. K.B. and I had a lot of conversations during that time.

"What happened, Kenneth? How did you wind up here?" He was the best friend I had had other than Doyle Wayne, and I just couldn't picture him murdering anyone.

"I was the oldest of seven kids; I dropped out of school and left home early," K.B. explained. "I joined the marines, but after a while I went AWOL from Camp Lejeune in North Carolina, and it all just went downhill fast from there. I was taking uppers, downers, and all-arounders, but my drug of choice was 'hospital heroin,' or Dilaudid. I got my hands on an old .22-caliber pistol. It had a hair trigger, but I never, even in my drug-crazed mind, ever intended on firing it. It was a prop to scare someone into giving me what I wanted—money for drugs. I should have removed the bullets, though. There are always a lot of things we should have could have done when it all goes bad.

"So I went into this store. I waited for the last person to leave and then I demanded that the man behind the counter—whose name I later found out to be Michael Sedita—give me the money. I showed him the gun. Everything would have been okay but wouldn't you know it, a Harris County policeman, showed up during the robbery. Of course he immediately called in the cavalry and soon they were all out in front of the store talking to me through a bullhorn, telling me to come out with my hands up.

"I went to leave the store, but outside the police cars were everywhere. Their pistols were aimed and drawn and all pointing at me. Across the street was a hurricane fence and lots of bushes for camouflage. I figured if I could just get there, I could get lost and get away. I stepped out of the door with the shopkeeper in tow, and I tried to negotiate, telling the SWAT crew that I would let him go in exchange for passage to the fence. 'No deal—Put down the weapon and lay facedown on the ground—*now*!' they shouted. That was the only deal they were willing to make. I saw all of those guns pointed at me and I just panicked. The next thing I knew the gun fired. Michael Sedita began to crumple in my arms and fall and I knew he was struck. I dropped him and took off running for those bushes. How I made it without getting hit by the volley of gunfire I'll never know. I hid for hours in a culvert until they finally found me. At the Harris County Jail I found out that he had died. The fault was mine entirely. I have regretted it daily, and if my execution could bring him back, I would have volunteered for it a long time ago.

"Unlike you, Kerry, I deserve to be here," K.B. said in a voice that was low with sadness. He readjusted his gold-rimmed glasses and neither of us said another word. I had never met anyone like Kenneth Albert Brock. He was honest, sincere, kindhearted, and a man of his word. His downfall was drug addiction.

After a while I broke the silence. "That was a tragic accident, Kenneth, one I don't believe you owe your life for. It's awful for the Sedita family—I can only imagine—but wasn't your lawyer able to offer up the weapon to show that it had a hair trigger, like you claimed? It could have been an accidental discharge . . ."

"I'm sure they knew, Kerry, but none of that mitigates the fact that I killed a man and ruined his family. That it was an accident matters little to me. I deserve to die for what I done."

K.B. and I spent all of our time with each other, be it in the cell or in the yard. We watched each other's backs in the dangerous theater where we both lived. As time marched on, K.B. knew

Through the Killing Fields ‖ 147

my case almost as well as I did. He believed I was innocent and victimized by a corrupt criminal justice machine that had sacrificed the scales of justice to win a conviction at all cost. We shared our whole lives from start to finish in that cell on H-17. He said he felt bad for never knowing me through the years or standing up for me. Now that he knew me, he wanted to make up for that—and he did. He provided me with an emotional support system I had never had on death row. In that world of hatred, bitterness, and anger, we stood together until the inevitable.

"NO MATTER WHAT, Kerry, you have to hold on—even without me—because you *will* be free," he said to me one day after he got a letter from his attorneys, putting him on notice that the prosecution was seeking the immediate scheduling of an execution date. By May 1986 K.B.'s appeal had wound down, and his attorneys could no longer stave off the State of Texas. K.B. worried not for himself, ironically, but for me: He knew that before I had met up with him, I would hurt myself whenever I was either sexually assaulted or needed to be physically moved because I was in fear of my life.

Then one morning the officer yelled, "Brock, pack your stuff. You're going on bench warrant." K.B. was convinced his long struggle was finally over and that it was time for him to follow the fourteen other Texas executions that had followed that of Charlie Brooks. I hugged him when they came for him. The cell door rolled open and, silently, the guard came into the cell, gently pulled K.B. away and led him through the cell door. That afternoon a Houston judge set K.B.'s execution date for June 19, 1986, a month away.

I told myself that the United States Supreme Court would stay his execution based on the claim that he had received poor legal representation. Anything was better than entertaining the dark notion he was going to be put to death, and that I was going to lose my best friend and be left here alone again. With this latest loss, I felt like Sisyphus, endlessly pushing the boulder up the mountain slope just to have it roll back down by the end of the day.

A few days before his scheduled execution, K.B. was moved to the Death Watch cell on G-13. The days came and went with no word on a reprieve of his sentence, and on the very last day, the Supreme Court in Washington, D.C., refused to halt his death. That sealed his fate. On June 18, K.B. was to be transferred to the Walls Unit for execution, and that night, Sergeant Peralez permitted me to go on G-13 and see him one last time. I was so grateful to Peralez for giving us that chance. He didn't have to do it, but he knew how close K.B. and I were. He said we could only have a couple of minutes, and then he stepped to the side of the door to give us a moment of privacy. I walked in and the door was rolled shut behind us.

I knew K.B. was holding in all that he felt inside because of the reality of his impending death. K.B. looked me straight in the eye with both of his hands firmly on each of my shoulders. "Kerry, you've always kept your word to me. I know I am leaving you in a few hours. I *know* you are going to get out. You will not know the room at the Walls Unit where I am going. I want you to promise me you will not give up. Promise me this." He took my hand, gripped it tightly. "Promise me."

"I won't, Kenneth. I promise I will not give up and will fight to the bitter end."

The door rolled open and Sergeant Peralez was there. "Cook, you have to go back to H-17 now."

K.B. asked me to write his sister, Nancy, and tell her and her husband how much their support meant through the years. I promised I would.

"Kerry, just walk out the door. Don't look back. I want you to remember me like this. If you look back, I swear I will lose it. Just go," he whispered even lower. "I am going to tell Michael Sedita I am sorry, face-to-face, Kerry. I love you. And I know it will not be easy for you, but remember your promise to me." I hugged him. I dried my eyes, stepped through the open doorway and into the hallway.

I didn't look back.

That night, I lay awake imagining what Kenneth must have been experiencing. When midnight came I put my headphones on and tuned my radio to KSHU. I was convinced Kenneth would get a stay of execution due to the circumstances that had come together near the end. Texas attorney general Jim Mattox admitted the pistol had a hair trigger and that it could very well have been an accident just as Kenneth said. His convicting prosecutor, George O. Jacobs, asked for mercy, saying, "If prison is designed for rehabilitation, Brock was an enormous success. He was a model prisoner." J. M. Sedita, Michael's father, in an extraordinary act of understanding and compassion, also joined in asking the Texas Clemency Board and the governor to commute his sentence to life imprisonment.

I was revisiting all of those events when the talking head on my radio spoke. "It's official. Kenneth Albert Brock has become the fifteenth inmate put to death in Texas since the United States Supreme Court reinstated capital punishment. Brock was convicted of the 1974 shooting death of. . . ."

Two days later mail was passed out. The guard placed a letter in the bars. I saw the letterhead. It read: "Kenneth Albert Brock, Ex: #522, Walls Unit. Huntsville, Texas. 77343." The time at the top of the letter said 11:50 P.M. He was finalizing his last thoughts: "I know I have been very lucky in life to have been loved so much. I had many chances and I threw them away. I am glad I did not throw away the one chance that was our friendship. The warden said I couldn't go into the execution chamber with my glasses on because it was against the rules. 'Why do you need those, Brock?' I told him I have made a lot of mistakes in life: I might need to see where I am going. Well, they're here for me, Kerry. I love you. Remember your promise to me."

In the days and weeks that followed, the KSHU disc jockeys were pretty busy, keeping up with the wrath of Texas: Soon Randy Woolls, Larry "Doc" Smith, Michael Evans, and Richard Andrade all followed Kenneth Brock.

WHAT IS HOPE but a belief something will change in the future? In June 1987, the Texas Criminal Court of Appeals (TCCA) left for summer recess—again—without a ruling on my appeal. Hope, I decided, had waited long enough. I wrote a protest letter to the editor of *The Texas Lawyer,* a respected law journal that most, if not all, Texas judges and legal scholars read. Next, I wrote Harry Heard and asked him to file a writ of mandamus to force the TCCA to rule on my appeal. A writ of mandamus was a rarely used legal instrument asking a higher court to demand a lower court to rule on a pending appeal. Such a writ was almost never resorted to, much less in a case involving the death penalty. It was considered the "nuclear option," because it risked alienating, embarrassing, and generally angering a lower court, which would still decide the case. However, I was dying a slow and agonizing death. Meanwhile the appellant system was growing more and more conservative. And I knew that the TCCA was playing politics with my Smith County debacle and did not want to rule on my appeal unless they were forced to.

Heard wrote back asking me to hang on; he still believed the court would do the right thing and throw out my conviction. He told me that his longtime friend defense attorney M. H. "Rusty" Duncan III had won a seat on the TCCA and would take his place on the court in January. Heard said he had told Duncan all about my case and that Duncan was going to be our loudest voice for justice on the court.

Meanwhile, *The Texas Lawyer* responded by dispatching a reporter named Walter Borges to interview me. On June 29, 1987, after eighty-eight months of waiting for the TCCA, my words were splashed across the front page, with the headline "Inmate Demands Decision." A smaller caption beneath read "Writ of Mandamus Requested on Longest-Dormant Appeal." Reading the article, I was surprised to learn that my direct appeal before the TCCA was the longest to go without a ruling from an appeals court *in American history;* the court had ruled on more than a hundred other death cases since mine was filed and presented in February 1980.

Heard was quoted in the article: "Anyone with common sense who read the transcript could tell this boy is innocent." For their part, the TCCA had no comment as to why they had withheld a decision on my case. The mandamus was considered suicidal—no one in their right mind would have done it. But I was not in my right mind anymore; after having patiently waited 2,640 days, my faith and trust had fully eroded.

Unfortunately, the article made a point of identifying the other death penalty cases that had been pending decisions. Most death-row prisoners, of course, were in no hurry to have their cases resolved—they wanted every hour of life provided by the court's indecisiveness. And so when this article appeared, not only were the eyes of the legal community focused on me, but so, too, were the eyes of all the other death-row prisoners whose delayed cases were mentioned along with mine.

Could life be any more unbearable here? Sadly, the next few months provided an answer.

ON A CHILLY day in early December I was sitting in my cell wrapped up in a woolen military blanket, reading a book a reporter had sent me, called *Last Rights: 13 Fatal Encounters with the State's Justice,* when an officer told me I had a legal visit. I thought it odd to have a visit—it was Tuesday and the TCCA published its death penalty decisions only on Wednesdays. *Maybe it's Doyle Wayne.* I wanted that almost as badly as I wanted a ruling setting me free.

I sat down on the wooden chair in the visitation room. After waiting a moment, I looked up and saw a ghost from my past: John S. Ament. "John!" I almost shouted. It felt good to see him. I liked him a lot, and he was honest with me before and during the trial. He and Larue Dixon had defended me with only five hundred dollars to work with. I knew they had done the best they could given the enormity of the police and prosecutorial misconduct.

Ament was going through Huntsville on business and stopped in to see me for a moment. We talked about the incredibly long time the TCCA had sat on my appeal. He expressed extreme confidence that this was a sign that I would go free. He said they just wanted things to die down because reversals of convictions for *any* reason were very political and used by conservative adversaries. I thanked him for everything he had tried to do at the trial.

"They are going to do the right thing when they rule, Kerry. Just hang in there," Ament said, as he scooted back his chair, stood up, and left.

The next day, just like the preceding 402 Wednesdays, I kept my headphones on and the radio tuned in for news of TCCA activity. By 6:00 P.M., I had begun to write a letter when the G-15 porter walked up to my cell. "David McKay said come to the dayroom door on the next in-and-out. He has something important to tell you." David was a friend I had met through K.B. and was my old cellmate on H-17 after Kenneth was executed.

The dayroom was nearly empty as I walked in. A couple of prisoners were in an animated game of dominoes, slamming the hard plastic down on the concrete table. I went up to the door that separated the G-15 and H-17 dayrooms and looked into the small window for David.

David tapped on the Plexiglas window, playfully trying to spook me. "Have you heard?"

"Heard what?" I said.

"The TCCA affirmed five cases today. One of the five was yours, Kerry."

I looked hard into David's face. "That's not possible. I've been listening to the radio all day—you know I do that—and have not heard of any rulings. The TCCA didn't rule on any death penalty cases this week. You have it wrong," I said. David just shook his head back and forth. "It's true, Kerry. I'm sorry."

I raced back to my cell and wrote Harry Heard. *Please, God. Don't let this be true. It just can't be true.* The next few days were excruciating. I filled out an I-60 trying to get special permission to use the phone so I could call Heard. *Surely if this rumor had any legs he would have called me,* I counseled myself.

I began reading a letter from an old friend from Jacksonville. "Kerry, I read from the AP wire service that the Texas Court of Criminal Appeals affirmed your conviction. I couldn't believe that so I called your mom's house. Doyle Wayne answered the phone. I asked him if he had heard the news about your case and he said 'Heard what news?' I told him. It sounded to me like he dropped the phone. I was calling out his name when your mama evidently picked up the phone. She wanted to know who it was and I told her. Your mama said when she walked up the phone was on the floor and she didn't know what was going on but she had to go now and find Doyle Wayne. She just hung up on me." My hands trembled as I held the paper. I still didn't believe it. *How was it even possible?*

I wrote Thomas Lowe, clerk for the TCCA, and asked him to please send me the court's opinion in *Cook v. State*, published on December 9, 1987. Two days later, a brown manila envelope arrived. There was no letter, just the paper on which the decision was printed. Writing for the 8–1 majority, presiding judge John Onion said the evidence was sufficient to sustain both a verdict of guilt and a sentence of death. The legal rationale was: I had confessed the rape and murder to a fellow jail inmate named Edward

Scott Jackson, and his cogent testimony before the jury "established the guilt of the accused" because he (Jackson) knew things only the actual murderer could have known. Nowhere did it say that he lied and was shown the crime-scene photos by A. D. Clark so they could bamboozle the jury into thinking I had confessed in intimate detail. Onion went on to write, "Fingerprint evidence also placed appellant in the apartment at the time the crime was committed"—and that Rudolph even identified me, thereby bolstering that point. Regarding the numerous inflammatory examples of prosecutorial abuses—such as Thompson making arguments that were not supported by any evidence, that is, telling the jury that the reason the victim's lips and vagina were missing from the murder scene was because "the defendant probably ate them"—Onion agreed there was prosecutorial misconduct. However, those abuses complained of were waived and not reviewable because Ament and Dixon had failed to properly object and thereby preserve them for the record. This included calling me a homosexual pervert and telling the jury I had "cult friends." The majority opinion did recognize the admission of Dr. James P. Grigson's testimony as a violation of my Fifth and Sixth Amendment rights, but Grigson's testimony was ruled a "harmless error" because Jerry Landrum's testimony and evaluation mirrored Grigson's, and Landrum's testimony was admissible. In summation the court affirmed my conviction and death sentence. I was convinced Onion and the other seven judges relied solely on Smith County's brief and did no independent examination.

There was, however, a dissenting opinion. It was twenty-two pages long and authored by a justice named Sam Houston Clinton. Noting that my case had drawn "instant notoriety," Justice Clinton observed that "no doubt, and commendably so, members of the law enforcement community, including the district attorneys, were anxious to solve the crime, and convinced they succeeded. But to me, at least, there are some troublesome aspects in this case." He argued that "a rational reviewer of all facts is left with serious questions whether a rational trier of fact could find guilt beyond a reasonable doubt." He highlighted how Rudolph had first identified James Mayfield the day she discovered her roommate's body, describing him as having silver hair cut above the ears—a description that fit him to a tee—and that evidence showed my hair was brown and shoulder-length; that she changed her testimony only after I had been arrested and then languished in jail for a year. Judge Clinton dissected the majority's opinion and replaced it with a more lucid version of reality. He pointed out that the most inflammatory evidence came from Robert Hoehn's narration of homosexual conduct, and that to secure this testimony prosecutors gave him immunity because homosexuality was a crime in Texas. The most incriminating testimony came from Edward Scott "Shyster" Jackson. Justice Clinton told the world what his brethren had incredibly failed to note—that Jackson had recanted his testimony and admitted he had committed perjury in exchange for a secret deal. Also, Justice Clinton pointed out that Tyler Dr. V. V. Gonzalez had changed the time of death and moved it forward to a time when I was without an alibi. Still, Clinton highlighted the glaring logistical error within the state's case—Paula Rudolph's eyewitness identification at the murder scene overlapped with the time that Robert Hoehn testified he was certain he dropped me off. Worse, Dr. Gonzalez's testimony regarding the victim's wounds stated that to inflict such damage "in this area here" alone probably took "five to ten minutes." The state's own time line of events, as given by their own witnesses, effectively ruled me out as a viable suspect. As my eyes came to the last line of his opinion, I wished the rest was just a bad dream: "For these reasons, I dissent. The conviction should be reversed."

I wasn't the only one whose understanding of truth and justice had been shattered—I never heard from Harry Heard again.

I know Harry was devastated as a lawyer by the TCCA's bizarre ruling. He had left my case, but not before doing much to advance my cause. It was Harry who first managed to turn the

Dallas Morning News onto my case. He gave me the only money I had to fight from the inside. Most of all, he got me to the next stage of the journey because he gave me hope. I loved him for that.

ON THE MORNING of December 27, my mind was still coming to terms with the TCCA's ruling when escort officers Bradley and Skeens came out into the garment factory where I was sewing on the second leg of a guard's uniform. I had a visitor, they informed me. My first reaction was that maybe it was Harry Heard. I had been jotting down notes from my trial incessantly, piecing together snippets of information. I was working on combining it into a comprehensive "case history" and planned to send it out to the media to try to get help. At the same time, I was also trying to deal with the hostility of a few very vocal prisoners who claimed I had put heat on their own cases by what I had said in *The Texas Lawyer*. It was okay to get my own case affirmed, they said, but I had no business "fucking with our cases." A lot of other—guilty— people were perfectly happy with their own dormant appeals and felt like their lives were shortened by my interview with Walter Borges. They made it clear that they wouldn't mind if someone else shortened mine a bit—with a homemade knife to the heart.

I walked over to the sally port and began to remove all of my clothes for the mandatory cavity search, the price for a visit. Officer Bradley waved it off. "Chaplain Timmons wants to see you in his office." *Chaplain Timmons?* I whispered to myself. He only does funerals and execution dates. *Damn,* I thought to myself. *I just got my case affirmed two weeks ago and already they were cranking up the process to put me in the ground!*

I had no idea what was going on as we made our way down the long hallway of the Ellis Unit. As we got to the end of the building I entered the chapel where a large Christmas tree stood—it was the first one I had seen in over a decade. I paused for an instant as a barrage of childhood memories flooded my mind.

A second later a prisoner passed me, whispering, "Sorry about your brother."

My brother? What about Doyle Wayne? My heart pumped furiously. My mama wrote me very few letters, but the ones she sent had said that my father had been having serious problems with colon cancer. *God, it's my daddy!*

The door to Chaplain Timmons's office opened and the escort officers prodded me in. The chaplain was sitting behind a messy desk, holding a beige phone with one hand and cupping the mouthpiece with the other. He motioned for us to sit down. Timmons spoke quickly into the phone, laid it down for a second, and stared right at me.

"Kerry, I have your father on the phone. He's at the funeral home. Here."

My daddy's voice spoke to me. "He's gone, son." It sounded like it had taken him a lifetime to build up the courage to say those words.

This was not making any sense. "Who's gone, Daddy? Who?"

"Doyle Wayne. He's dead, son. He was shot and killed by a man in Longview last night, son. Your mama's all torn up. We're here at the funeral home. He looks so handsome." The room began to spin.

Hot tears marched down my flushed face, each one a symbol of surrender. Somewhere in the distance, my daddy was talking from the earpiece. "Doyle Wayne would not have wanted you to give up now, son. He wanted you to fight on, go free, and help take care of your mama and me, give us a grandson to take into the sunset of our lives. You'll get out, if you just hang on and fight," daddy was saying, but I was unable to absorb his words. Officer Bradley gently took the phone out of my hand and handed it back to Timmons.

"Mr. Cook?" Chaplain Timmons said into the phone. "He's going to be okay, but he can't talk anymore."

As I was led back down the center lane of the Ellis Unit hallway, I felt death all around me, inside of prison and, now, outside of it, too.

My sanity had only been as strong as a cardboard box, and when I got back to my cell, it finally collapsed. As loud as I could force my body, I screamed for my brother. Smith County finally had nothing to take. For two more days I receded deeper into myself than I had ever gone before.

MR. DUFF, THE supervisor of the garment factory, gave me an indefinite "lay-in." After three days and three nights without showering or accepting meals, I went to the shower that morning when my door rolled open. I meandered down the hallway. With everyone at work, the cellblock was empty, except for Leon King, the porter, who was picking up the prisoners' dirty laundry and sweeping.

I was staring past the shower faucet at the brown sandstone walls as the hot water spit onto my swollen face. In a split second, a hand emerged from nowhere and went over my mouth.

"Daddy will make it all right, baby," Leon King's raspy voice said.

I stood with the water cascading over me, talking to Doyle Wayne—he was standing vibrant and alive, sitting on a rock; we were taking a break from the steep uphill climb going to Honecken Castle, perched atop the mountain when we lived in the army complex of Vogelweh, a housing area at Coffey Barracks in Kaiserslautern, Germany.

Not even the pain of King's penis ripping and pushing inside me could steal my attention from where I had gone. I bent over and Leon King fucked me.

A few days after, the cellblock was abuzz with King's story of sexual conquest. Amid unrelenting jeers, I decided to escape. I broke open a razor and made the most serious lacerations of my tour of duty on Texas death row: I sliced into my wrist, legs, and penis without consequence or feeling. The shame of what was happening to me in prison had taken its toll, and the humiliation I felt inside far outweighed anything I felt physically. I longed for a place to go within so I could shut it out and hide.

For years I had resisted stepping into the darkness that constantly pulled at me. On the other side of the prison doorway always had been Doyle Wayne and the belief that my innocence would eventually be proven, if I just didn't give up. Now my brother was gone, and the highest court in Texas had said nothing was wrong with my conviction and that I should die. Now, without anything holding me back, I slipped across in the darkness.

I was found unconscious, then sewn together and shipped back to the Ellis II Unit Psychiatric Center. A few days later I spoke with the head doctor, Dr. Morgan. I told him about Doyle Wayne's murder, the rejection of my appeal after an eight-year fight, my daddy's cancer, and finally—after making him swear that he would not tell the prison administration—I told him about what had happened in the shower stall with Leon King. If I could just not go back to death row, I told Dr. Morgan, I would be okay. I was a constant target on death row, day in and day out. Hurting myself was the only way to get temporary relief from the permanent madness of death row. The mandatory strip searches kept me constantly vulnerable and in the crosshairs of sexual predators. And if it wasn't a sexual predator, I became the bane of everyone else's hatred, prejudice, and anger at the world for having landed themselves on death row facing execution.

Dr. Morgan recommended that I be admitted to the treatment center.

———

"AFTER YOU LEFT, Kerry, he went crazy."

My mama and daddy visited me a few days later and pressed pictures of Doyle Wayne in his casket up against the glass. "When the court in Austin said your conviction was okay a few weeks ago, Doyle Wayne sat in his room playing the same song, 'Carrie,' over and over. It really tore Doyle Wayne up," my daddy said.

Soon after their visit, Charles Underwood, a friend I met when we first moved to Jacksonville in 1973, sent me a letter and enclosed an article by the *Jacksonville Daily Progress* covering my failed appeal. I opened up a newspaper clipping and a very small second clipping fell out. I unfolded it—it was Doyle Wayne's obituary.

"Sorry to hear about your brother, Kerry. I can only imagine how you feel."

It said he died in Longview, Texas, and was survived by his parents, Earnest and Evelyn Cook of Jacksonville. Even in death I wasn't allowed to be a part of my brother. My mama's shame of me being sent to death row was more important than my pain as a brother, and I knew this was why I was excluded. She didn't want to remind the Jacksonville community that we were related.

I had to find out how Doyle Wayne came to be in a coffin. I wrote a reporter named Bob Howie of Longview Newspapers, who had authored the lengthy piece on my story in 1979. "Help me, Mr. Howie. Tell me anything you can about my brother's death. Please," I wrote.

A week later Howie filled in some of the blanks. Doyle Wayne was at a club in Longview with a man named Jeff D. Woolverton from Tyler. From the information he had managed to collect, Howie said that this club had a bad reputation—other shootings had occurred there.

"Your brother got into an argument with another man who then followed him out into the parking lot and shot him with a

.44-caliber, Charter Arms, five-shot, snub-nosed revolver. He died in the parking lot waiting on the ambulance at 2:30 A.M."

That wasn't enough. I had to know more; I had to know *all of it*. I knew Doyle Wayne would not just be at some club in Longview—especially one with a bad reputation. From the police report Howie summarized for me, I obtained Jeff Woolverton's address in Tyler, and on October 22, 1988, I wrote him a letter. He promptly responded and narrated for me the story of how my brother's life was taken that night.

Jeff first met Doyle Wayne while they were both working at a restaurant in Jacksonville in 1986. One night they were at Lake Jacksonville having a few beers, and though Doyle Wayne never talked about me, this night he was somber and spoke about what had happened to me. Staring out of the car into the darkness with the music down low, he told Jeff, "You remind me of Kerry sometimes." Jeff thought that was one of the reasons they got to be such good friends. They both loved to play pool and they would either go to a club in Jacksonville and play pool, or drive to Tyler and play.

The night Doyle Wayne was killed, they went to a club in Tyler called the Foxy Lady. They played pool for money and were really hot that night, and Jeff suggested a club in Longview he knew called The Rainbow Connection. In Longview, the two of them were running the tables and were on fire, but also getting good and drunk. When the PA system announced closing time, Jeff left to go start the car while Doyle Wayne was finishing up one last game.

As Jeff made his way through the club toward the exit, two men were sitting side by side on a pool table near the door. Jeff reached up, snatched the sunglasses off the head of one of the men, and put them on and mimicked Stevie Wonder. The man's friend, Ben Franklin Williams, immediately jumped down from the table and demanded that Jeff return the glasses. About this time Doyle Wayne walked up and Jeff handed my brother the sunglasses and then walked out.

"Give 'em back, motherfucker," Williams said.

Doyle Wayne had no idea what he had walked into. He handed the glasses back, "and I guess they had some words, I don't know," Jeff wrote. Out in the parking lot, Jeff was trying to get the key into the keyhole to unlock the driver's-side door but it was so cold the lock was frozen. Doyle Wayne stood holding the metal handle of the passenger-side door waiting to be let in. Over the roof of the car Jeff could see a pickup truck pull up and Ben Franklin Williams get out.

"Watch out behind you, Doyle," Jeff called out.

When Doyle Wayne turned around, in front of him stood an angry twenty-eight-year-old black man with one arm behind his back.

"What you gonna do for me, white boy—all this motherfucking shit you done caused embarrassment. Huh, muthafucka?" he said to Doyle Wayne.

"Look, we've all been drinking. We're all gonna wake up tomorrow and laugh about this. It's nothing to get all bent out of shape about. It was a pair of sunglasses—you got them back. You need to get back in your truck and go home before you make me have to hurt you."

They were not the words he was looking for. Nobody could have told Ben Franklin Williams what he needed to hear that night in his anger and own drunkenness. "Fuck you," Williams said, and in one fluid movement raised a cannon from behind his back. He pointed the .44 Magnum revolver and fired. He shot at Doyle Wayne from about ten feet away, but he narrowly missed him as my brother ducked. But then Williams ran up to him and placed the pistol against his neck and shot him at point-blank range. He then ran and jumped into his truck and sped off into the night.

Doyle Wayne rose up to his full height of six foot one and stared blankly straight ahead. "'Doyle, you okay? You okay?' I couldn't even tell he had been shot. It was weird. He just stood there looking straight ahead," Jeff wrote. Then the blood poured from his nose and like a tree cleanly chopped, he fell forward. Jeff said he caught him and lowered him to the ground. Soon the blood stopped gushing from his neck and the stare was lifeless. Jeff closed his eyes. Doyle Wayne was thirty-three years old.

The police captured Williams about a mile away on Eastman Road, and found the murder weapon in his possession. There were ten eyewitnesses to the murder. Jeff said that when the case came up for trial months later, he did not agree with the plea bargain my mama and daddy agreed to. Ben Franklin Williams pled guilty to the reduced charge of "voluntary manslaughter, with a deadly weapon." He was given a sentence of sixteen years in the Texas Department of Corrections. "Your mama felt with you being on death row and all, they could lose the case before a jury. I didn't believe that, but it wasn't my son that was murdered, so I really can't say anything. He was just my friend."

The bullet Ben Franklin Williams fired that night ended my brother's life, but it also shattered something in my own. For the first time, I knew the hatred felt by a victim's family member when they are left to deal with what remains of their loved one after a senseless crime. Believe me, I understood.

MEN I COULD TRUST

When I rejoined death row, I began finishing my notes dismantling the appeals court ruling. I tried to put down the whole story of how I thought Smith County had gotten me convicted and onto death row. I hammered feverishly night and day on a vintage Royal typewriter that I had bought off a prisoner on J-21. As I typed, the letters on the paper became fainter and fainter—I had no money to buy typing ribbons from the commissary. But I was able to recycle the ribbons with mineral oil I got from the clinic. I found that pouring the oil on a ribbon, coupled with rubbing carbon paper over it, rejuvenated it and gave me the precious black ink I needed.

I finished my case for innocence in January 1988 and sent it to the editor of the *Dallas Morning News*. I couldn't believe my luck when the editor wrote back to say that he felt my case history had merit and that he was assigning my story to a reporter named

David Hanners to look into the facts and circumstances that led to my arrest, conviction, and death sentence. He wrote that he had thought the appeals court ruling would be swift back then and had planned to resume the articles after the court ruled. Meanwhile, the *News* had been investigating other instances of corruption in Smith County. The articles grabbed the national media's attention and became the subject of a *20/20* prime-time special entitled "Crime and Corruption Marks the Small East Texas Town of Tyler, Texas—Runaway Justice." The exposé highlighted the framing of Tyler club owner Kenneth Bora on trumped-up drug charges. The Tyler police chief, Willy Hardy, had instructed two undercover officers, Craig Matthews and Kim Wozencraft, to create a phony "stash" case against Bora. The piece clearly showed how corrupt the criminal justice machinery was in Smith County. Though I wasn't mentioned, I drew tremendous hope from the airing of this show. I felt it would make it easier for me to argue the facts of my case.

At the end of the previous month, December, I was in the visitation room talking with a woman who provided legal advice to death-row prisoners, when a tall, slender-looking man walked by. She told me it was Atlanta attorney Robert McGlasson. There was a rumor on the row that McGlasson and another attorney named Jim Rebholz were trying to start up a Capital Punishment Project to cope with the deficit of legal counsel for death-row prisoners. Lack of adequate counsel had become epidemic in Texas and pandemic to those under sentence of death in America.

"Mr. McGlasson? Do you have a moment," I called out. He was moving fast and many people were trying to get his attention.

"No, I don't," the busy lawyer said. "Is it important?"

"Yes, sir, it is to me. My name is Kerry Cook. My direct appeal was affirmed a few weeks ago by the TCCA. I've been framed for a rape and murder I didn't commit out of Tyler, Texas. Please read the twenty-two-page dissenting opinion written by Associate Justice Sam Houston Clinton."

"Who's your attorney?" Robert asked, as he stopped and turned to me.

"That's what I am trying to tell you. I don't have an attorney."

McGlasson yanked a pen out of his front shirt pocket. "Give me your name and the date of the opinion. I am really busy right now, but I will look into it."

I gave him the information, then added, "I know everyone says they are innocent in a place like this, but I am. The *Dallas Morning News* has been looking into my case. They have written stories. If you'll just take a few minutes to please look—"

"I'll get back to you. In the meantime, *stop* talking to the media and don't send them anything else." The group of people waiting to talk with him swallowed him up and he was gone. I knew from experience that every attorney's rule of thumb was to just keep your mouth shut. However, I was alone in my battle, and I no longer had blind faith in the legal profession. If I was going to die, I was going to go kicking and screaming all the way into the death chamber, and I wasn't going to allow my life to be exclusively in the hands of an attorney. I kept approaching the media because I knew that I needed to keep making people aware of my story.

On the morning of February 19, 1988, an attorney named Scott Howe came to visit me. A colleague of Robert McGlasson, he was handsome and athletic-looking, with red hair and a red mustache. I guessed that he was only in his early thirties. When assigning Howe, McGlasson had told him about the details of my case but also made a point of saying that the passion and sincerity with which I had spoken made me different. Howe and I talked from 11:00 A.M. until 5:00 P.M. "You need an attorney, Kerry. Smith County is going to set an execution date and you need someone to file a stay of execution with the United States Supreme Court. You need representation for the upcoming execution date." The mere use of the phrase "execution date" made me dizzy. People had been executed for years all around me, but I never thought I would be one of them. I shook my head at the thought of it.

"I am innocent, Scott. Maybe that is a stretch to believe, but it's true. I need someone to fight for me in the courts."

Scott softened his tone. "Kerry, you need to understand something about the process: The appeals court only cares about the *legal* errors that may or may not have occurred in your 1978 trial. They are not going to be interested in your assertions of innocence. That is irrelevant at this point."

"But the trial was all about trying to find out if I was guilty or not. Now you're telling me that no one is going to be listening to whether I am innocent?" I loudly said.

"That's right, Kerry. The appeal of your conviction is not about your innocence or guilt. It is about procedural matters and whether or not you were given a fair trial, nothing more." I really liked Scott's genuine honesty. He was kind to me, yet under that nice exterior I could discern a fierce lawyer who would fight for me.

"Scott, will you represent me?" I looked him in the eyes and asked.

Without hesitation Scott said, "Yes. I will do everything I can, Kerry, but understand, I can't make any promises. I can only promise to give you my very best. I will say this: I think Justice Clinton's dissenting opinion is going to be what saves your life." He paused for a moment and continued: "You are different, you stand out. You are very smart, not like anyone I have ever met or represented in prison."

"Your very best is good enough."

AFTER A THOROUGH and exhaustive investigation into the facts and circumstances that led to my arrest and conviction, the *Dallas Morning News* ran a front-page story on Sunday, February 28, 1988, with a headline that said it all: "Inmate Was Railroaded." The article criticized police and prosecutors for manipulating or embellishing the facts to gain a conviction, including the Shyster Jackson story, the secret agreement with A. D. Clark and the prosecution, Rudolph's new and improved in-court identification, and many other instances of overreaching.

But for me what stood out the most in the story was that Randy Dykes "now says that his testimony was incomplete and that prosecutors told him what to say on the witness stand." I knew all the way to the bottom of my soul that this was true. Nothing else could explain the lies told from the witness stand by Randy and Rodney Dykes, Robert Hoehn, Shyster Jackson, Doug Collard, and so many others.

Finally, someone was listening, and that someone was the state's most conservative newspaper—the *Dallas Morning News*.

BY MARCH, SCOTT Howe had called and arranged for the former supervisor of the FBI's fingerprint division, George Bonebrake, to examine Lieutenant Doug Collard's trial testimony. Bonebrake gave Howe an affidavit stating that there was no way to scientifically age a fingerprint. In short, Collard had lied so Smith County could obtain an arrest warrant to satisfy "probable cause"—during the September 1977 examining trial, at the bond hearing, to the grand jury that indicted me and held me over for trial, and finally, before the jury that convicted me. I always knew it; now everyone else would, too. It was a huge development.

Next, Scott obtained a certified copy of my driver's license photograph from the Department of Motor Vehicles in Austin, taken on June 10, 1977, the day of the murder. It showed my hair was brown, long, and to my shoulders—a far cry from silver and touching the ears. He had a professional photographer blow it up in order to potentially display it before a jury.

Scott wasn't done yet. He went to Tyler and interviewed a tenured professor of psychology named Dr. Frederick "Gary" Mears. He was a forensic psychologist and had written numerous articles in his field, including works in the areas of psychopathology and forensic psychology. He had been qualified to testify as an expert in psychology in Texas courts over a hundred times. In an affidavit submitted to Howe, Dr. Mears stated that he had served as chairman of the department of psychology at the University of Texas at Tyler from 1973 through 1985, and that he was acquainted with James Mayfield, Linda Jo Edwards, and Paula Rudolph, who were all fellow employees at the university. More than a year prior to Edwards's murder, Dr. Mears was reviewing the psychology titles in the university library and came across a forensic book that was almost exclusively made up of police crime-scene photographs depicting female mutilation murders. In his opinion the book held no academic value and should never have been placed in the university library in the first place. He learned from the library staff that none other than James Mayfield, the dean of library resources, had ordered it.

Mears's affidavit said that a day or two after Linda Jo Edwards's murder, Mayfield walked into Mears's office and asked him if he could tell him how he could "beat" a lie detector test. Mayfield knew that Mears had a polygraph machine in his lab, but Mears refused to help Mayfield. Mears described Mayfield's demeanor as "upset and worried." Mears knew that Mayfield had been romantically involved with Linda Jo Edwards and that she had tried to commit suicide when he left her to go back to his wife. As a result of this behavior, Mayfield had been asked to resign. Soon afterward, Mears heard reports that Edwards had died from multiple stab wounds. Mears decided to confront Mayfield about the book on sexual mutilation killings. Mayfield looked worried that the book he had ordered had been discovered, and Mayfield told Mears that he had other books like that one. Mears advised him to hire a lawyer, at which time Mayfield left.

A few hours later, Mears telephoned the Tyler Police Department and asked to speak with the chief. He was transferred to a high-level official whom he believed was the chief, maybe a detective. Mears identified himself and told the official of the mutilation book and what had transpired in his office with Mayfield. No follow-up questions were asked; the voice simply said the police would get back to Mears and then the person quickly hung up. The police never did get back to him.

The day after Mears called the police he saw Mayfield in the hallway and asked him if he had hired a lawyer. He acknowledged he had and that the police had informed his lawyer about what Mears had told the police in the phone call. Mears was startled that the police had given this information to a possible suspect's attorney.

"My lawyer has advised me not to talk with you," Mayfield said, and stormed off.

"COOK, PACK YOUR stuff. You're going on bench warrant."

It was May 20, 1988. Scott Howe had warned me that Smith County likely was going to grandstand and bring me back to Tyler to set an execution date. I didn't trust the deputies, so I spoke as few words as necessary during the three-hour drive.

When we arrived, I was escorted up to the second floor, and soon I was facing the two double oak doors of the 241st Judicial District courtroom. I saw myself nearly ten years earlier, face ablaze with tears, being pushed out through those same doors after being sentenced to death. Now the halls were silent, but I couldn't help looking over to where my mother would have been standing, shielding her face in shame. I entered the familiar courtroom, and instead of lawyers John Ament and Larue Dixon, it was Robert McGlasson, Scott Howe, and Eden Harrington who greeted me from the defense table.

"Kerry, we anticipate Judge Tunnell is going to set an execution date for you today. They are going to do this even though the United States Supreme Court hasn't ruled on our certiorari petition. It's just posturing for the media," Scott whispered while Robert nodded matter-of-factly.

Thankfully, it all happened quickly. Rolling into the courtroom through the side entrance just as Judge Phillips had done so many times before, Judge Joe Tunnell rapidly read a statement proclaiming that I was now scheduled to be put to death no later than sunrise on July 8, 1988.

I had scarcely heard those words before I was hoisted out of the courtroom, stuffed back in the sheriff's car, and driven to Huntsville. I was back on death row before dinner.

ON A TUESDAY afternoon in June—eleven days before my scheduled execution—the U.S. Supreme Court in Washington, D.C., stayed my pending execution based on Scott's petition for writ of certiorari. The Court recessed for the summer and pledged to review the substance of the petition as the first order of business for the fall term.

It was a long, hot wait, but in the first week of October, the Supreme Court granted our certiorari petition and sent the case back to the Texas Court of Criminal Appeals for reconsideration in light of another Supreme Court case called *Satterwhite v. Texas*.

In the Satterwhite case, the Court found that a prosecutor's use of psychiatric testimony aimed at predicting a defendant's future dangerousness was a constitutional violation unless the defendant had first been read his Miranda rights against self-incrimination before being interviewed. Dr. Grigson had never informed me that I had the right to have Ament and Dixon present during the meeting. In my case before the Court, the question was not so much that Dr. Grigson's testimony was a violation—the state readily admitted that it was—but whether or not Grigson's testimony had contributed to the jury's verdict of death and, if it did, whether it could be construed as harmless, as it was possible that other evidence—i.e., Jerry Landrum's testimony—that was admitted before the jury at the same time could have sufficiently established that I was "a future danger to society."

Finally, there was a basis for real hope. But I also knew it could just as easily be fool's gold. Other death-row prisoners around me had gotten their cases reversed on the same technicality, but their respective counties had merely requested that the governor commute their death sentence to life imprisonment in order to avoid the expense of a retrial. To me, facing a life sentence in the Texas prison system hardly seemed to be an improvement on execution.

A week later, on October 9, David Hanners and the *Dallas Morning News* ran another front-page story entitled "Key Testimony in Cook Case Said to Be False." Every time I read an article, my heart raced to hear what had been discovered in my case by investigative reporting. The truth was slowly coming out.

A policeman's testimony about the fingerprint that helped put Kerry Max Cook on death row was mostly false and misleading, according to two experts who have examined the print. . . . The fingerprint is the only piece of physical evidence linking Cook to the scene of the crime. . . . Jurors told 'The News' earlier this year that they had considered Collard's testimony crucial in the case against Cook.

Now, the whole state knew how Collard and the prosecution had falsely "aged" my fingerprint in order to make me appear guilty. Rudolph, Gonzalez, Randy and Rodney Dykes, Shyster Jackson, and Hoehn: as incredible as it sounded, the police and the District Attorney's Office had manipulated every witness.

But unfortunately, my fate was still in the hands of the Texas courts, which thus far were resistant to admit that an innocent man had been railroaded onto death row. Still, on January 18, 1989, when Scott Howe argued my case again before the Texas Court of Criminal Appeals in Austin, I could not help feeling hopeful.

A YEAR LATER, we would find out that the U.S. Supreme Court didn't hold much weight in Texas after all. On January 17, 1990, my former attorney Harry Heard's "magic weapon," Judge "Rusty"

Duncan III, authored a 7–2 majority decision reaffirming my conviction and death sentence. Justice Duncan wrote, "After reviewing the evidence at both the guilt/innocence and punishment stages of the trial, and taking appropriate account of the vile, offensive, and sordid facts, we find beyond a reasonable doubt that the improper admission of Dr. Grigson's testimony did not contribute to the appellant's punishment." In other words, it was an error, but because of the testimony of Jerry Landrum, a harmless one that did not merit a reversal of the jury's verdict.

Howe had fifteen days in which to file a motion asking the court to reconsider their ruling, which upheld my conviction for a second time. It was only a perfunctory measure, one that was likely to be summarily denied. Even Scott Howe, who had been so optimistic, was resigned to the fact that there was no justice in the Texas Court of Criminal Appeals.

BUT I BEGAN to realize that it wasn't just the criminal justice system, the prisoners, or the prison administration that I had to find ways to overcome: My fight was also internal.

The jealousy over the *Dallas Morning News*'s attention to my case brought hardships and depression. I was taken back to Ellis II Unit, the psychiatric facility, and placed on suicide precaution on E-1 wing. I was given no clothes, mattress, soap, toothpaste, toilet paper, or underwear—my cell was as naked as I was. None of the mostly female medical personnel wanted to come near a convicted rapist. Lying alone, I had to develop better ways to cope with my circumstances. Doyle Wayne was gone now, and it was easy to close my eyes and allow myself to be swallowed by the darkness that forever lurked inside me. But I knew that if I ever stopped fighting and allowed myself to be consumed by that despair—then I would never find my way back. To fail could still mean death, but I had to try. *I will never give up,* I whispered to myself.

I *was* allowed mail, and I stared at a cream-colored envelope in my bars. It was a letter from Centurion Ministries that had been forwarded from Ellis I Unit, death row. I first wrote the organization after seeing a *60 Minutes* program regarding a Texas janitor named Clarence Lee Brandley, who Mr. Jim McCloskey, a lay minister, had gotten freed from a wrongful rape/murder conviction. Centurion was a New Jersey–based, nonprofit investigative organization, composed of volunteers from the Princeton University community—faculty, lawyers, doctors, administrators, social workers, seminary students, and other learned people who lent their time investigating the thousands of letters received each year from prisoners across the United States who had substantive claims of innocence.

Centurion had very narrow criteria for considering cases: You had to be factually innocent, that is, you had absolutely *nothing* whatsoever to do with the crime you were convicted of. And you had to be serving a life sentence, or death sentence and have exhausted all appeals. If their preliminary investigation supports complete innocence, they then hire a competent attorney and an investigator to further develop the case. Then the attorney will submit a habeas corpus petition and try to free you based on the accumulated evidence of innocence.

Reporter David Hanners met McCloskey while he and an attorney named Paul Nugent were working on the case of Clarence Lee Brandley, whom they freed from Texas death row. Jim was on his way back to New Jersey when Hanners told him, "I think you're leaving another one behind." David sent Jim a thick envelope containing his award-winning investigative stories on my case. On Hanners's recommendation, I also wrote Jim. I had hoped that McCloskey could do for my case what he had done in Brandley's. Yes, I now had Scott Howe, but he was spread thin with other cases—and it looked like we had reached a dead end in the appeals process. Besides, until I was freed, nothing could be considered enough.

A week passed and then the mail carrier came. Inside an envelope there were a set of forms and, attached by a paper clip, a hand-scrawled note by Jim McCloskey. The note read:

> Thank you for your letter. Before I commit to any case, I require an honest, detailed account of your life, from childhood to present; a detailed description of your conviction. It should be as long as it takes for you to tell me everything about you. An innocent man named Matt Connor, he once wrote us 60 pages. I know that is a lot, and that was an extraordinary case. I look forward to reading your story.

All during the day, into the night, and through the middle of the next day, I worked feverishly. With a cramped hand, I pressed the dull point of the pencil into the paper to make the last period, then straightened my stack of paper and read it back to myself.

> Dear Mr. McCloskey: You said a man named Matt Connor once wrote you 60 pages. Enclosed please find my 61-page biography, detailing my conviction as well as life before arriving to death row. I am one page more innocent than he was.

I stuck the envelope between the bars for pickup on Saturday, February 24, 1990, and slept soundly until the next day.

Meanwhile, February moved into March, April, May, and then into June without word on Scott Howe's last appeals court motion. But on June 13, 1990, the Texas Court of Criminal Appeals stunned the legal community and *granted* Howe's motion for rehearing. I was shocked speechless.

THE MORNING OF November 2, 1990, Jim McCloskey paid me a personal visit. We talked intensely for five hours straight—

McCloskey grilled me heatedly, and demanded to know every scrap of detail I could think of relating to the case. McCloskey made notes as I spoke, but then he got right to what he had really come for: "I want to know about the fingerprint," he said, looking at me through the glass. Still afraid to admit that I had known Linda Edwards, I repeated the theory that had been originally advanced at the 1978 trial—that I had seen Edwards nude from the sidewalk and had walked up to her patio door to get a closer look. It would take me another year to admit to McCloskey that I had met Edwards at the pool and had been invited into her apartment several days before her murder.

McCloskey wanted to grill me on one last issue. He asked about a 1988 *Dallas Morning News* story entitled "Ex-D.A. Says Inmate Confessed." After the newspaper ran its first front-page article in February 1988, "Inmate Was Railroaded," A. D. Clark responded by manufacturing a story that I "confessed" the murder during a break in the jury selection proceedings. I told Jim that it was an incredible lie. It did not shock me: I had also been on the receiving end of Clark's vile and unscrupulous misconduct since my arrest.

"Talk to my trial attorneys, Jim," I said. "They were there. They will tell you A. D. Clark is a liar."

"That is protected by the attorney-client relationship, Kerry. Ament is prohibited from discussing with me anything you may have confided in him. However, if you are *really* telling the truth, and this Clark is that corrupt—prove it to me: Sign a paper and waive your right to the attorney-client confidentiality clause and clear the way for me to talk to John Ament so I can get to the bottom of this."

"Get me the form, I will sign it and send it back to you immediately," I said.

A week later McCloskey returned with an investigator named Richard Reyna.

"We met with John Ament. He confirms your rendition of events. You've been telling me the truth; he said you never confessed to them or to any member of the District Attorney's Office. This and other pieces of our investigation to this story prove you are telling the truth. This portion is behind us, Kerry," Jim told me.

I HAD BEEN assigned a record-breaking two years at the Ellis II Treatment Center. In that time my entire treatment team turned over. Under great scrutiny, the team of Kathy Oden, Dr. Joanne Johnson, and Tina Gougler had courageously ignored administrative pressure and kept me off death row and assigned to the Treatment Center. This was in part because of the ongoing front-page investigative articles in the *Dallas Morning News*, Justice Clinton's dissenting opinion, and the addition of Jim McCloskey and Centurion Ministries to the fight. They believed my conviction would undoubtedly be set aside and that it would be inhumane to keep me on death row, especially with "Good Pussy" carved on my ass.

Considering me a model prisoner with a spotless two-year record since arriving, Kathy Oden and the rest of my treatment team persuaded the building major to remove me from the punitive E-1 cellblock of suicide precaution to the general-population intermediate wing of B-1, and they changed my automatic death-row classification of "A" status to that of "B," or nonassaultive, prisoner. This had never been done before. It meant I would no longer have to wear handcuffs while on the unit. It also meant I could go to and from the chow hall, therapist meetings, visitation, arts and crafts sessions, without an escort. Kathy Oden called me "Christopher Columbus" of the Texas prison system because of the new ground I had broken. I had made a lasting impression on tough prisoncrats who believed in me enough to take a risk. I vowed that I would not let them down.

That evening I was moved into the first cell at the front of the wing with David Franklin Hunter. David had also been on Ellis and knew about my story before I arrived. Hunter was about twenty-four and also had been sent to the psychiatric facility for depression—he had a lot to be depressed about: Hunter had been convicted of a string of armed robberies and sentenced to an aggravated sentence of 149 years. Pending direct intervention from God, he wasn't likely to see the light of day until he was elderly. During the brief time we shared the cell on B-1 together, the *Dallas Morning News* was continuing to put my story before the Texas public in detailed, revealing stories. Late at night, obsessed with the trickery and prosecutorial malfeasance that had railroaded me to prison, Hunter read all the stories, and expressed sympathy and shock at the extent to which prosecutors had gone to place me there.

Hunter had been receiving visits from a twenty-two-year-old girl named Amy Joanne Ticer. She was from Chandler, Texas, just outside Tyler, and her mother and a lady named Betty Mathews founded a local prison ministry called Standing in the Gap. Because I rarely received visits, Hunter pushed me to let Amy visit me for emotional support. Finally I did. The truth is, I was alone and desperate for any kind of human contact or companionship. After Doyle Wayne's murder, I felt empty, and so I began to visit with Amy Joanne. Meanwhile, Hunter was shipped back to the Darrington Unit—a rough and tough maximum-security unit that held the prison system's more notorious white supremacist gangs.

Before long Amy was convinced I was innocent, and wanted to get more involved with my case. She also began to express more than a platonic interest in our friendship, and she informed me one afternoon that she felt compelled to tell David. Hunter's letters trickled to a stop and his jealousy grew. Hunter began visiting with Amy's mother, Susan, instead.

I loved Amy Joanne—or maybe I was in love with the *thought* of not having to be alone anymore. It was difficult to separate my emotions. Either way, I surrendered to my feelings and we began visiting and writing as a couple. In fact, she was so convinced that I was going to get out that we talked about getting married.

Texas had a law that made allowances for those who were incarcerated, and therefore unable to attend their own marriage service, by allowing a prisoner to obtain a legally binding marriage by proxy. It was a wedding ceremony with all of the appearance of normalcy, but instead of the groom standing before the minister, a man of the prisoner's choosing stands in for him and says "I do." In my case, I chose Daddy, though he could barely stand.

On the Fourth of July, 1991, Amy drove twenty miles to Jacksonville, where Reverend Moore from Mama and Daddy's church performed the wedding ceremony at my parents' house.

I PERSUADED MY psychologist, Dr. Don Gottney, to discharge me from the treatment center so that I could return to death row and live out the final days of my death-penalty struggle—win or lose. I would not be alone now. I had Amy Joanne. I was discharged and I returned to death row in early August. I was put on G-15, next door to Vernon Satterwhite, John Satterwhite's cousin.

Soon David Hunter wrote me a letter. In an angry tirade, he delivered an ultimatum: If I didn't stop writing and visiting Amy immediately, he was going to contact the Smith County District Attorney's Office and inform them I had confessed the murder to him in intimate detail while we shared a cell together. I was given three days to acknowledge by a return letter.

The next day I went out to the visitation room and looked Amy in the eyes. "Do you really love me?"

"Why do you ask?" she said, laughing.

"Just tell me, Amy. I have one of the most important decisions of my life to make."

"Yes, I do," she said.

"Then, we will weather this storm. I will never leave you, Amy. Not for Hunter, not for anyone." I told her of Hunter's letter. For the first time she told me of the letters she, too, had been getting from him, telling her I had confessed to him and that she had no idea how sick I was. She said she knew it wasn't true, but her mother, Susan, whom I had never met, didn't share her beliefs. Her mother would return from weekend visits with Hunter and apply enormous pressure on Amy to return to Hunter and stop seeing me, because I was extremely dangerous and guilty of the murder of Linda Jo Edwards. Amy Joanne refused, and not long after that, "Mom" turned into "Susan," Hunter's new girlfriend. Soon they were married.

David Hunter, out of the madness of his hatred and jealousy, did write the Smith County District Attorney's Office, claiming I had confessed the murder to him. Eventually Detective Eddie Clark and Assistant District Attorney Kevin Henry went to Huntsville and secured a sworn statement from him attesting to that fact. Hunter believed if Shyster could go free for *murder*, surely a few armed robberies could be overlooked and a deal could be worked out to set him free as well.

Every week, Susan Ticer told Amy a new horror story about me and more details of the sick way I purportedly tortured, raped, and murdered Linda Edwards. To make things worse, Susan was now in contact with Smith County Assistant D.A. Kevin Henry on David's behalf trying to secure a deal.

"He's the sickest man imaginable. He belongs to a satanic cult and he is a devil worshipper," Susan screamed at Amy one night before she was to visit me the next morning. "Kevin Henry is an officer of the state—he wouldn't *just lie*! You have to stop this nonsense before it's too late. He's a *monster*, Amy!" She demanded her daughter annul the marriage.

Amy had me write her every single day—no matter what was going on, because of the pressure her mother was putting on her. I spent my first few days back on the Ellis Unit curled up on my metal bunk writing novels of love and encouragement to my brand-new wife.

Susan called the Smith County District Attorney's Office often because she was trying to negotiate a deal for Hunter in exchange for his testimony against me. Amy said Hunter knew the extraordinary lengths they went to to get the testimony of Shyster Jackson.

"My Kerry, I am under constant pressure at home. I need you to write every day so I can stand and not fall against it."

And I did. But she didn't stand long.

Only a few weeks after exchanging our wedding vows, Amy disappeared from my life. I wrote frantically but each night, the guard passed my cell without a word from her in return.

ALTHOUGH I TRIED my best to forget death row during the two years I was away, death row hadn't forgotten about the guy with "Good Pussy" carved on his backside.

"What does that bitch look like," a voice on the first row said.

"I don't fuck around. Man, no matter what, that bitch still got a dick. I ain't doing that rodeo," someone said mirthfully.

"I dunno, but I heard Leon King fucked that bitch in the shower on '15."

I had been cooped up for two weeks, refusing recreation each afternoon. I had finished writing Amy a nine-page letter and this time when the guard stopped at my cell I finally said yes to recreation. I knew that an old friend named David Harris was in my recreational group. I liked him a lot, and I thought I would go out and talk with him, since I hadn't seen him for years.

I never made it out to the yard from the dayroom.

I met James Russell's eyes briefly before they darted to see where the guard was on the wing. "No, Russell, don't know what you heard but I am not like that," I said as I tried to back away. Russell cornered me by the urinal and pushed himself against me. He shoved his hand into the back of my pants and then pushed a thick, dry finger inside me.

I panicked and didn't know what to do. My mind did nothing. He climaxed into the urinal and the sick sexual whispers stopped ringing in my ears.

Looking around while he fixed himself up, he said, "You're all right, Cookie. Hey, come out tomorrow—let's talk! All right?"

One after the other the prisoners from the outside yard came in. To my shock the guards had reverted to implementing a full strip-search policy on return from recreation. Ice raced up and down my spine. They had stopped this strip-searching policy before I left, but every time there was an outbreak of renewed violence, they reinstituted it. I looked on as two guards took each article of clothing and ran it through their hands before handing it back.

"Turn around, bend over, and spread 'em," the officer said.

Oh my God. What am I going to do? I can't strip in front of everyone.

"Cook? Let's go!" a female yelled. I walked up to the G-13 door and tried to whisper to the female guard about the stuff on my butt and how traumatic it would be to have to strip with an audience behind me.

"Strip. Let's go. You got the same thing everybody else's got—let's go," she barked. I got down to my underwear and pleaded with my eyes. Their eyes told me to do like everyone else had to do.

As I did, I heard the familiar catcall whistles from behind.

I was handcuffed and the guard put me in my cell.

Soon a porter threw a note on my bed. "James Russell sent that to you," he said and slipped away.

I opened it up and he had outlined his penis. It was wet and sticky.

That night I took a full pack of the prescription Dimetapp cold medicine that I had gotten from the clinic. I set a broken shard of mirror in the cell bars so I could see if and when the guard or anyone else was coming down the row. Then I broke up three commissary razors. I ran the first blade over my arm, and then deep into the back of my legs. Heat flowed down my body. I grabbed a piece of typing paper.

I really was an innocent man, Amy Joanne, Mama, Daddy, Doyle Wayne. I can't do it anymore. I love you.

My rectum still stung from the plunging finger of Russell. Images of me just standing there, paralyzed, doing nothing, darted in and out of my mind, causing me to shake my head violently from side to side. After losing my rights as a male and having scratched my way to survival tooth and nail to make it just to suffer further, I looked down at the penis that, according to prison programming, I shouldn't have. I broke open a new blade, closed my eyes, and began cutting deeply into the soft flesh.

I slipped the note into my typewriter as a way to hold it.

The darkness screamed at me, and instead of fighting it, I embraced it, stepped into it, and finally felt no more.

"I'm coming home, Doyle Wayne" was the last thought I remembered saying, as I cut my arm and leg and ran the blade against my throat. Only later would I learn that the prison officials had videotaped me as I lay bleeding to death in my cell.

I woke up two days later at the UTMB (University of Texas Medical Branch) Hospital in Galveston, Texas. Dr. Karen Caroti was staring down at me.

"Welcome back. You're quite a lucky man."

I was at this prison medical facility for several days before being discharged and returned to death row. Though I had been patched back together, I returned to a life made worse by what I had done. Also, I finally did hear from Amy. It was brief and to the point. Richard Reyna, the investigator hired by Centurion to look into my case and who had uncovered more evidence that tended to establish my innocence, told Amy that he was beginning to believe I was a homosexual because of what a prison guard said to him one day as he was leaving the unit after visiting me. Amy became convinced that I had married her under false pretenses, and she was going to seek an immediate annulment of the marriage. She hired a Tyler attorney and I was served divorce papers.

LATER THAT SUMMER, a guard walked by doing a routine counting of heads. Near panic, I stopped him and thrust the precious piece of paper through the bars. The guard pushed my hand back into my cell.

"The warden approved this call! It's my father. He's dying—I have to talk to him."

"After we feed chow. I'll see what I can do," he said coolly.

I paced up and down the cramped quarters of my cell. I could feel the tension in my face. In my hand, I clutched a piece of paper that was my only hope of speaking to my father again. It was a prison form called an "I-60," or an Inmate Request Form. It was a prisoner's only means of communicating with the warden. Warden Peterson had signed this particular I-60 and authorized me to be taken to the office to call my daddy at Nan Travis Hospital in Jacksonville, where he lay on his deathbed. Daddy had asked my mother to make arrangements through the warden, so that we could talk over the phone one last time. My father had requested that the morphine and other pain-reducing drugs be lessened because he wanted to be lucid when he and I spoke—he had something to tell me, something he wanted to leave with me, and I desperately wanted to hear it from him.

Every moment passed like a lifetime as I waited for the guards to take me from my cell to the phone. It was, in my mind, one less second Daddy had for me. The mobile "chow cart" had come and gone, and the cleanup process for the evening meal was completed. I tried to catch the guard's eye to remind him I was still waiting. I continued to pace up and down my cell. Another guard walked by to get my next-door neighbor, Rudy Hernandez, who was diabetic and was taken over to the clinic across the hall from G-15 every day and given an insulin injection. I raced to the green bars, thrusting the piece of paper through, pleading, "My father is dying, I need to use the phone. Please! The warden approved it."

"We're aware of it, Cook. After count time." With that, the guard walked away with Rudy. A few minutes later, guards brought Rudy back, put him in his cell, took the cuffs off, and left. I fought back my panic and remained silent as I watched the two guards walk away.

Hours later my hands were still clutched around the bars of my cell, my knuckles white and cramped, as I stood looking for any sign of a guard. Seeing no one and hearing nothing other than the mundane sounds of prison, I shouted into the nothingness: "The warden approved this call. My daddy's dying!" The other prisoners banged their metal cups on the bars in protest because the noise was bothering them.

Suddenly a guard materialized from nowhere. "Cook, you're not going to get your phone call raising all this hell and creating this disturbance. Knock it off or you won't get a phone call, period. Just sit on your bunk and someone will come to get you."

Reluctantly, I released the bars and sat on the corner of my bunk, facing the cell door so I could watch for them to come and get me.

Soon it was 10:00 P.M., and guards changed to the graveyard shift. The new guard on watch walked up to my cell for a routine TV vote. "Officer," I frantically said, as I again thrust the I-60 form through the bars to show him, "I have had this phone call approved from the warden. My father is on his deathbed—I have to call him. It's my last chance to ever—"

The guard cut me off. "Cook, you know there's no phone calls after 10:00 P.M." Mute tears fell from my face. I told the guard I urgently needed to see Sergeant Pruitt, the graveyard supervisor. He said he would look into it. With that, he stepped to the next cell and asked, "TV vote?" I was situated on the bottom row of the G-15 cellblock. Two tiers were above me. The guard had fifty-nine more cells to go, and as he moved from cell to cell his robotic question grew fainter—and with it, so did any hope of ever hearing my daddy's voice again.

I waited and waited until sleep somehow overtook me. The next sound I heard was the startling kick of my cell door. I had lost all sense of time. My eyes burned as I tried to adjust them to the morning light hitting my face. A tall, clean-cut figure wearing a tan blazer looked down at me. It was the new Ellis Unit chaplain, Reverend Taylor.

"Are you, Cook?" he said casually.

I looked into his face and responded, "Yes, sir, I am. Are you here to take me for my phone call?"

"Your father passed away at 7:30 this morning. Your mother is at the hospital. I can bring you to my office to use the phone, if you want," he said stoically. Every bone in my body seemed to crack. The chaplain motioned to a nearby guard. I backed up to the bars and was handcuffed for the trip to his Ellis Unit office.

I sat motionless in the metal chair in the chaplain's small office. One handcuff was removed and the other attached to the arm of the chair. The chaplain dialed the phone and handed it to me. "Mama," I cried. "I'm sorry."

"Why didn't you call him? He asked for you over and over through the night. Why didn't you call?" My mother's hostility washed over me.

The only words I could find were "I tried, Mama, I tried."

As I trudged slowly back to my cell on G-15 that day, my mind could not see or feel death row any longer. My mind was inundated with images of my daddy's pain-filled face. I had long ago come to the cold reality that my country and my government could place me on death row for a crime I hadn't committed. Ironically, my daddy had given his youth and his entire twenty-one-year career in the military because of his love for his country and government.

I longed to hear the words my daddy would have spoken to me.

I now know from his sister that he knew I was innocent and that I would one day prove it. He worried that after Doyle Wayne was murdered and his passing, I would give up and die. He wanted me to take care of Mama. My struggle brought misery and despair in the days, weeks, and months following my father's death. It haunted me to know what his last words would have been to me. But for just an ounce of compassion, I could have known.

It began to feel like I was drawing strength from an empty well.

8

THE MORE THINGS STAY
THE SAME: PRETRIAL, 1992

Congratulations, Kerry. I had just heard the news. The appeals court reversed your conviction and death sentence—and themselves. What a story!"

One year and three months after the TCCA had granted Scott Howe's motion for a rehearing, on September 18, 1991, while out in the visiting room, a reporter for the *Houston Chronicle* leaned over and interrupted my visit to tell me.

In a historically grueling legal fight, Scott Howe had scored the match point and prevailed, stopping Texas from putting me to death. My case was reversed on a punishment phase technicality, yes, but it was nevertheless a reversal of the conviction and would give me the chance to go back into a Smith County courtroom with a clean slate, armed with all the information the *Dallas Morning News* and Centurion Ministries had uncovered—and with Jim McCloskey and a competent death penalty attorney at my table defending me.

The *Dallas Morning News* had completely dismantled the entire case against me, revealing it to be a huge embellishment and systemic instance of police and prosecutorial misconduct. The legal criterion to deny me a reasonable bond was that the proof of guilt had to be "proof evident." There was no way to meet that burden of proof now. *If there is to be a second retrial, I will get to go home to await it,* I thought to myself.

On Wednesday, October 30, 1991, God caused lady luck to point her smile my way when the TCCA denied Smith County's attempt to have my conviction reinstated. This ruling put the lights out on Smith County's efforts. Still, they went back to the U.S. Supreme Court, to argue that the TCCA was in error in reversing my conviction.

"Scott," I said when he came to visit me to tell me the TCCA had rejected their petition to reinstate my death sentence, "why are they appealing?"

"Because they are stalling for time, Kerry," Scott said. "Their backs are up against the wall and they are just trying to buy time to reconnoiter so they can send a wing and a prayer up to the Supreme Court in the hope that a miracle will happen," Scott replied. "Kerry, in a case such as yours, rife with so much police and prosecutorial misconduct, they can't ever admit a mistake was made. They won't let go. You'll have to fight them every inch of the way."

AS AN OUT-OF-STATE attorney licensed in Washington, D.C., Scott Howe could not try a case in Texas. Scott relinquished all legal responsibility in my case and handed it over to Houston attorney Paul Nugent in December 1991. I trusted Scott Howe with my life, and I loved him for the respect he showed me. It was difficult knowing he was not my counsel of record anymore. I was going to have to switch over to a complete stranger, handpicked by Jim McCloskey, who would be paying all of the bills. But I trusted Jim, and he had complete faith in Nugent. When Paul was fresh out of law school in Boston, he moved to Conroe, Texas, where he exposed widespread racial prejudice and police misconduct. He also helped Jim exonerate Clarence Brandley from ten years of wrongful imprisonment on Texas's death row.

Paul Nugent had studied all the information Jim accumulated, including the 1978 trial transcript. On a Sunday morning, he called and told Jim he would take on my case because he, too, was convinced that I was wrongfully convicted. Jim said Centurion couldn't pay him a lot at this point, so Paul took my case pro bono—in the interest of justice. Scott and Paul worked on the response to Smith County's brief before the Supreme Court together. Although it was Scott's last official act as my attorney, it was far from his last as my friend.

We did not know it yet, but the combined efforts of John Ament, Larue Dixon, Harry Heard, and Scott Howe would pale in comparison to what Paul Nugent and Jim McCloskey would go through in joining my battle.

JIM COMPLETED HIS initial investigation in December 1991 and wrote a report entitled "Why Centurion Ministries Believes Jim Mayfield Killed Linda Jo Edwards."

More than fifty friends, neighbors, relatives, and professional colleagues of Jim Mayfield were interviewed. None of these people had been individually interviewed by the Tyler Police Department. Three of the interviewees, including Dr. Mears, were colleagues of Mayfield and had taken it upon *themselves* to contact the Tyler Police Department because of information they had regarding Mayfield and the Edwards murder—none was ever called back or contacted again by the police. Everyone interviewed in the report believed that Mayfield could very well have killed Linda Jo Edwards.

The report began with Paula Rudolph's description and identification of the killer. All the people to whom Centurion spoke agreed that Mayfield's build matched Rudolph's description—sleek and slender, a very trim figure with a broad face, broad shoulders. The height and complexion as consistently described by Rudolph also fit Mayfield. He was around five feet seven inches and during June had a nice tan from playing tennis. The hairstyle as described by Rudolph matched Mayfield's silver cut—medium length and styled in a "touching-the-ears fashion."

McCloskey's report contained a critical observation regarding Rudolph's eyewitness identification. After a reenactment of Rudolph's observations at the crime scene with District Attorney Dobbs, McCloskey wrote in the fall of 1991:

> Rudolph told the jury that for a split second she and the man were face to face. She viewed the figure while standing in a dark foyer and looked at the figure who was standing in the well-lighted room. This is an ideal lighting situation to accurately see someone. David Dobbs and I reenacted Paula's view in the same apartment with the exact same lighting conditions at night just a few weeks ago. David, playing Paula, looked at McCloskey playing the killer. David mentioned to me that my hair was getting gray on the side. I pointed out to David that's because my hair *is* starting to gray on the sides. Dobbs also revealed something startling and stunning, confiding that he (Dobbs) didn't believe Paula Rudolph saw Kerry Cook at all.

The report also described Mayfield's character and personality. According to those who knew him best, Mayfield had an explosive temper. Each of the nine women who worked for Mayfield at Midwestern University, as well as the women who worked for him at Texas Eastern University, described him as a vindictive and abusive personality whose mood swings were unpredictable and frequent. At home, Mayfield completely domineered his wife, Elfriede, and ruled over his family with an iron hand.

Mayfield's former primary assistant, head reference librarian Olene Harned, also gave an affidavit. Rudolph called Harned shortly after she called the police the morning she found Edwards. Harned drove over and picked up Rudolph and took her to the police station and then home to her house that weekend. Rudolph confided in her that she thought the murderer was Mayfield. On the Monday following the crime, Mayfield came to work shaking and crying. He told Harned that he had failed a polygraph test several times and he had hired Buck Files as his defense lawyer. Harned stated that she was shocked the police had never interviewed her about Mayfield during their initial investigation.

Mayfield's secretary, Sophia Lenderman, reported her boss had talked about wanting to break off his relationship with Linda, but still had some reservations about leaving her. After Edwards's suicide attempt, Lenderman was aware that Linda had written a suicide letter to Mayfield. Lenderman also stated she was surprised that no police officer ever contacted her during the course of their investigation.

Pam Post, who was a clerk in the Office of Admissions and Records in 1977, said in her affidavit, "Linda had just returned to her employment at the university soon after her suicide attempt. She appeared puffy eyed, nervous, and high strung. When I asked her what was bothering her or what was the matter, she told me she was having problems with 'Mayfield.' She referred to him by his last name. I then asked her what do you mean. She responded by saying 'I am going to get him back, no matter what.' She made that same comment to me at least twice or three times that day; that she was going to get him back no matter what."

Peggy McGill, a recent widow when she worked for Mayfield in the library from 1975 to 1977, told Centurion that Mayfield was a "wild animal on the prowl." He was "like a wolf"—trying to trap her in the library book stacks or in his office alone with the door shut. Eddie Clark called her after the murder and asked her what the atmosphere was like at the library, and she told him that it was like "a time bomb." Even so, Detective Eddie Clark had never asked any questions about Mayfield. In fact, *no one* from the Tyler Police Department interviewed her one-on-one. She stated she couldn't believe they didn't do this.

Dr. Judy Freeman, a colleague and neighbor of Mayfield, was also a confidante of Linda's. According to Freeman, Linda told her that Mayfield was "jealous and possessive" of her. As soon as they heard that Linda had been murdered, Freeman and her husband went to the police station to tell them that they thought Mayfield could have committed the murder because he was so jealous. Professor Andrew Szarka and his wife, Tamara, also went to the police station as soon as they found out about the murder. Both were colleagues of Mayfield and neighbors on Lake Palestine. Earlier on the night of the murder, Edwards came over to their home after conversing with Mayfield outside his house around 8 P.M. She told the Szarkas that Mayfield was angry with Linda because she had informed him that she wanted to date other men.

Ann White, another employee working under Mayfield's supervision, gave an affidavit stating that on the morning of June 10, 1977, she received a phone call from Dick Harned, Olene Harned's husband, telling her that Edwards had been badly beaten. White informed Mayfield of this a few moments later, as he arrived to work. He telephoned Linda's residence, identified himself, and asked about her condition. White stated, "It did not appear as if the person told Mr. Mayfield anything concerning Miss Edwards because after Mr. Mayfield hung the telephone up, I clearly remember him looking at me and commenting on how calm he had behaved and how he didn't lose his temper." They drove to the Embarcadero Apartments and sat in the car and watched the police, the ambulance, and the media. White said that Mayfield "became angry and told me that Miss Edwards had ruined him, that she had cost him his job and had caused a lot of problems for him."

Later, after Mayfield said that he was no longer a suspect, White's husband told her that during a conversation they'd had, Mayfield had commented, "No matter how serious the trouble you're in, you can get out of almost anything if you have enough money." After the murder, White spoke to Jerry Landrum and his wife at the library. Landrum then told White that Mayfield had been the number one suspect but that the police had not been able to break his alibi.

On the night of the murder, Mayfield claimed, he was at home with his wife and his sixteen-year-old adopted daughter, Louella. Mayfield hired attorney Buck Files after leaving the police station on the day of the murder. According to police reports, Files telephoned the police immediately and advised them that they were not to interview Mayfield, his wife, or his daughter. Files also told police that Mayfield would not be taking the polygraph test he'd agreed to take when he spoke with the police the day of the murder. In effect, Mayfield's "ironclad alibi" was that he simply told police he was at home with his family. No corroboration was ever sought by authorities.

McCloskey also attached to his report copies of the various forensic pictures found in the book *The Sexual Criminal: A Psychoanalytical Study,* which had been ordered by Mayfield. I compared them with the pictures of Linda Jo Edwards's partially nude body that had been blown up in large color pictures during my trial and that were burned in my mind. The similarities were downright eerie, and a few of the poses were identical to the way Edwards's body was found.

WHILE THE UNITED States Supreme Court was considering the District Attorney's Office's petition arguing that the stay of execution should be lifted, prosecutor David Dobbs had extended an olive branch to Jim. Dobbs said he was willing to reinvestigate the case, and if the evidence warranted it, recommend that the criminal district attorney, Jack Skeen, drop all charges. Jim took the position that the evidence Centurion had unburied against James Mayfield was of such a convincing magnitude that it warranted such a recommendation. Jim also took Dobbs at his word.

I didn't—and Scott Howe agreed with me.

"If this were true, why would they continue on with the appeal to the United States Supreme Court trying to get my conviction reinstated?" I asked.

But Jim met with Dobbs, and in an attempt to show that Smith County had convicted the wrong man, he turned over his report; the affidavit given by Dr. Mears; the Bonebrake affidavit that challenged Collard's fingerprint analysis; my June 10, 1977, driver's license photograph proving it was impossible for me with my shoulder-length brown hair to have been the person Rudolph saw in the apartment; and the affidavits Jim had secured from Mayfield's university colleagues. David Dobbs reciprocated by providing Jim with copies of the grand jury testimony and signed statements by Robert Hoehn, James Taylor, and the Dykes brothers. The Smith County district attorney's office had possessed this critical evidence since 1977, but had hidden it from my defense team for the previous fifteen years. (Upon reviewing this new discovery, it became apparent that Robert Hoehn's 1977 grand jury testimony was inexplicably missing pages 37, 40, 42, and 44.)

THE TEXAS COURT of Criminal Appeals officially vacated my conviction, and on the morning of March 4, 1992, I left death row for the Smith County Jail.

As I left the place that had been my home for fourteen years—and at times, I thought, would be the last home I would ever know in this world—I was charged with a sense that my departure from death row was the beginning of the end. The *Dallas Morning News* had championed my story in front-page story after front-page story, exposing a case that had been manufactured by overzealous police and corrupt prosecutors. In addition to what those investigations had brought to light, McCloskey and Centurion Ministries had dug up even more. Most important, I had a seasoned trial lawyer now in Paul Nugent. Armed with so much information and the tools to finally deal with the prosecution, *I will never see this gulag again,* I thought.

I was received at the Smith County Jail like a specimen to be displayed at the local zoo. I was booked in, and a red armband—printed with my name, date of arrival, and the number 7642—was snapped around my right wrist. I exchanged my death-row uniform for an orange monkey suit.

A short man with glasses and an air of supreme self-confidence strode up to me, thrust out his hand like he wanted my vote, and said, "Hi, Kerry. My name is David Dobbs. I'm the chief felony prosecutor for Smith County." He came across not as a prosecutor out to kill me, but as Ed McMahon, surprising a winner of the sweepstakes.

I refused his hand.

"I know your attorney, Paul Nugent, is in trial in Arizona," he continued, "but I would like to know how your fingerprint got on the door. That's the only problem I have with this case."

I was stunned and scared, and at first said nothing. Dobbs, perhaps sensing an opportunity, quickly peppered me with other questions about my case and asked if I would take a polygraph test.

"I won't ever talk with you, and I wouldn't trust you if you were the last man on earth. I need to call my attorney—please just leave me alone. Can I use the phone?" I finally blurted out, telegraphing a look of sheer panic. I didn't know how to get ahold of Paul, so I called Hanners of the *Dallas Morning News* instead. I told him that Dobbs had met me at the jail. I was afraid he would use the opportunity with no witnesses around to say I had confessed to him, or something else equally incriminating. Hanners was shocked and couldn't believe that the District Attorney's prosecutor had met me at the jail and tried to interrogate me—which is exactly what Dobbs had tried to do.

I was whisked into an elevator and up into the jail, placed in a tiny cubicle with a solid steel door. Even before the door of the side cell slammed behind me, I thought to myself, *Bad just got worse.* It was August 8, 1977, all over again.

The next day the *Dallas Morning News* published a story by Hanners that said Dobbs had met me at the jail illegally, cornered me, and tried to get me to discuss the facts of my case. McCloskey denounced Dobbs in strong language, asserting Dobbs's unethical actions were reprehensible and illegal. Once the article came out and I had so publicly blown the whistle on Dobbs, I knew the battle lines would be drawn and they would bury me so far in a hole, they'd have to pump in sunlight.

And they did. Using the ruse it was for my "own protection," I was stuffed once again in a side cell, which was primarily used for disciplinary purposes to deter and control unruly prisoners. I celebrated my thirty-sixth birthday in solitary confinement.

Two weeks later, on April 20, 1992, the U.S. Supreme Court denied Smith County's request to reinstate my conviction and death sentence.

FOR THE SECOND time in sixteen years, the Smith County District Attorney's Office convened a grand jury in the rape and murder of Linda Jo Edwards. It was an improper use of the grand jury system, since I was already indicted under the original 1977 indictment. While the Supreme Court had reversed my conviction, the reversal did not throw out the original indictment that had first brought me to trial—thus calling a new grand jury was both superfluous and an abuse of the power of the District Attorney's Office. Dobbs had subpoenaed the individuals who had provided affidavits to Centurion, requiring them to appear before the grand jury. Paul filed a motion attempting to immediately stop Skeen and Dobbs from using the grand jury system as a means of previewing the new witnesses who, after all, tended to incriminate Mayfield. By subpoenaing these witnesses to appear at the closed-door grand jury hearings, Dobbs was gaining the ability to interrogate them on the record, without Paul Nugent being there to represent our interests. Whatever Dobbs bullied them into saying became the "minutes of the grand jury" and, despite their affidavits, would become the official record and would be used to undermine their testimony.

Paul's motion to force Skeen and Dobbs to stop calling the Centurion witnesses was eventually granted, but not before they had grilled Mears, White, and others on the record. Sometime later, Paul Nugent was able to get the grand jury transcript, and it revealed Dobbs indeed had tried to force Mears to back away from the original force of his statements to Jim.

Dobbs also called ex–Ellis II Unit Treatment Center prisoner David Hunter. Through Hunter, Dobbs advanced yet another "jailhouse confession" story to replace the one lost by Edward Scott "Shyster" Jackson's recantation. Based on the copy of the transcript that Nugent later was able to obtain, Hunter told the grand jury that I had confessed the murder of Linda Jo Edwards to him.

ON MAY 8, 1992, before a packed courtroom and the surviving family of Linda Jo Edwards, the Smith County District Attorney's Office announced their intention to retry me for the rape and murder of Linda Edwards. Judge Tunnell set an October 5, 1992, date for the case to be retried. Later, solely on his own motion, Tunnell moved that retrial to Georgetown, Texas. Georgetown was known to be one of the toughest places on crime in the state—a haven for prosecutors.

When the hearing concluded, Jim, Paul, and I met in a jail conference room for the first time as a defense team. Paul reassuringly set the tone as our leader. "The Smith County District Attorney's Office has proven that they cannot be trusted. They lied and cheated to falsely convict Kerry in 1978. They are now embarrassed that the *Dallas Morning News* has exposed some of their misconduct. They are not interested in seeking the truth or prosecuting the real killer. Only by killing Kerry can they hope to save face. We are in a war to save Kerry's life." Jim understood. He had successfully freed twelve people from wrongful convictions from prisons and death rows around the country. He was a serious-minded man of integrity, a decorated Vietnam War veteran who had been awarded the Bronze Star for his valor and service to his country. Jim rolled up his sleeves that day and knew he was involved in a fight that was going to be like none he had ever encountered.

IN THE SUMMER of 1992, while I sat alone in the side cell, Paul Nugent made an appointment to meet with Dobbs at his office. Paul insisted that he personally inspect all documents related to my case. Dobbs placed a storage box on his desk, then pulled out a folder containing a crime-scene photograph of former district attorney Michael Thompson's dead body, lying crumpled up with a gunshot wound to the head.

"Isn't this terrible—he killed himself," Dobbs remarked.

"Where?" Paul asked.

"At his sister's house, in her closet," Dobbs said. "Isn't it sad?"

"I think it's pretty chickenshit that he killed himself in his sister's house," Paul said.

All the blood drained from Dobbs's face.

"I feel sorry for his sister, but not for him: He would have been disbarred if he hadn't killed himself," Paul continued. "He lied to a jury, suppressed exculpatory evidence, and put an innocent man on death row." With that, Paul set the tone for their meeting; he made it clear that he was there for business.

Dobbs was coy about the cardboard box, not really letting Paul see that much of its contents. Paul saw a tab marked "Doug Collard" and reached for it. Seeing where his hand was going, Dobbs tried to interfere, saying, "That's nothing." But Paul quickly pulled from the box what appeared to be some kind of a report. Dobbs continued to downplay the document, dismissing it as nothing of any significance. Sensing from Dobbs's reaction that the report might be important, Paul demanded a copy. On the way home to Houston, Paul scanned the thick document at a stoplight—what he saw caused him to pull over and carefully read the entire report on the shoulder of the road. He was holding a written "response" by Douglas Collard, now a captain, to a complaint filed by the International Association for Identification (IAI)—"the oldest and largest forensic organization in the world," which certifies forensic professionals in order "to ensure all specialists maintain the highest levels of integrity and professionalism." After having read an October 1988 front-page *Dallas Morning News* article entitled "Key Evidence in Cook Case Said to Be False," a member of the IAI had filed an official complaint against Collard for testifying falsely as to a specific age of a latent print—mine. At the time of the 1978 trial, Collard was seeking his certification with the IAI.

Collard's May 1989 response to the complaint was written on City of Tyler letterhead. In the opening remarks Collard implored the IAI to keep the contents of his response confidential. Paul lit up when he read the following admission by Collard, regarding the precise aging of my fingerprint to the time of the murder:

I knew when this first came up [at the first hearing], it was a mistake on my part to have openly made the statement. I did not make the statement with the intent it was to be used. I attempted to prevent this from going any further, but met with full and continued resistance. I did so each time I had the chance, and before anytime I testified. I could not under oath deny I made this statement, but only defend it to my best ability.

If this case should be returned to any court for further hearing and I am called to again testify, I will still testify the same. I will guarantee [as I have done each time] that I will still request that I not testify to this issue, that it be included that 1) it is my opinion, 2) only my opinion, 3) no other examiner will confirm this opinion, 4) that this opinion does not represent the IAI or any of its members.

In the rambling thirteen-page document, Collard admitted that he committed perjury throughout the course of my case. In his closing paragraphs Collard wrote, "I did not originally have desire to oppose this Complaint, but at the request and with the support of my Chief, the police department, Criminal District Attorney, I feel I had to make the best effort."

Jack Skeen Jr. wrote a letter that accompanied Collard's response. Skeen corroborated that Collard's testimony would have ended by June 28, 1978. This was to support Collard's claim that since he did not receive certification from the IAI until November 1978, the complaint filed against him for aging a fingerprint should not be considered. Skeen ended with, "If you have any questions, do not hesitate to call."

From the Texas Court of Criminal Appeals all the way up to the United States Supreme Court, Skeen had argued that I should be put to death—he told the media and the courts that my fingerprint was six to twelve hours old based on Collard's expert testimony. Now here was proof that he knew this was a lie. And he kept it secret and hidden, all the while fighting for the reinstatement of my conviction and execution. Skeen never thought this document would see the light of day. But it became the first evidence of what I knew all along: They had framed me.

I HAD GROWN a lot since 1977 when my daddy told me to keep my mouth shut about having known Linda Edwards. When I whispered to him through the small portal of my side cell that I had been invited to her apartment several days before her death, he said firmly, "If you tell *anyone* else about being in that apartment or knowing this girl that was killed, you might as well have committed the murder, because they are going to pin it on you. You talk too much, son—*keep your mouth shut.*" Those words had welded the truth within me ever since. Had I just told Ament and Dixon this from the beginning, I wonder how things could have been different—or how A. D. Clark would have worked around it to still make me look responsible for the crime. It's a question I knew I would never know the answer to. But many nights on death row, I wished I had just told the truth. My daddy wasn't here anymore, and I had to trust my own instincts now. I decided that the very next time I saw Jim, I had to tell him about my relationship with Linda Jo Edwards. He might leave me for not telling him before, but I had to do it.

In August I was called down to the conference room where all attorney-client visitations were conducted. It was Jim and he looked like he was loaded for bear. Whatever Jim had on his mind would have to wait.

"Jim, I need to tell you something that's been weighing very heavily on me," I said, cutting him off.

"Come on, then I have something important I've come to talk to you about," he said.

I told Jim about my arrest, and the first visit with my daddy at the Smith County Jail. Surprisingly, a look of relief washed over Jim's face, and he lit up.

"Did you ever tell anyone else this other than your father?" Jim asked. "Anyone back in 1977?"

"Yes. I told Hoehn as we made our way to the swimming pool that night he came over. I didn't point out the window for him to go and peek inside it like he had told the jury in 1978. That was a lie. I told him I met the girl that lived there at the swimming pool. I told him her name, Linda."

"Uh-huh. Is that it?" Jim said as he sat listening, poker-faced. I was waiting for him to explode in anger.

"I don't remember exactly how I told them, but, yes, Randy and Rodney Dykes lied to the jury in 1978 when they testified along the same lines as Hoehn. When they saw the passion marks on my neck the day they came over, I told them where I got them—from a girl I had met at the pool named Linda. I didn't point out some window and make it appear I had been peeking into it to *watch a girl undress.*"

"Kerry, I know you are telling me the truth now. I had uncovered this after trading files with David Dobbs, and this is what I came to speak to you about today." Jim had read the long-secreted 1977 grand jury testimony, including the sworn statements of Robert Lee Hoehn, Randy Dykes, Rodney Dykes, and James Taylor. All of them had testified before the grand jury that I told each of them that days before she was found murdered, I had met Linda at the complex swimming pool and that she had invited me back to her apartment, where we made out and she gave me passion marks. This meant that A. D. Clark's administration had known with certainty—through their own witnesses—that I had met and known Linda Jo Edwards and thus had occasion to use the patio door where my fingerprint was found.

After we talked that day and my heart stopped racing, Jim looked me right in the eye. "Kerry, if you ever lie to me again—for any reason—I am just going back to New Jersey. I mean it. One time—that's it, Kerry. Do you understand?"

"I won't, Jim."

MISCONDUCT HEARINGS

On October 15, 1992, Paul Nugent filed an application for writ of habeas corpus, seeking to prevent another retrial under the principles of double jeopardy, due to egregious and systematic prosecutorial misconduct spanning fifteen years and two different administrations of the Smith County District Attorney's Office—from A. D. Clark III, on through his first cousin, Jack Skeen Jr. Paul explained to me the constitutional provision called "double jeopardy," which protected someone from being tried twice for the same crime. Though it was an unprecedented argument, Nugent held that my case had been so tainted with egregious police and prosecutorial malfeasance that Smith County shouldn't be allowed to have a second opportunity to wrongly convict me.

The hearing was held in Tyler on October 19 and 20. Paul called witness after witness revealing what had been hidden for over fifteen years—including that Hoehn, the Dykes brothers, and James Taylor (and the prosecution and police) *knew* that I had been an invited guest in Edwards's apartment prior to the murder; that Doug Collard's IAI response proved he had falsely testified as to the age of my fingerprint; and that the police and prosecution had failed to adequately pursue James Mayfield as a suspect. In addition, Paul asserted that Hoehn's and Paula Rudolph's testimony established that at 12:30 A.M. on the night of the murder, I was dropped off outside the complex, when at the same time Rudolph was in her apartment and saw the murderer— a man she initially identified as James Mayfield. Clearly, I could not have been in two places at the same time.

Paul also put into the record that A. D. Clark and Michael Thompson had lied in 1978 when they argued to the jury that I had "left Tyler like a bat out of hell" immediately after the murder. While they pointed to this as a sign of guilt, in truth they knew from the grand jury testimony of James Taylor that Taylor had forced me to leave his apartment that Sunday, acting upon his jealousy after he learned that I had been with his best friend, Robert Hoehn. And Randy Dykes admitted to the *Dallas Morning News* in 1988 that although he did drive me to my brother's house in Jacksonville that Friday, June 10, after job interviews, I had asked him to do this days before and the request was not a reaction to a news broadcast about the search for a suspect in the Linda Jo Edwards murder investigation. I returned that Sunday—and the police and prosecutors knew this. James Taylor told the police and prosecutors—and included this in his grand jury testimony—that he had kicked me out and had driven me to Houston. It was just another example of how the prosecutors had suppressed everything that got in the way of the script they wanted to present to the jury.

Robert Hoehn told officials in 1977 that although he was an avowed homosexual, he was unable to ever persuade me to have sexual relations with him. And like the Dykes brothers and James Taylor, among Hoehn's other sworn statements was the revelation that on the Monday before her murder Linda and I had ended up back at her apartment, where she gave me passion marks on my neck. To support Hoehn's previously hidden testimony, Paul showed the judge a document dated June 8, 1977, entitled "Texas Eastern University Employee Application for Leave," showing that Edwards was off from work for Monday, June 8, 1977, the same day we had met at the pool. Instead of this truth—that as a twenty-one-year-old man I had happened to see a young woman in a sexually stimulating situation, became interested in her, later introduced myself at the pool, and had been invited back to her apartment where we made out—the prosecution cut, copied, and pasted through willing witnesses a false script, hiding all of this and advancing the suborned perjury of me being a boozing, sexual deviant who was living off his gay benefactor and bragging about having snuck up to Linda Edwards's window to watch her undress.

Paul later called my former defense attorneys, Larue Dixon, now a judge, and John Ament. Both testified that A. D. Clark had stood up in open court in 1978 and said Hoehn had not made any prior written statements, and that there was no exculpatory evidence in the case. They testified that they were never provided the 1977 grand jury testimonies of Hoehn, the Dykes brothers, and James Taylor, as required by law.

Nugent also placed into the record that on March 4, 1992, David Dobbs had met me at the Smith County Jail while I was without counsel and proceeded to interrogate me about the fingerprint on Edwards's patio door.

One of the more eerie examples of the police and prosecution's negligent investigation regarded James Mayfield's alibi, his adopted daughter, Louella. Two weeks *before* the murder of Linda Jo Edwards, Louella Mayfield had donned a police cadet uniform and impersonated a Tyler police officer. She went around to apartment complexes in Tyler claiming she was investigating a murder involving James Mayfield and Linda Jo Edwards. The apartment managers at the Embarcadero and Casa de Oro Apartments became suspicious and telephoned the Tyler police, who called her to the police station. Sergeant Gerald Hayden created a supplemental offense report and turned it over to Detective Eddie Clark, documenting Louella's conduct at the apartments, and also how "Louella was going around the school [then called Texas Eastern University, where Mayfield and Edwards worked] threatening to kill Linda Edwards" and that Louella had "reportedly called Linda Edwards up on the phone and threatened to kill her about three to five days before she was killed." Sergeant Hayden ended his report by stating, "I personally know Louella to be mentally and emotionally unstable, very hyperactive and a pathological liar." However, when Paul Nugent subpoenaed Sergeant Hayden and brought him to testify in the misconduct hearing, he resisted Paul's questioning, saying whenever possible, "I don't recall."

Paul put in the record other instances of official misconduct, but after the two-day hearing was over, Judge Tunnell straightened his glasses and told Paul, Jim, and me that he would take Paul's double jeopardy claim and all the supporting evidence "under advisement," and adjourned the proceedings.

Thirty-six days later, Paul petitioned Judge Tunnell to reopen the prosecutorial misconduct hearings because Edward Scott "Shyster" Jackson had been found in a Missouri State Penitentiary doing time for another murder. Jury selection had already commenced in Georgetown when I was transported back to Tyler. On November 25, in Tyler, Jackson was brought into the courtroom and admitted his 1977 testimony was not only a total fabrication, but that District Attorney A. D. Clark III and his staff had coached him on how to testify effectively. I felt my heart jump.

Jackson made it clear it was A. D. Clark III—not Michael Thompson—who made the tacit agreement with him that in exchange for his perjury, Clark would arrange for his murder charge to be reduced to *voluntary manslaughter,* and he would be given a sentence of two years, time served. He would be in and out in no time.

"I got exactly what I was promised," Jackson told the hushed courtroom. Indeed, he was released on August 28, 1978, roughly forty-five days after I had arrived to Texas death row.

David Dobbs angrily attacked Jackson's recantation. Now that he was no longer *their* witness, Dobbs brought out the full extent of his criminal history in order to try and discredit him. It was the same criminal history that in 1978 prosecutors denied having any record of to supply my lawyers. After his release by Smith County officials he was convicted in Carthage, Missouri, of selling a controlled substance, and then in July of 1981 he was arrested for capital murder, pled guilty, and was sentenced to life imprisonment.

"They let a murderer out, and he murdered *again*. That blood is on the hands of A. D. Clark and the Smith County District Attorney's Office," Jim McCloskey whispered over to me.

Dobbs shouted, "You don't have much to lose in coming down here and talking about someone else who was sitting in the penitentiary on a murder charge, do you?"

"No. I have something to gain, though: peace of mind," Jackson said.

Despite Dobbs's intense badgering, Edward Scott Jackson looked at the judge, into the faces of the packed courtroom, then directly at David Dobbs. "Sir, there are a lot of things in my past that I am not proud of but I have to live with. Those things are immutable. A hundred years from now when I am dead, those things will show up on your computers and in your records. But the lie that I told on that man that sent him to death row is not immutable, and I'm here to change that."

In this very courtroom I had looked at my mama's face, huddled down just a little more during the commanding testimony of Edward Scott Jackson. I looked to where her seat would have been. I whispered inside, *I wish you were here now, Mama.*

After adjourning the hearing, Tunnell announced that he still would wait and rule on Paul's claims until *after* the second trial was over, and the jury had reached a verdict. I could not make sense of that decision. It contradicted the very reasons we had submitted the double jeopardy claim—to prevent Smith County prosecutors from having the right to put me on trial a second time and make an innocent man look guilty again.

ON OCTOBER 30, 1992, Deputy Captain Bobby Garman and a lesser deputy drove me to the Williamson County Jail for the start of jury selection. I sat quietly in the backseat, letting my thoughts wander and mingle with the barren trees and strip malls that littered the highway along the way to Georgetown. Behind the painted

brick buildings I knew children scampered to get ready for Hallow-
een the next day. I thought briefly of the good memories of Doyle
Wayne and me together as kids—and about how those memories
had constantly been there through the years, and even after his
death, to help me face this often incomprehensible fight.

Before I knew it, the car was pulling into the sally port of the
Williamson County Jail. I exchanged my orange Smith County
jumpsuit for a brown, two-piece suit with the logo WILLIAMSON
COUNTY JAIL stenciled on the back and a pair of old rubber flip-
flops that were too small. On the orders of Smith County, they
placed me in yet another freezing, suffocating solitary confinement cell. It had another solid steel door, gray walls, a table stuck
to the wall, and an open shower. The first thing I did was investigate the shower. It shot out a hard blast of icy water. I stood holding it for several minutes, waiting for the hot water to arrive. It
never did. After the shower, I couldn't ever get warm because of
the frigid air cascading down from the air-conditioning ducts in
the ceiling.

PROSECUTOR'S MOTIONS
TO SUPPRESS EVIDENCE

The morning before the jury selection commenced, Skeen filed a
barrage of motions that were clearly designed to control a version of
the trial that could be presented before a jury. The judge gave the
prosecution everything they wanted.

Most damaging of all, the judge agreed to prohibit the defense
counsel from mentioning any of the documented history of egregious police and prosecutorial misconduct that had been put in
the court records just two weeks earlier in Tyler during the misconduct hearings. Skeen had argued that it would deny the state

the right to a fair and impartial trial. That meant that Doug Collard's response to the IAI would not be available. Also the jury could not hear that James Mayfield asked Dr. Mears for assistance to pass a polygraph exam on the day Paula Rudolph was identifying him at the police station. Mears would not be allowed to mention the police forensic book *The Sexual Criminal*, which showed forensic police photographs depicting, in some pictures, exactly the way Linda Jo Edwards was found.

Tunnell also ruled that the defense could not present the evidence that Randy and Rodney Dykes and Robert Hoehn had told the police and the first grand jury that three days before her murder I had met Linda Jo Edwards at the swimming pool, had been invited back to her apartment where we made out, and had called the girl by name, "Linda," as opposed to having simply pointed out the window of a nude stranger whom I had watched "undress" from the sidewalk like a voyeur. Even though this testimony explained why my fingerprint—the only evidence linking me to the crime—was found on Edwards's patio door, the judge granted Jack Skeen's motion. It was a crippling blow.

Tunnell made it loud and clear, if we wanted to show the jury that the prosecution witnesses were lying, I would have to waive my rights as a defendant and testify on my own behalf. It was an outrageous ruling. Of course, it would also provide grounds for an appeal should I be reconvicted, for under the statute known as "Optional Completeness," once a witness gives new testimony that contradicts a previously sworn statement (such as statements made to the police or sworn testimony before a grand jury) their previous testimony becomes admissible to illustrate the inconsistency. Of course, I didn't want to go back to death row and wait another ten years, hoping and praying that lightning would strike twice and another appeals court would have the courage to reverse my conviction.

Dobbs also told the judge that they would be calling Louella Mayfield to the witness stand, and he asked the judge to restrict the scope of what Paul could ask her about her past. The judge agreed and ruled Paul was prohibited from asking Louella about her 1985 conviction for aggravated assault in the November 10, 1984, near-fatal shooting of her husband, Michael Valentin. Police records obtained by McCloskey and Nugent showed that she pointed a shotgun at point-blank range and fired, in an attempt to kill him. She blew off his arm instead of his head only because he jumped at the last second. The judge further ruled that Paul could not question Louella about a June 9, 1991, complaint made against her by a Baytown police officer, R. Ward, who claimed she committed the felony offense of "making a terroristic threat" against her brother, Charles Edgar Finley. The police report shows that she busted out two windows at his home and threatened serious bodily injury to him and his child. She was reported as saying to her brother, "Watch out for your baby—if I don't get her first, I'll be back with my Winchester."

For our part, Judge Tunnell ruled there would be absolutely no introduction of any homosexuality in the trial, despite the prosecution's determined efforts. Unlike in 1978, Tunnell ruled the inflammatory portions of Robert Hoehn's testimony relating to alleged homosexual acts would be excised from his testimony and the jury would not be permitted to hear it.

NOTIFICATION OF EXTRANEOUS OFFENSE—AMBER NORRIS

After Skeen had finished with his motions to exclude all evidence of past prosecutorial misconduct, Assistant D.A. Deborah Tittle walked over and handed Paul a paper, informing him of an "extraneous offense" that they were prepared to present before the jury if I were to take the stand. An "extraneous offense" is a legal term that meant the prosecution wanted to place an unproven, alleged criminal offense before the jury in addition to the one I was on trial for. In this instance, the extraneous offense was a brand-new story from my former roommate, Amber Rita Norris.

I had met Amber at a club in Houston. She said she had a friend who owned a bar in Port Arthur and that she could get me a job as a bartender there. It became an altogether different story once I arrived in July 1977. Through my own efforts, I wound up getting hired by Fred Hollis and working at the Holiday Club on Gulfway Drive. After I was arrested on the night of August 5, Detective Eddie Clark privately questioned Amber. A reading of his official police report shows Clark tried everything he could to get Amber Norris to play along and fit me into the persona of a sadistic, misogynistic, confused, impotent, woman-hating, homosexual male—their standing profile of Linda Jo Edwards's murderer.

Amber Norris originally told police—in response to loaded questions about homosexuality—that she had no direct knowledge of any type of homosexual behavior on my part. She told Detective Clark we had intercourse a few times and it was normal and uneventful. No, she said, I never roughed her up during sex. And, no, I didn't become violent.

Detective Clark had hit a flat zero. But even with nothing, I had learned, they could always shake out something. Over fifteen years after I had been convicted, Amber Norris gave authorities a different statement, one that completely contradicted what she said in the original police report. She told them that one night while driving home from the Holiday Club, I pulled over to the side of the road, yanked her out, and underneath the silhouette of a cross, had savagely ripped off her clothes and raped her. Then Amber Norris, who was no less than 255 pounds, and I got back in the car and drove home to resume the normal routine of our short life as roommates.

It was an extraordinary tale. Amber had obviously been pressured by Skeen's administration to help keep me behind bars. Unfortunately, the fact is that when you have been on death row for a decade and a half, people tend to believe the worst about you, no matter what. This story was completely manufactured, just like Shyster Jackson's. But now I watched Amber nervously walk into the courtroom and deliver this new tale into record.

NOTIFICATION OF SECOND EXTRANEOUS OFFENSE—TOMMY WILBANKS

Next the prosecution handed Paul the sworn statement of a Dallas man named Tommy Wilbanks, whom they also intended to call against me. I sat quietly and read the statement that Dobbs had obtained from him. Wilbanks claimed he knew me when I lived in Dallas in 1977 and worked as a bartender at the Old Plantation Club. He told Dobbs I had "an extreme obsession with lips," especially his lips and women's lips. One day, he said, he came over to my apartment, and while I was purportedly in the shower, I asked him to go to a drawer and bring me a pair of underwear. Wilbanks stated that when he opened the drawer, he found women's panty hose, stockings, a two-headed dildo, and a *Playboy* magazine with the large centerfold of a nude female with her nipples and vagina cut out. Wilbanks also claimed I had mutilated and murdered another girl and placed her body at a place called Mountain Creek Lake in Dallas. His ramblings continued to a fifth page, but I stopped reading at the point where he wrote I allegedly pulled a switchblade knife on him and a girl in the country and threatened to cut her nipples off.

Not surprisingly, Wilbanks had a past criminal history of "making a false report." But the judge ruled that should Wilbanks's testify, he would not allow that information to be told to the jury to establish Wilbanks's proclivities for lying. Through the years, I had been shocked by so many things that the prosecution had done to obscure my innocence. But Tommy Wilbanks took the cake. The prosecution's use of such charlatans as Wilbanks, Shyster Jackson, Doug Collard, Gonzalez, and others had turned my quest for truth and justice into something akin to the search for the Holy Grail.

Tunnell, in a small victory for us, ruled the prosecution could not call Amber Norris or Tommy Wilbanks to the stand unless we either reached the punishment phase of the trial, or I took the witness stand in my own defense to refute the prosecution's allegations against me.

Under the law, Paul explained, once I took the stand to dispute the charges, everything became admissible to attack me before the jury and impugn my credibility. "You don't have to be convicted of a crime, or even legally charged, for prosecutors to exploit supposition or mere innuendo, to be permitted to put the appearance of wrongdoing before the jury," Paul explained. Only in the rarest of circumstances does a defendant take the stand in his or her own behalf. With these extraneous offenses that the prosecution now held over me, taking the witness stand was no longer an option.

Given Tunnell's pretrial rulings, the trial was practically over before it began. Outside the courtroom, the media reported the normal routine of jury selection; all the while, inside the courtroom, a nightmare was unfolding.

9

THE 1992 RETRIAL

THE PROSECUTION PRESENTS

Smith County District Attorney Skeen basked in his starring role in which he projected himself as a champion of victims' rights. We were in a large courtroom where the more than four hundred potential jurors had been summoned for the capital murder trial of Kerry Cook. All eyes seemed to be looking at me.

Believe it or not, to qualify as a juror in a death penalty case in Texas, it was required by law that you be in favor of capital punishment. Anyone who indicated he opposed or was even undecided was ineligible to sit as a juror. So from the calling of the very first witnesses, the jury of your peers, as it is called, was constituted of twelve hard-core proponents of the death penalty.

The prosecution team—Jack Skeen Jr., David Dobbs, Deborah Tittle, and Detective Eddie Clark—sat at the table nearest the jury. I was seated in between Jim McCloskey and Houston attorney Chris Flood, whom Paul had recently asked to assist as co-counsel. Both Paul and Chris were working pro bono for Centurion Ministries. The gallery of the courtroom was filled with a number of people who had walked in off the street for a peek at a well-known capital murder case involving a possibly innocent person. Those who were loyal to the prosecution pressed in behind Dobbs's table. Smith County had paid the expenses for Linda Jo Edwards's brother and father to stay in Georgetown for the duration of the trial. They were placed in the most visible location, right behind the state's table on the first row, so that the jury could view their reactions to testimony. I glanced over at them but turned immediately away—they were staring directly at me, hard and mean. While my mama did come once, she really wasn't able to make the trip due to her failing health. So our side of the aisle had just a few loyal observers. Until the actual trial started, that is; then, loyal or disloyal, people just wanted a seat.

BY EXCLUDING THE prior inconsistent statements of Robert Hoehn, Rodney and Randy Dykes, James Taylor, and Doug Collard, Tunnell had crippled our case. Through these witnesses, the prosecution, as in 1978, advanced the theory that Linda Jo Edwards and I were complete strangers and that the only time I had ever seen her before I allegedly murdered her was when I snuck up to her bedroom window in a voyeuristic episode to "watch her undress." Without being able to establish that I had been in Edwards's apartment or to present Collard's damning IAI admission that it was not scientifically possible to precisely date fingerprints, the prosecution was able to place extreme emphasis on the fact that my fingerprints were found on her rear patio door—fingerprints Doug Collard falsely swore were the murderer's calling card by aging them to coincide with Rudolph's testimony and Gonzalez's altered testimony regarding the time of death.

Jack Skeen, like A. D. Clark before him, got away with simply suppressing all evidence that contradicted the state's compellingly scripted case. For example, in a sworn written statement of Randy Dykes dated August 3, 1977, Randy—like his brother Rodney, Robert Hoehn, and James Taylor—told police how three days prior to the murder of Linda Jo Edwards, I had explained to him how I had "met her at the pool and went to her apartment with her and she had given [me] the passion marks." Instead of this the jury only heard about an alleged Peeping Tom incident. Jack Skeen had persuaded a judge to keep the truth, not from the defense as had been done in 1978, but from the jury.

Paula Rudolph

When Paula Rudolph was called, her memory had gotten even better. As I tried to focus on Dobbs questioning Rudolph while she relayed the same stale lies, I couldn't keep from remembering what Jim had told me after he and David Dobbs had met at the Embarcadero apartment complex, where together they reenacted what Paula Rudolph saw the night she entered the apartment. Dobbs acknowledged to Jim that the light could not have made the hair silver nor could it have "cut" the murderer's hair—as common sense would dictate. Yet, now, before the jury, David Dobbs sponsored Rudolph's identification of me as the murderer she saw that night in 1977. She told the jury she was certain it was me now because she and her sister got on an elevator with me one day after a hearing in 1978 and she knew right then and there I was the man. Her sister never came in and testified—because her sister was never in the elevator.

James Taylor

James Taylor was called to make his first appearance in my case since his secret appearance on October 3, 1977, before the grand jury. There, he testified under a grant of immunity, meaning nothing he said could be used against him in a court of law. Still protected by that legal freedom, Taylor and the prosecution now introduced brand-new stories. For instance, Taylor said I had run off before he returned to the apartment on June 10. He testified that I allegedly called him from out of town and, in response to his questions, specifically told him I didn't know the girl who was found dead and that I had never been inside her apartment before. Prohibited from confronting Taylor with his contradictory 1977 grand jury testimony, Paul, frustrated, could do nothing but submit his objections to Taylor's testimony for the record. Tunnell reinforced his ruling that I would have to agree to testify before the jury could hear this exculpatory evidence. Last, in response to Dobbs's question, Taylor testified that I was "sexually ambivalent," a euphemism for homosexuality.

The Dykes Brothers

The prosecution bench-warranted Rodney Dykes from prison where he was doing time on convictions for delivery of a controlled substance and burglary. Dykes was shown a picture of Linda Jo Edwards and confirmed that this looked just like the girl he had seen at the pool Wednesday afternoon before the murder. He claimed I had sent him over to her poolside table to try to get me an introduction. He said two girls were seated by the pool—"one of them was a large woman, not as in fat, just big framed, with long, black, dark hair" (Linda Jo Edwards)—and they didn't just reject me but laughed with disinterest, he said. This was brand new and something I knew the prosecution had gotten Rodney to invent for them. I never sent him over to introduce me to Linda Jo Edwards at the pool. In fact, Randy Dykes had admitted to the *Dallas Morning News* in 1988 that the prosecution had pressured him to create his 1978 testimony before the jury. Now, sponsored by Skeen, Dobbs, and a permissive judge, the Dykes brothers were allowed to do it all over again. Due to the pretrial ruling, Paul Nugent was not allowed to inform the jury that they were lying.

Dobbs asked how my hair looked in 1977. Rodney described my hair as short and brown in a touching-the-ears fashion. "Did he ever in the time that you knew him have shoulder-length hair?" Dobbs asked.

"No, sir," Rodney said.

"Is there any doubt in your mind about that?" Dobbs pushed for finality.

"No, sir."

Rodney testified he spent the night with me that Wednesday. He said I had been out drinking with a male friend at the pool, and eventually we all ended up back at his uncle's apartment, with me and the male friend still consuming beer. He claimed the friend left, and sometime later, I left the apartment as well. After midnight, Thursday morning, June 9, he claimed, I returned to the apartment, shirtless and in just shorts. He said I asked him to massage me, and that was when he saw the passion marks all over my neck.

This was a bald-faced lie.

Because of the new insinuation that I had gone out into the night and came back with passion marks, with the inference being that I had gotten them from a homosexual man, Paul argued to Tunnell that Dobbs had opened the door and he should be allowed—finally—to confront Rodney with at least his 1977 sworn statements and grand jury testimony that revealed the passion marks had come from a girl I had met at the pool named Linda. Dobbs objected and they ended up at the bench. "I'm not going to allow that," Tunnell told Paul.

Randy Dykes regurgitated his 1978 testimony regarding me allegedly pointing to a window in which I had once seen a naked woman fondling herself. He also testified that when he and his little brother came over to the apartment the morning of June 10, I had asked him the day before if he would take me to a couple of places to fill out applications for a job. We were out and about when he said a news flash came on his truck radio about police investigating a woman found badly beaten in her Southside apartment. He told the jury I looked shocked upon hearing about the search for a suspect.

One of the only issues Paul was allowed to ask him about was taking me to the Department of Public Safety station in Tyler that morning to get a duplicate driver's license. Randy said he did not remember taking me to the DPS station that morning. *But he remembers this "news flash," and my apparent reaction of "surprise"?* I thought to myself.

Robert Hoehn

Though he had died of AIDS in 1988, Robert Hoehn was very much alive at my retrial. Assistant D.A. Deborah Tittle read selections of Hoehn's words to scenes of *The Sailor Who Fell from Grace with the Sea*, the movie that the prosecution had maintained precipitated and incited the brutal rape and murder of Linda Jo Edwards. As in 1978, the movie was projected on the courtroom wall.

And despite the judge vowing that I would not be tried on the issue of homosexuality, nor would he permit *any* testimony of it, the prosecution waltzed by the judge's pretrial ruling and read Hoehn's allegations that I masturbated on the carpet while facing the television. While the judge claimed he was sanitizing the scene of any homosexuality, the prosecution was establishing that

the movie whipped me up into a sexual frenzy, one that later cul-
minated in the lust murder of Linda Edwards. Tittle read Hoehn's
account that I then got dressed, putting on a pair of blue Everlast
swimming trunks, with a thick, red stripe running down the
sides. We then drove to two different places to get cigarettes, and
Hoehn later dropped me off in front of the apartment complex,
by no later than 12:30 A.M.

All Hoehn's contradictory sworn statements to police, and his
prior grand jury testimony from 1977, were excluded—including
Hoehn's admission that, although he was homosexual, he was
not able to persuade me to have sex with him that night; that I
didn't just abruptly ask to go to the pool and on the way point out
the window of a girl I used to watch undress, but told him of a
girl named Linda whom I had seen nude, met a few days later at
the pool, and went back with her to her apartment where we
made out.

Hoehn's time of dropping me off that night all by itself made it
impossible for me to have first run and changed out of my shorts;
run over to Rudolph's apartment; rape, stab, and murder Linda
Jo Edwards; clean up the crime scene; and still be the one seen by
Rudolph when she entered the apartment around 12:30 A.M.

The prosecution called Eddie Clark to the stand and Detective Clark said he did that trip to the Kroger and later the Williams Grocery and it took him half that time. So their case-in-chief
witness, Robert Hoehn, was wrong when he testified he dropped
me off at 12:30 A.M.

But Hoehn's testimony again made me appear as a dysfunc-
tional homosexual pervert, one enraged by an inability to sustain
an erection, and inspired by a movie to go out and rape and kill
someone, stealing her stocking, packing it full of body parts, and
sneaking out into the night. *All this was based on homosexual dysfunc-
tion, and some dumb movie I never even saw. And we were not allowed to
show the jury he was lying with the truth of what he first told authorities!*

Doug Collard

The State called Danny Carter, the supervisor of the Latent Fingerprint Laboratory for the Texas Department of Public Safety in Austin. After first delivering testimony for Dobbs that my fingerprint found on Linda Jo Edwards's sliding glass patio door had to have been left while opening and closing the door, Dobbs questioned Carter on my fingerprint. Carter was emphatic that a fingerprint cannot be aged, and that it would be inappropriate for any fingerprint examiner to age a fingerprint for *any* reason.

Tunnell had the bailiff herd the jury out of the room and out of earshot. Then Tunnell took it upon himself to cross-examine the state's fingerprint expert witness. Under intense questioning by Tunnell, Carter disagreed with Tunnell that the freshness of a fingerprint could be determined, and instead Carter told the judge that the use of the word *fresh* to describe a latent fingerprint was inappropriate as well. Carter told the judge that a reputable fingerprint examiner could not determine how long ago a fingerprint had been left. Danny Carter was the first ethical member of law enforcement called by the prosecution to ever make an appearance in my case and testify.

The prosecution called Bill Watling of the Treasury Department. Watling had no problem ignoring science and ethics and agreed with Dobbs that Collard could determine and say a fingerprint was "fresh" if he wanted to. Tunnell, based on Watling's testimony, reversed his ruling and allowed Dobbs to recall Doug Collard and bring forth the testimony that my fingerprint was "extremely fresh."

Still, when Collard testified, Paul exposed him as a hack who was incompetent and poorly trained. The prosecution, through Collard, had theorized that I carried the missing body parts out in the stocking, and on the way out the door, a drop of blood soaked through the stocking and dropped onto the lid of a terrarium that was near the sliding patio door. Only the missing stocking and the drop of blood found on the terrarium supported this "theory." When Nugent questioned Collard on what basis he derived these findings, especially since he had never sent this blood evidence to a lab for testing, Collard replied that he didn't send it to a lab because the blood at the crime scene was "all the same color." More evidence of incompetence was shown by the police never testing a pair of wet jeans along with a green leafy substance that were both found in the trunk of Louella's car against the green leafy substance found alongside the murder weapon in the victim's closet. All fingerprints discovered at the crime scene except for the thirteen introduced in court were destroyed also. And a hair—presumably the hair Eddie Clark was talking about the night he arrested me—found on Linda Jo Edwards's buttocks was finally tested. It was neither mine nor hers. However, that hair was never tested against James Mayfield's or Louella's.

The Mayfields

"Do you swear to tell the truth, the whole truth and nothing but the truth, so help you God?" the bailiff said to James and Elfriede Mayfield as they sat down one after the other and told stories to derail any suspicions. Fifteen years after the murder, James Mayfield's ironclad alibi was finally checked out by Tyler police when his wife, Elfriede, signed a sworn statement and averred that her husband was at home the night Edwards was killed, and so was their daughter, Louella. On the seventh day of trial testimony, the prosecution called the rotund Louella Mayfield to the stand; it was her first appearance in the case. Even the police knew Louella at sixteen years old to be mentally and emotionally unstable, and a pathological liar. Yet, they still had her come into a courtroom and swear under oath her father was at home, asleep, the night Linda Jo Edwards was being raped and murdered. She said she didn't remember wearing a police cadet uniform while visiting area apartment complexes—including the Embarcadero—"investigating" the murder of Linda Jo Edwards two weeks before it occurred, nor did she remember Captain Findley of the Tyler Police Department bringing her down to the police station to question her because of the complaints from apartment complex managers. And while she did admit to threatening Linda Jo Edwards's life, she testified that she didn't mean it. They were really like sisters, she said.

The attention shifted to James Mayfield. He stated he had left his wife of twenty-three years and moved into an apartment with Linda Jo Edwards on May 14, but on May 20, the day before his wife's birthday, he moved out and back in with his wife. According to Mayfield, he saw Linda Jo Edwards the afternoon of June 8, when he went over to Rudolph's apartment to see her on his birthday. She gave him a tennis outfit as a gift. He asserted that their relationship was broken off and that they were not having any type of sexual relations. The last time Mayfield claimed he saw Linda alive was at 7:45 the night she was murdered. She had come by his house on her way home.

Paul established that Mayfield would come and go whenever he wanted from his house, without any explanations. He would go to see Linda on the weekends Paula Rudolph was out of town, which was every other weekend. In fact, Mayfield's wife didn't know of the affair until May 1977, even though the affair had been ongoing for some time. He denied telling Ann White, a fellow university employee who drove him to the Embarcadero Apartments the morning Linda was found dead, "she ruined me—she cost me my job!" He did lose his job—his forced resignation was accepted June 6, 1977. In response to questioning, Mayfield told Paul that Louella was furious when she learned he had moved out of their house and into an apartment with Linda. He clearly remembered Louella telling him that she was going to murder Linda Jo Edwards if they didn't stop their love affair.

Paul asked the judge at the bench if he could at least ask Mayfield about going into Mears's office the morning of June 10, expressing concern that Rudolph was identifying him at the police station as they spoke. "Court is not going to allow it," Tunnell ruled.

Mayfield denied he had become explosively angry the evening of June 9, 1977, when Linda Jo Edwards stopped by his lake home and informed him she was going to date other men. In fact, Mayfield said he encouraged her to see other men. Again, Mayfield claimed she was like a daughter to him and no sexual relationship existed between them at the time of her murder.

Though polygraphs are not admissible in a court of law, James Mayfield admitted that he had taken "several" privately administered "lie detector" tests in 1977 and had failed them all. He was asked to take a polygraph exam in 1992 by David Dobbs and, through his attorney, F. R. Buck Files, he refused.

James Mayfield's testimony and appearance concluded with the stoic assertion that he did not rape and murder Linda Jo Edwards.

Dusty Hesskew

Next—despite the court's ruling barring psychological profiling—Dobbs called criminal profiler Sergeant Dusty Hesskew, under the guise of being a blood-spattering expert, to the stand. Hesskew testified there was no struggle: When the victim was first struck on the head with a blunt instrument, the victim was lying down asleep—this despite her being fully dressed, and wearing earrings, and with both an iron and the television turned on. It was a crime against women in general, Hesskew theorized, and not against Linda Jo Edwards. He categorized the murder as a disorganized "lust murder." It was a stranger-on-stranger sexual homicide and was not a crime committed by someone intimate with the victim. It was a crime of sexual intent in which the perpetrator had watched the victim for some time—and may have peeped through her window. The perpetrator of this type of lust murder will take souvenirs, like the stocking, the lips, and the vagina.

Paul objected that Hesskew's testimony was spurious psychological profiling and amounted to junk science. The judge overruled Paul's objection, saying, "He ain't profiling anybody. I know a profile when I see it."

Robert Wickham

The prosecution called former volunteer sheriff's reservist Robert Dean Wickham. He said he was in the restaurant business and helped the sheriff's department on the side as a reserve deputy. In 1978 he claimed he was called in to handle a prisoner during the jury selection process—that prisoner was me. Wickham stuck with a September 1991 sworn statement he had given Dobbs after my conviction had been set aside:

> The sheriff [J. B. Smith] took me to the jail elevator himself and told me to take Cook upstairs to the courtroom and keep him handcuffed at all times and not let him out of my sight. He said if he tried to escape, shoot him. I took him around to the public elevators and we got on to go up to the courtroom. On the elevator Cook looked at me and said, "Do you think I killed her?" I said I don't know but I guess we'll find out in court. He said, "I killed her, and I don't give a shit what they do to me."

Tyler detective Erik Liptak, Wickham's longtime friend, had notarized the document. Later in his statement Wickham explained that he never told prosecutors about the "confession" because he didn't think it was admissible because my attorney was not present. Now, after my case was reversed and the prosecution lost their only "confession" witness, Shyster Jackson, Wickham had decided to come forward. In the pretrial hearing he said he had kept the alleged remarks to himself but now, before the jury, he testified that he *did tell* someone about it after all: former Texas state trooper Glenn A. Miller.

"You're a liar!" I screamed from the defense table. The judge immediately excused the jury. He then told me that if I spoke another word that he would have me gagged and handcuffed to the chair for the remainder of the trial.

Wickham grinned. He continued testifying that they brought me down, in handcuffs, from the jail in a brown Smith County Jail jumpsuit. The fact was that in 1977, prisoners were responsible for their own clothing and there were no standard-issue jumpsuits, with the exception of those worn by the trusties. Second, I was never handcuffed going to or from the courtroom, as old video footage showed. Wickham responded to these inconsistencies by stating that he made no notes of the alleged incident. I wondered how Robert Wickham could function in normal society—*Can someone capable of manufacturing a lie of this magnitude blend in with regular people?*

Jim McCloskey investigated Wickham's story as best he could. He found out that Wickham owned a restaurant that was a cop hangout. We were sure that Wickham had commiserated with his police friends over the *Dallas Morning News* stories, which tended to paint the Tyler Police Department in an extremely negative light, and that this was how he came to offer his story. One of the officers, Glenn Miller, even testified that Wickham had informed him of the "Kerry Cook confession" a few days after it occurred in 1978. This alleged conversation occurred while Wickham was riding around with Miller. When Paul asked why he did not fill out a report—especially since he was in his trooper car at the time—Miller said that it had occurred after the trial was over.

When Paul stated that "a few days" after the incident would have been right in the middle of the trial, Miller changed his story midstride and stated that he meant a week to ten days. The *Dallas Morning News* reported that Miller had been found guilty of forging the signature of a judge on a search warrant. But predictably, Judge Tunnell ruled, at Skeen's insistence, that any mention of the conviction, which established Miller's penchant for dishonesty, was inadmissible. Wickham and Miller were both liars.

V. V. Gonzalez

Skeen called Tyler pathologist Dr. V. V. Gonzalez to the stand. As presented in 1978, his original autopsy report indicated Linda Jo Edwards died between 9:30 P.M. and 11:30 P.M. Because their chief witness, Robert Hoehn, gave me an alibi during this time, Gonzalez simply changed the time of death and testified that Linda Jo Edwards was killed during a later two-hour time period for which I didn't have an alibi.

Paul pressed Gonzalez and he agreed he was not board certified in clinical or forensic pathology. He admitted that he never made any notes in his official autopsy report that the vagina, lip, or anything else was cut out and missing—just that multiple wounds had caused her vagina to become macerated and destroyed. According to Gonzalez, the assault and murder of Linda Jo Edwards took "five to ten minutes," or longer.

David Hanners

In the end, the most damning testimony came from one of my strongest advocates, David Hanners, who had written almost forty articles on my case for the *Dallas Morning News*. I had denied knowing Linda Jo Edwards in an interview with David Hanners and this information understandably had made its way into one of his stories. Dobbs had the article blown up to poster size and set on an easel before the jury to read. It was ironic that my lie was seemingly the only truth ever uncovered and used by the prosecution.

The state rested.

DEFENSE WITNESSES

My defense would call twenty-three witnesses, including Olene Harned; Ann White; Dr. Frederick Gary Mears (made to testify outside the presence of the jury); Andrew Szarka and his wife, Tamara; fingerprint expert George Bonebrake; Doris Carpenter; Dana Gregory; Sunny McMakin; Dr. Judy Freedom; Orlando Padron and his wife, Alma; and the Dallas County forensic medical examiner, Dr. Linda Norton.

Dr. Judy Freeman, a colleague at East Texas University and a neighbor of the Mayfields, was also a close friend and confidante of Linda's. Freeman testified that Linda told her Mayfield was "jealous and possessive" of her. As soon as Freeman heard that Linda had been murdered, she and her husband went to the police station to tell them that they thought Mayfield could have committed the murder because of his extreme jealousy.

Professor Andrew Szarka and his wife, Tamara, also went to the police station as soon as they found out about the murder. Both were colleagues of Mayfield and neighbors on Lake Palestine as well. Earlier on the night of the murder, Linda Edwards came over to their house after conversing with Mayfield outside his house around 8:00 P.M. Linda told the Szarkas that Mayfield was angry with her because she informed him that she wanted to date other men.

Orlando Padron lived at the Embarcadero apartment complex as well, and he and his wife, Alma, had known Linda Edwards about two years. Padron told the jury he saw Edwards at the tennis courts the evening of her death and that his wife had invited Linda to come over to their apartment for drinks around 10:00 P.M. He said Linda appeared nervous and apprehensive about something. Linda left, excusing herself, saying she had to go back to her apartment to meet someone, Padron testified.

Alma Padron said that Linda kept glancing nervously at her watch several times and was sitting on the edge of the sofa while fidgeting her leg up and down. Finally she looked at her watch one last time and said she really needed to get back to her apartment.

Former FBI latent fingerprint supervisor George Bonebrake testified that it was impossible to determine the age of a fingerprint found on any surface, and also that the term "freshness" was an inappropriate term for a fingerprint examiner to use.

Paul called Doris Carpenter, the property manager for the Embarcadero apartment complex in June 1977. A few days after the murder, while Rudolph's father was packing up all of her things from the apartment because she was moving out, Rudolph was in the office waiting. Carpenter said she had heard that Rudolph had gotten a glimpse of the killer and asked her about it. Carpenter testified that Rudolph told her it was James Mayfield she saw. Rudolph went on to say that there was no way she could have gone to bed that night had she not been sure of it.

Dr. Linda Norton, the Dallas County forensic pathologist, cogently testified that a pathologist—or anyone else—could not determine from looking at the crime-scene photographs whether or not Linda's vagina had been removed; therefore, one had to trust the man who conducted the autopsy. V. V. Gonzalez never made any hint, or a notation, of any "missing body parts." Dr. Norton told the jury that something as significant as missing body parts from a victim and a crime scene would have such incredible forensic importance to the case that the failure to note such a fact would be criminal and incompetent. It was more than safe to assume that the reason no such findings were ever mentioned in Gonzalez's autopsy report was that no such evidence of it existed.

Paul called a former resident of the Embarcadero Apartments, Marc Wilcox, who owned a chain of launderettes in Tyler. Wilcox told the jury that on two separate occasions while he lived at the Embarcadero apartment complex in 1977, he had witnessed Linda Jo Edwards's exhibitionism as she paraded nude in front of an open bedroom window. He said he observed this clearly from the sidewalk—the very same sidewalk I had seen her nude from as I made my way to the community swimming pool in the summer of 1977.

Next, Paul brought former Longview reporter Bob Howie to the stand. He told the jury he visited a friend at the Embarcadero Apartments in May 1977; while on the balcony with other friends, they would "watch the show" of a woman walking nude in front of her open bedroom window. That woman was Linda Jo Edwards. Wilcox's and Howie's testimonies were immensely cathartic: For years the police and prosecution had manipulated the truth so that they could cast me as a sinister Peeping Tom who snuck up to Linda Jo Edwards's bedroom window to allegedly watch her undress.

Though we subpoenaed Edward Scott "Shyster" Jackson and he was bench-warranted from the Missouri State Penitentiary, Judge Tunnell would not permit him to testify as to what astonishing lengths the prosecution had gone to in order to secure a phony confession story.

IT SHOULD NEVER have come to it, but I was faced with the biggest decision of my life—the life-and-death decision of whether to take the stand or not. My greatest fear was Dobbs and Skeen and the extent they would go to to destroy me before the jury with trumped-up stories such as those of Amber Norris and Tommy Wilbanks.

Paul said the jury would be instructed in the court's charge that my failure to take the stand in my own defense could not be used against me and that the burden of proof to establish guilt beyond a reasonable doubt rests solely with the prosecution.

The question was deceptively simple: Should I take the stand to explain how my fingerprint came to be on the patio door, while risking the prosecution's dangerous penchant for misconduct, or do I leave the fingerprint unexplained, trusting instead on the legal precept that it was the prosecutor's burden to establish guilt beyond a reasonable doubt? In the end, it was the history of the police and prosecutorial misconduct that made me listen to the counsel of Paul Nugent, Chris Flood, and Jim McCloskey, who urged me not to take the stand.

The defense rested.

CLOSING ARGUMENTS

In their final time before the jury, Skeen and Dobbs argued thunderously for conviction. Dobbs talked to the jury for forty-five minutes. He told the jury that if they had seen the movie *The Sailor Who Fell from Grace with the Sea*, they'd probably say, "I don't know what that movie had to do with any type of trial." But if they reviewed the testimony of Robert Hoehn and compared it with the movie, then it became critical to their case. There was a scene, Dobbs said, where a boy is peeking into his mother's bedroom, spying on her as she masturbates in the nude. Dobbs claimed that after watching the scene, I expressed a desire to go look in the window of Linda Jo Edwards.

"Do y'all remember that? When the little boy comes into his mother's room and picks up the stocking and holds it like that? It does not make any sense unless you take a look at the facts of this case and see what is missing from Linda Jo Edwards's mutilated body. Interesting, isn't it?" Dobbs said, referring to the prosecution's theory that I had stolen one of Linda Edwards's stockings and filled it with part of her vagina.

He reminded jurors of a scene in which a cat is purportedly dissected—or "mutilated"—by a group of boys. Hoehn, he said, had left to use the restroom while it aired. Dobbs made it appear—as Michael Thompson did in 1978—that while I was alone watching this particular scene, I was getting turned on, such that when Hoehn came out of the bathroom I was waving a bread knife, saying excitedly, "Let's cut it up!" Hoehn testified he clearly understood me to be talking about a pizza that I was taking out of the oven in the kitchen—*not* standing in the living room watching a cat being dissected on television. However, Dobbs asserted that this was what I was doing not thirty minutes after having peeked into Linda Jo Edwards's apartment, and an hour and a half before she was murdered. Dobbs claimed I was in a sexual frenzy by the end of the movie, in which the boys are "just about ready to cut [the sailor] up," and said I masturbated on the carpet in view of the television.

"Don't pooh-pooh this movie," Dobbs argued to jurors. "Mr. Nugent wants to tell you it's a rabbit trail. You take a look at this movie."

Dobbs finished his time with the jury telling them that, in order to believe the theories of the defense, then "you have seen a parade of perjury from this witness stand. James Taylor lied. Rodney Dykes lied. Randy Dykes lied. Bob Wickham lied. Glenn Miller lied. Paula Rudolph lied. You have been a witness to a parade of perjury."

That was one of the few times David Eugene Dobbs told the truth before the jury, or in my case.

Jack Skeen closed out the prosecution's show. He told the jury that there was no evidence I had ever known Linda Jo Edwards, and that the only time I was ever in her apartment was the night I allegedly raped and killed her. Doug Collard, he said, had proved that I was the murderer by precisely aging my fingerprints to the time of the crime. Without the IAI document or the previous statements of Hoehn, the Dykes brothers, and James Taylor, these claims were left unchallenged.

JURY DELIBERATIONS

After two days of intensive deliberations, the jury still had not reached a verdict. Meanwhile, I waited in the small holding cell adjacent to the courtroom. Each and every time Captain Gorman walked by or tapped on my window, pain shot through me, thinking the jury had made a decision.

On the third day of jury deliberations, Paul Nugent found David Dobbs in the back of the courtroom on a bench reading from what appeared to be an original trial transcript. Paul was suspicious, so he went over to Dobbs and pulled the transcript out of Dobbs's hand. Paul dispensed with niceties because he knew that any attempted explanation by Dobbs would be less than the truth. The transcript Dobbs was reading from was the 1977 grand jury testimony of Robert Lee Hoehn. When the prosecution had finally turned over Hoehn's grand jury testimony in 1991, Skeen and Dobbs had vowed that they didn't have an original copy of the testimony and that, unfortunately, the page missing from the copy they gave us was missing from theirs, too. Paul repeatedly asked for the missing page as the months passed, and he was always told the same thing: The page was lost forever. Now Paul snatched the transcript out of Dobbs's hand and began leafing through it, stopping on page 41—the missing page. Paul read it for the first time. It was an exchange between Robert Lee Hoehn and a 1977 grand juror:

Grand Juror: "You said that after you all watched this movie that he then wanted to go to the pool and you wanted to watch—"
Robert Hoehn: "No, no, the movie was on and he wasn't paying any attention to it."

Finally, here was evidence that I had not been watching the movie that prosecutors claimed was the motive for the brutal rape and murder of Linda Jo Edwards. Paul brought Hoehn's incredible admission—and the fact that Skeen and Dobbs had hid it from the defense—to Tunnell's attention, and he asked that the jury be brought out of deliberations and informed of this startling revelation.

However, Tunnell denied Paul's motion to permit the jury to see this crucial new evidence. But what happened next was beyond even Tunnell's control.

"I DARESAY NO judge in Texas has ever been confronted with a situation like it. But come and read the note," Tunnell said, his voice breaking.

Tunnell, looking whiter than the whitest ghost, looked up at Jack Skeen, David Dobbs, and then over at Paul, Chris, Jim, and me. All the attorneys ran up to the bench. Dobbs and Skeen were visibly shaken. Chris Flood laughed and shook his head back and forth.

The note read: "We have found the nylon stocking in the jeans of Linda Jo Edwards."

Apparently, while examining the evidence, the jurors had—for the first time since 1978—broken the seal of the police bag that contained Linda Edwards's bloodstained jeans. In an attempt to gauge the victim's physical height, they shook the jeans and out fell the stocking, which prosecutors had said I had stolen and used to carry away Edwards's missing body parts.

"Incredible," I mumbled from the table.

———

AFTER TWO MORE days passed, the jury began sending out notes saying they were hopelessly deadlocked. On the fifth day Tunnell finally ruled that the jury was unable to reach a verdict and declared a *mistrial*. I wanted to race up to the rail of the jury box and hug the jurors as they filed out one by one. I could not know which ones had voted "not guilty"—they had been split six to six—but to make sure I got to hug one of them, I would have hugged them all.

According to the Texas Penal Code, "Bail may be denied by the court when the state has produced proof evident that the accused is guilty of capital murder and the jury would return a sentence of death." Under the "proof evident" law, the only way a reasonable bond could be denied is if the evidence showed I had committed the rape and murder of Linda Jo Edwards. To deny me bond, the evidence had to be so convincing that not only would twelve jurors vote unanimously to convict me of capital murder, but also vote to sentence me to death. Well, I had just had six jurors vote that Smith County's case was insufficient to establish guilt beyond a reasonable doubt.

Tunnell announced he had absolutely no doubt Smith County prosecutors would seek to retry me a third time, and in the meantime, bond would be *denied*.

"The court finds that it would be manifestly unjust that this case not stand for trial another day before another jury."

THE NEXT MORNING I boarded the same Smith County command bus used to chauffeur the jury to and from the courthouse and was transferred back to the Smith County Jail. Seated next to me were David Hunter and Rodney Dykes, being returned to the Smith County Jail as well. Hunter told me he was sorry for what he had done, that he had just gotten depressed and hopeless with the anvil of his 149-year sentence. He didn't mean for it to go as far as it did, but once he made up the story and wrote Smith County about it, they became the proverbial snapping turtle that refused to let go.

Once at the jail I was again placed back in the dreaded side cell. But this time, after the hung jury, I entered with a lot more hope than I had left with.

10

GEORGETOWN REMATCH, 1994

Near the end of January 1993, Judge Joe Tunnell announced that he was withdrawing as presiding judge for unspecified reasons—but not before he left a final mark on the case. On Paul Nugent's double jeopardy, habeas corpus petition, which Tunnell incomprehensibly had deferred ruling on until after the jury had reached a verdict in the last trial, thereby defeating its intent. The judge ruled that, although there was a history of police and prosecutorial misconduct, it was not egregious *enough* to bar prosecutors from trying me a third time.

Then, in a shocking paragraph, Tunnell admitted that the sworn statements to police, and sworn testimonies before the grand jury—those of Robert Lee Hoehn and Randy and Rodney Dykes and James Taylor—were exculpatory and *should* have been turned over to my 1978 defense attorneys for cross-examination purposes. And yet, Tunnell, under the prodding of Skeen and Dobbs, had suppressed the same testimony from the jury in the 1992 retrial.

In his final order, he scheduled a third trial for March 29, 1993 (it would be rescheduled and not begin until 1994), again in Georgetown. Robert D. Jones was appointed to preside over my case. A couple of years earlier, citizens of Travis County voted Judge Jones out of office. But under Texas's "visiting judgeship" program, he was allowed to travel around the state hearing cases as a "substitute" judge. In April 1993, the *National Law Journal* would publish an article entitled "Have Gavel, Will Travel," exposing the lack of accountability in Texas's visiting judgeship program. Because of the heavy court loads, regional administrative judges can appoint visiting judges to their area. All judges are eligible for the program, even if they had been turned out of office by voters or retired for years. The article specifically mentioned Jones under the heading "Immune from Democracy." After finishing third in a three-candidate race, Jones then became a visiting judge and had been busier than ever. One of the opposing candidates stated, "The electorate of Travis County turned him out, and now the people of some other county are subject to his inappropriate behavior." The article also quoted a longtime Austin courthouse observer who said that Judge Jones's reappearance under the visiting judge program was "frightening," and also said "he was out of control as a judge here." Nevertheless, Judge Jones was appointed to preside over my retrial. It was an ominous development.

ONE OF THE first things Jones did was adopt all of Tunnell's rulings on the admission of evidence that had been so debilitating to my defense in the last trial. Once again, there would be no mention of *any* evidence of police and prosecutorial misconduct. Jones called my retrial a "two-script" case. He put Paul on notice that the script he would be going with was the script used by the 1978 prosecutors and again sponsored by Skeen and Dobbs at the last trial. Collard, for instance, could say that my fingerprint was "extremely fresh," but Paul would not be allowed to discredit him with his admissions before the IAI.

Next, seeking compensation for representing me and funds to rehire the same experts used in the last trial, Paul filed a motion with Jones asking the court to appoint him to the case because I was indigent. Centurion had thrown everything it had in the kitty fighting for my life at the 1992 trial, and now my defense was bankrupt. Up to this point, Paul and Chris had worked over a thousand hours without compensation, with all monies having gone toward essential witnesses.

In a ruling that left us virtually speechless, Jones thanked Paul Nugent and Chris Flood for doing a commendable job representing me, but "having reviewed the defendant's affidavit of indigence I hereby find the defendant to be indigent and entitled to court-appointed counsel. I accordingly appoint Bill Wright of Smith County, Texas, and Jim Brookshire of Williamson County, Texas." So it was that, over Paul Nugent's strenuous objections, Jones fired Paul and Chris on the eve of the third trial in January 1994 and appointed two strangers who lived and practiced law at opposite ends of the state. Both lawyers were public defenders, more apt to "go along to get along" than to fight tooth and nail for my innocence. If Paul Nugent wanted to remain as counsel of record in my case, he would have to do so pro bono, without compensation from the taxpayers of Smith County. And that's just what he did.

Nor would there be any continuance: The Texas justice system had taken a beating in the "Kerry Max Cook case" with all of the allegations of prosecutorial misconduct and judicial abuses, and it was time to get to another trial and have it resolved once and for all. Because Jim and Centurion didn't have the funds to hire a second chair to assist Paul, we were forced to use court-appointed George-town lawyer Jim Brookshire, who knew practically nothing of my legal debacle and seemed eager to learn even less in the short amount of time before the trial began. He just sat at the defense table as Paul picked the jury and later questioned all of the witnesses.

"YES, SIR, MY name is Kerry Cook. I have court this morning. I need a razor to shave, please."

The Williamson County Jail made the Smith County Jail seem like paradise lost. It was run like a military stockade, and to go through it a second go-round was awful. Again I put on the drab brown uniform and slipped on a pair of plastic sandals two sizes too small. I went back to the second floor and into the ice bin. Each day was as grueling as the one before. It began by having to get up at 3:00 A.M., when I would slip out from under the thin blanket that was the only protection from the freezing temperature, push the intercom button, and wait shivering for the scratchy metallic voice that sat in a different world from mine—one of warm clothes and freedom—to respond.

When the flap of my portal opened, the plastic razor was shoved in with the fiat, "You have five minutes with the razor—done or not," said by a guard whose face I could not see. I would step in the shower stall, pressing the silver nozzle with one hand, and trying to shave with ice-cold water pounding me in the face with the other. I was only allowed one disposable razor a week. My head always itched because I could never really get all the soap out of my hair.

At about 4:30 A.M. a jailer escorted me downstairs to the property room and I would change into my court clothes. Paul Nugent had given me Clarence Brandley's tie, the one he had worn when he went free. Dressed, I would go into a tiny holding cell by the book-in area. There was nothing but a low concrete bench that was so cold my legs would go numb if I didn't get up and pace the small tomb. I had to wait there for *hours* until Captain Gorman came to get me a few minutes before the 9:00 A.M. court sessions.

The highlight of jury selection was a juror questionnaire Paul showed me. Though he was excused for having a predisposed opinion about the case, juror number 21 had written a note on the back of his form:

> *I worked for the prison system of Texas for eight years before retiring. I was a guard at the Ellis II Unit (Treatment Center) and worked around Kerry Cook for two years. Due to this association I don't think he did this crime.*

Court would adjourn around 5:00 P.M., and I was brought back to the main building, through the underground tunnel. I went back into the cold storage that was the holding cell to wait for a jailer to be freed up to take me first to change out of my court clothes, then back upstairs to my cell. Sometimes that didn't happen until after ten o'clock at night.

THIS TIME IT felt different—the entire courtroom atmosphere. I was running on empty, barely able to stay awake, and my defense was bankrupt. Paul and Jim's dedication was there, but this go-round, Paul would have the entire case on his own. Even though Jones appointed Brookshire, he would not be involved in the trial. David Dobbs, Jack Skeen, and Detective Eddie Clark were seated at the prosecution's table.

Judge Jones granted Dobbs's motion asking that neither side be allowed to tell this jury that the previous jury had found the missing ankle stocking. They simply dropped this "theft" from the indictment. As in Judge Tunnell's trial, Jones said there would be no "criminal profiling." And no evidence of homosexuality would be allowed in the trial.

OLD PLAYERS, NEW PLAYS

With several significant exceptions, the trial that opened on January 31, 1994, was a carbon copy of the one before it. Collard once again regurgitated his finding of the fingerprint on the patio door frame the morning of June 10, stating it was "extremely fresh," making it the killer's calling card.

Dobbs called Dusty Hesskew again, under the guise of being a blood-spattering expert; but what he really came to do was sneak under the radar as a profiler and to dispel any notion that James Mayfield could be the killer. Hesskew said the same thing—the murder was a "stranger-on-stranger, lust murder," one not committed by someone who had been an intimate-lover, or jealous-lover type or—or anyone that knew the victim.

Despite the judge's ruling that the junk science of psychological criminal profiling would not be allowed in the trial, David Dobbs called David Gomez, an FBI agent formerly assigned to the National Center for the Analysis of Violent Crime (NCAVC). Gomez labeled the murder of Linda Jo Edwards as "lust-murder, stranger-on-stranger" crime, as opposed to one committed by a jealous lover. Gomez said this was a murder of sexual intent, and the killer was "sexually inadequate," and "sexually ambivalent," a code word for homosexual. He said the person who raped and killed Edwards had previously engaged in voyeurism and had fantasized about her.

Dobbs asked, "How important would it be for you in making your determination to know that less than an hour before the murder, Kerry Max Cook had pointed out the window of Linda Jo Edwards, engaged in relations assuming the female role, was unable to sustain an erection, and was unable to perform?"

"It would be *very important*," Gomez said.

In early December 1993, Jim McCloskey and Paul Nugent had met with Gomez and discussed the Linda Jo Edwards murder with him. At that time, he agreed with Jim and Paul that the murder appeared to be a "domestic homicide" committed by a jealous ex-lover, and *not by a stranger on a stranger.* Yet sometime later, Gomez told them that owing to the policy of the FBI, agents were prohibited from testifying for the defense. And on Paul's cross-examination, Gomez denied he agreed that it was a domestic homicide, and told the jury that the reason he didn't testify for the defense was that he disagreed with their analysis of the murder.

There was very little Paul could do. But he told me not to worry; Jim had spent innumerable hours with a world-renowned behaviorist expert named Robert K. Ressler—Gomez's former boss—who would neutralize Gomez.

RUDOLPH TESTIFIED THE same, only adding that she was "in shock" when she gave her initial sworn statement of June 10, 1977, to Detective Nelson Downing at the Tyler police station. In other words, she didn't know what she was saying. (There is overwhelming evidence that a witness's recollection doesn't get better with time but is best immediately after the crime.)

"Was James Mayfield in any way sexually ambivalent?" David Dobbs asked, as if the very question was preposterous.

"No, of course not," Rudolph said, laughing at the very question. Paula Rudolph then said under oath for the very first time that she distinctly remembered telling Detectives Eddie Clark and Nelson Downing that the person she saw was not James Mayfield. She explained her "the-light-made-his-hair-silver" theory. Equally inexplicably, Rudolph said the light in Linda's room made "my" hair look shorter.

To bolster Rudolph's identification, the prosecution called in more junk scientists, this time Allen Weckerling of Weckerling Laboratories in Dallas. He claimed he conducted an experiment with a hundred-watt lightbulb that showed that lights could give hair the appearance of a silver halo. His experiment, however, didn't address how the light could "cut" my shoulder-length hair by six inches.

Detective Nelson Downing testified that he thought Paula Rudolph was in shock when he took her statement. Downing told the jury that he basically wrote what he *thought* Rudolph meant—her statement wasn't actually her words at all, just his own interpretation of what he thought she was trying to say.

AGAIN ROBERT WICKHAM testified I confessed during a seventeen-second elevator ride to jury selection, and again I was overcome with emotion and screamed out.

"He's lying!"

Acting bailiff Toby Young, Captain Bobby Garman, and Deputy Steve Channey immediately surrounded me. Jones retired the jury. He warned me that one more outburst and he would have me gagged and handcuffed to the chair. He told Nugent if I spoke again, he would waive my Fifth Amendment right and force me to the stand to testify. Nothing they did or said could surprise me anymore.

Rodney and Randy Dykes retestified the same, with Rodney, however, now saying that I had very short hair. Paul asked Rodney to describe my hair one more time for the jury. He readily complied, saying how short it was. Paul turned on a tape recording that was obtained during discovery. The voice of Rodney Dykes could be clearly heard in an interview on November 10, at the Lubbock jail, to prepare and refresh his memory so he could be called as a witness for the third trial. Eddie Clark was asking about my hair, and Rodney responded by saying my hair was "Mexican dark brown and very long."

The June 10, 1977, driver's license photograph was shown to the jury, depicting me with long, brown shoulder-length hair.

Dobbs disputed the authenticity of the license, taking it and saying he wanted to have it tested to see if it was a fake. What he never explained was that this license came from the Texas Department of Public Safety in Austin, Texas.

The ghost of Hoehn's testimony was the same—but so was Jones's ruling, and again Eddie Clark was called to dispute the time Hoehn testified originally in 1978 he dropped me off in front of the apartments.

Despite the discovery of the stocking, the prosecution was still very much vested in the inflammatory "missing body parts" theme that had carried their campaign through the years. Retired medical examiner Dr. Charles Petty came in for the prosecution and testified that after having reviewed photographs, it was his opinion that the lip and vagina were removed and missing from the scene.

Eddie Clark plugged the hole that was made when another jury "during a prior proceeding," as they said, found the missing stocking. Clark admitted that he could have been more thorough in his investigation of the crime scene by running his hands up the inside of the pants legs of Linda Jo Edwards's blue jeans. He told the jury that he did, however, reach inside and check each pocket for any keepsake he may have been able to turn over to the victim's family.

On that note, the state had completed its case. Unlike the jury in 1992, when I noticed that several members had puzzled looks, as if to say "Is that it?"—this jury showed nothing.

ON OUR SHOESTRING budget, we were only able to bring the most important of the university witnesses to testify in Georgetown, including Mears, Harned, and Szarka. Several new witnesses also appeared. For instance, Doris Carpenter, the property manager of the Embarcadero apartment complex in June of 1977, testified that after the murder, Paula Rudolph and her father came back to collect some of Paula's things from the apartment. Rudolph did not want to reenter her former apartment so she waited in the office while her father retrieved her belongings. Carpenter's assistant said to Rudolph, "I understand you saw the man in your apartment that night. Boy, weren't you scared?" Carpenter testified that Rudolph responded by saying, "No. I knew him. It was James Mayfield."

Robert K. Ressler

Paul also called Robert K. Ressler, the founder of the FBI's Behavioral Science Unit, in Quantico, Virginia, and the coauthor of the FBI's *Crime Classification Manual on Violent Crime* that Gomez had used to reach his conclusions about the Edwards murder. Ressler was beyond reproach as one of the world's leading experts on violent crime. Nugent began to lay the groundwork for the rendering of his expert testimony by asking him what he had familiarized himself with that would enable him to give his opinion on the type of crime the Linda Jo Edwards murder was, and the type of person who would or wouldn't commit it. Ressler stated he had reviewed crime-scene photographs, Dr. V. V. Gonzalez's trial testimony, police reports, and—

Jones immediately interrupted and sent the jury away. Dobbs asked Ressler to detail all that he had reviewed to reach his conclusions in order to testify. Ressler listed a litany of documents and exhibits and was nearly finished when he stated that he had reviewed the testimony of David Gomez. Then David Dobbs addressed Jones and objected to the testimony of Robert K. Ressler, based on the fact that he had reviewed the sworn testimony of another witness, under the rule that forbids one witness from hearing the testimony of another. *But,* Paul Nugent argued back, this rule does not apply to expert witnesses, since, theoretically, their knowledge is known and is not supposed to be influenced by what another said.

However, while acknowledging that he could very well be creating a reversible error, Jones sustained David Dobbs's objection and ruled that Robert K. Ressler would not be allowed to testify in my case. He had the jury brought back into the courtroom and firmly instructed them to act as if they had never heard from Ressler. It was another serious setback to our case and denied our ability to disprove the testimony of Dusty Hesskew and Dave Gomez.

In his closing arguments to the jury, David Dobbs alluded to the psychological profile testimony of David Gomez thirty-eight times, arguing that this was a "lust murder" committed by a "sexually ambivalent" person—or homosexual. Both Tunnell and Jones disallowed the prosecution from using the word *homosexual*, but allowed everything else that went along with it. It was bizarre.

"It is not innuendo, it is going as far as we can—as far as we are allowed to go—to tell you something about this defendant, so that you can understand how this defendant fits into the motive that Dave Gomez told you about, the type of individual that will commit one of these lust murders, one of these stranger-on-stranger crimes."

JURY DELIBERATIONS

After five hours of deliberations, jury foreman Thomas Winn wrote a note stating that jurors were "divided on the guilty/not guilty issue." The jury foreman advised Judge Jones that there were jurors holding out for acquittal. He requested to be given the portion of David Gomez's testimony that identified and distinguished this as a "stranger-on-stranger lust murder" as opposed to a "domestic homicide" by a jealous lover. Though the jury asked for only one small piece of Gomez's testimony Jones decided the jury needed to hear all sixty-two pages of his testimony and have it read back to them.

Paul knew the damage the judge was inflicting by reinforcing Gomez's testimony—especially when we were prohibited from having Ressler dispute Gomez. The jury struggled for the next three days. Paul finally moved for a mistrial, arguing that the jury had been deliberating for twenty-five hours and was unable to reach a verdict. Jones denied it. After Gomez's testimony was re-read to the jury, Judge Jones recessed again and sent me back to the holding cell to await further movement from the jury.

Jim came back to my cell. "It doesn't look good, does it, Jim, the jury asking for Gomez? Judge Jones excluding Robert K. Ressler is going to be too much to overcome, isn't it?" I almost whispered.

"Kerry," Jim said, "we need to pray. Here, take my hand."

"Merciful God, don't let Kerry be handed over to this jury by this parade of lies and deceit that has been launched against him. Take this jury by the hand, guide them, help them to see the truth that Kerry is an innocent man and has been a lamb among wolves. You know his heart. You know his suffering. Lord, we ask this in Jesus—" A tap on the windowpane cut off Jim's words.

I looked up, in dread, and saw the face of Bobby Garman. "There's a note—a verdict. The judge wants us all back in the courtroom." The words rushed from him. I squeezed Jim's hand and released it.

Jim and I walked to the defense table and joined a weary-looking Paul Nugent. His face told the story. I sat between Paul and Jim and took each of their hands.

"No matter what happens here today in the next moment, thank you for fighting so hard for me and never letting go. I love you both," I said.

"Has the jury reached a verdict?" Jones said.

"We have," Thomas Winn said.

I stared into the jury with all of my might, all the while clench-ing Jim's and Paul's hands tighter. The jury would not look at me. I thought of all of those grueling weeks of selecting the jury and the promise they made to "hold the state to their burden of proof."

"We the jury find the defendant, Kerry Max Cook, guilty of capital murder." The world was moving in slow motion. I was numb.

THE NEXT MORNING we met in Judge Jones's chambers for Paul to make a "bill of exception"—a record of what Robert Ressler would have testified had he been allowed. Paul put Ressler's affidavit into the record and then told Jones that Ressler would have told my jury that he analyzed the crime scene, and that based on his expert opinion, the murder of Linda Jo Edwards was not a "disorganized sexual homicide"—this was not a lust murder. This was a *"mixed sexual homicide"* with elements of a "staged domestic homicide." The murder could very well have been a "domestic homicide." Ressler would have defined a domestic homicide as a killing involv-ing sexual intimates—whether they were boyfriend, girlfriend, or a man and a wife—as opposed to stranger-on-stranger murder.

Ressler would have said that the murder scene in this case sup-ported great anger toward the particular victim—not females in general. The head wounds and the stab wounds to the neck, throat, and back region were designed to kill her and indicated extreme anger toward the victim and intent to kill her, and also the injuries to her vagina and pelvic region showed intent to de-stroy the area of previous interest. That damage indicated anger toward Linda Jo Edwards, and it signified that a previous rela-tionship existed between the victim and her assailant. The three breast wounds could have indicated an attempt at staging—trying to make it appear like a wanton sexual attack.

Ressler had never encountered, in all of his experience, pieces of missing body tissue taken from a crime scene. In his expert opinion, even if in fact there was tissue missing, it had no significance to this particular case unless they would be found in the possession of a suspect.

Ressler would have told the jury that voyeurs or Peeping Toms are not confrontational, and they don't engage in this type of violent assault. They don't have the courage for this type of confrontation. Ressler said that masturbation diffuses excitement and lessens the likelihood of a confrontational attitude.

Ressler would have told the jury that an expert cannot state, based on a review of the crime scene, that sexual inadequacy, sexual immaturity, or "sexual ambivalence" was or is a motivating factor, or played any role in forming the intent and basis for this crime. Crimes of such interpersonal violence are not necessarily committed within the same age group. Last, Ressler had formed his opinion in the murder of Linda Jo Edwards before he had heard David Gomez was a witness in this case.

He was a twenty-year veteran of the FBI, including sixteen years in the Behavioral Science Unit. He was also the FBI's first program manager for the Violent Criminal Apprehension Program. His vitae was twelve pages long, replete with specialized training, education, research, and he had been consulted by prosecutors around the world. Robert K. Ressler has authored three books: *Sexual Homicide: Patterns and Motives*, coauthored the very book David Gomez told my jury he used in order to reach his conclusions in profiling, the *Crime Classification Manual,* and more recently, *Whoever Fights Monsters*. The first two books were written with Gomez's current supervisor, John Douglas.

Ressler's crime-scene analysis would have seriously questioned the motives and validity of David Gomez's and Dusty Hesskew's analyses of the murder of Linda Jo Edwards and testimony for the prosecution.

THE PUNISHMENT PHASE

My August 1991 suicide tape was shown to the jury and was used by Dobbs to show my propensity for violence. After the camera had followed me on a gurney into the Ellis II Unit clinic, it went back to my cell. Everywhere the camera lens panned was covered in blood—on the bunk, the floor, the ceiling, and even flowing like a river out into the hall. The camera stopped on a note I had written and left in my typewriter. It read: "I was an innocent man. Good-bye Mama, Daddy, Amy Joanne."

David Dobbs also finally got Amber Norris in front of the jury. Jacksonville police officers came in and said my reputation in the community was bad. A Tyler psychologist named Tom Allan, whom I have never seen or spoken to, testified that he reviewed my prison records (including citations for fighting in self-defense) at the request of the prosecutors and he formed the opinion that I was a violent and dangerous person and would be a continuing threat to society if not put to death.

Even Jerry Landrum was called in to testify against me. He told the same stale self-serving lies, and Jones ruled Paul could not go into the *Dallas Morning News* front-page stories that called his 1978 testimony perjury. Landrum said that, as recently as 1973, I had a fascination with alleged "self-mutilation," because a Rusk State Hospital record showed me with sores on my body when I was brought there from the Cherokee County Jail to determine my competency to stand trial on the car theft at seventeen. Unable to bathe and in the hot Texas sweatbox of the Cherokee County Jail throughout the summer, I had broken out in itchy sores. I scratched them. Landrum stated that this was evidence of my penchant for self-mutilation. He told Hanners once on the phone before he slammed the phone down in his ear that he would have the last laugh.

And he did.

Despite their verdict, Paul Nugent continued to argue my innocence to the jury, and the holes in the prosecution's case.

AS IN 1978 at the first trial, the jury answered the three special questions that have to be affirmed unanimously, and I was again resentenced to death. Jones asked me whether I had anything to say before he pronounced the jury's recommendation of death. I stood up, and against the advice of Paul, I looked at Jones.

"With respect to the court"—I looked into the empty seats where the jury had sat—"with respect to the jury"—and then turning and looking into the faces of Ray and Jimmy Edwards—"and with respect to the victim's family, I am an innocent man. God forgive them, for they know not what they do."

Jones then sentenced me to death.

I was pulled and pushed to the same holding cell where I'd sat waiting out the results of the two retrials. Behind me the heavy steel door opened and Jim McCloskey and Paul Nugent came in. Before any of us could speak, the door unlocked again, and a smiling Doug Collard sauntered in, carrying a small attaché case.

"I need to fingerprint Kerry Max because of the new conviction," he said as he began setting up the portable inkpad kit. He rolled my fingers one by one on the identification card as Paul, Jim, and I observed in silence. After Collard left, I wiped the black ink on the tan suit pants Paul had given me for the trial. By this point, Paul's work had long been pro bono, with all monies going toward investigations and the hiring of expert witnesses.

"Paul, you're responsible for keeping me alive. When you go back to Houston, please tell everyone, from your paralegals Blanca and Elena, to your law partner, Mike DeGeurin, how profoundly grateful I am for their role in helping me stay alive. I know you did everything legally possible."

I turned toward Jim. His shoulders were slumped in a way I

had never seen before. I had never seen so much pain concentrated on a single human face as was on that of Jim McCloskey. I took two steps and enveloped him with a hug.

"Jim, I love you. You replaced hopelessness and despair with hopefulness. It is you and only you that brought me to have not one, but two trials. I am going to miss you the most."

Outside the door, Captain Garman stood ready to open the door at any second.

"This is far from over, Kerry. I am not going to rest until the world knows you are innocent. I will not give up until you have been freed and vindicated!" Jim said.

"It's over, Jim. Just get on that elevator and walk away, and don't look back. There is nothing more that can be done. First reversal by the Texas Court of Criminal Appeals was a miracle. Lightning will never strike twice in that court of Kerry Cook. I have to make this last walk by myself. You have to let me go," I said as the tears fell from my eyes.

"No, I am going to be talking to Paul later on to see if we can work something out so I can afford to pay him to represent you on appeal, since nobody besides us knows the case as well as he does. It will be reversed again, Kerry. There is no way in my mind I can ever, ever believe this travesty of justice can stand," Jim said with both arms on my shoulders. I had once heard almost those exact words from another warrior, Harry R. Heard.

"I will not rest until you are free."

The door opened, and it was time to go. It was the moment I had dreaded most of all. My greatest fear was to be alone with it all once again, back on death row.

I hugged Jim one last time.

"I will never let go, Kerry. Never. It's not over—not until I walk you out of here a free and vindicated man," Jim said as he walked through the doorway with Paul behind him. The steel door slammed behind them.

I pressed my face to the portal's pane of glass and watched them walk to the elevator, step in, and the doors closed behind them. Even the silence held an echo. With my back to the window, I broke down. My body gave way and I fell to the floor. It was March 3, 1994, nearly two years to the day I had first been bench-warranted to the Smith County Jail for a new trial.

THE VERY NEXT day I was put into a Smith County sheriff's car and returned to death row. Halfway there Bobby Garman spoke. "You know, Kerry Max, now that it's all over, I have to tell you, I never thought they'd ever be able to reconvict you again. But you gotta admit, Skeen and Dobbs put on a much better case than they did in '92."

I whispered, "Yeah," and remained silent the rest of the way to the row.

PURGATORY

I made the long walk all the way down to the north end of Ellis Unit until it met a brick wall, where we took a left and entered the cellblock of J-23. We called it "the dungeon" because of the heavy steel screens welded across the cell doors, with a hurricane fence, and a Plexiglas shield to walk prisoners to and from the shower. It was dark and dirty, and the more violent the prisoners coming into death row became, the more J-23 became a cellar to lock in that hatred and violence.

The cell door rolled open, and it rolled shut behind me. It took a few seconds, but as I scanned the dull, yellow painted dirty walls, my eyes rested on the homemade calendar I had etched into the wall sixteen years before; I had just returned to July 18, 1978, and the cell Assistant Warden Lightsey first assigned me to. This time, the tears just wouldn't come.

———

"**YOU HEARD ABOUT** the Lionel Herrera case before the United States Supreme Court, huh, K.C.?" Troy Ferris asked one morning.

"No, Troy," I said. "I haven't heard. What's going on with that case?"

He explained that the Supreme Court had ruled that it was not unconstitutional to execute an innocent person, provided that they were given a fair and impartial trial. Herrera had been put to death May 12, 1993.

Meanwhile, the political bed of coals on which I slept was heating up fast. Gubernatorial candidate George W. Bush defeated Democratic incumbent Ann Richards to become the forty-sixth governor of Texas, and he was keeping his campaign promise to speed up executions. His first order of business was signing a bill into law designed to shorten the amount of time a person was on death row. Senate Bill 11.071 combined the mandatory direct appeal with the state habeas appeal and added stricter filing deadlines. It gave an attorney representing a death-row prisoner "one bite of the apple," meaning prisoners could only file one state habeas petition for relief. What it really did was greatly diminish reviews of a death penalty claim, and it meant that death-row prisoners faced a faster, more definite destiny with the executioner.

It was with this in mind that, two days after I returned to Texas death row, a supporter from the outside sent in a copy of the *Dallas Morning News,* with the headline "Cook Again Sentenced to Death." I looked upon the smiling faces of Jack Skeen and David Dobbs, with the sun going down behind them, walking out of the Williamson County courthouse and into the evening with arms interlocked like exhausted heroes. Because of the nationwide exposure my case had generated, everyone claiming to be innocent on death rows across the country—including Texas—either wrote to me or put in for a legal visit to speak with me. I ended up referring several cases to Jim McCloskey.

The prisoners who passed my cell each day, some of the guards, and the medical personnel who passed out meds, all expressed shock and disbelief that I had been reconvicted and sent back. They had kept up with my trial through the electronic media. When the jury found the missing stocking, Region 56 News interrupted the soaps with the "breaking news." Officials who, before my two retrials, had looked upon me with the standard disdain shown one of those facing the needle now saw me in a different light.

On April 5, 1994, I turned thirty-eight years old. I spent most of my time reading and writing. I received between ten and twenty letters a day. I wrote letters throughout the night and until the sun poked through the darkness. My motto was "Nothing came to a sleeper but a dream." My mama took up a collection from family members until she finally got enough for a new word processor they had begun selling in the unit commissary. The day the commissary officer brought it to my cell was one of the happiest moments of my death-row stay.

TO AVOID THE daily strip searches, I took a job on the "paint crew." Another death-row prisoner, Randy Greer, and I would be dispatched to paint the cells on J-21—as soon as one became vacant by an execution. Sometimes, we'd be sent all the way to the other end of the building to the solitary confinement cells for the general prison population. Occasionally, a guard would put us in the pipe-chases—the space in between two cellblocks where the plumbing was located—to dust and clean. If we were placed in the "J-wings" pipe-chase, that meant we had access to everyone on both cellblocks.

Another fellow prisoner, Alvin Kelly, told me in church one morning about a person on the row named Anthony Graves, who he believed was innocent. Kelly wanted me to talk to Graves and look through his legal material. If I thought Graves was indeed innocent, Kelly wanted me to write a letter to Jim McCloskey and Centurion Ministries on his behalf. I agreed to at least go to the dayroom one evening and meet with Graves. We ended up talking for a few hours, and many more over the course of a few days. Graves told me he was innocent of the shooting and stabbing deaths of two women and four children of which he had been convicted, and that Robert Carter, a former prison guard who was also sentenced to death for the same crime, was solely responsible. I found this incredible, but it *had* happened to me; I believed it could happen to someone else. I already believed it had happened to James Beathard and Ernest Willis.

Graves asked me to try to talk to Carter the next time Greer and I were on the J-wings to see if Carter would tell me anything significant or perhaps even admit to what Graves had alleged.

After Christmas 1996, Greer and I found ourselves cleaning the pipe-chases in between the J-wings. We went inside the wing first to wet our cleaning rags. I looked on the wooden board that listed the prisoners' cell locations and spotted Robert Carter's name. He was almost in the middle of the cellblock. The only guard nearby was busy upstairs running showers. Greer and I were alone to do our work, and I made my way down to Carter's cell.

The Texas Department of Corrections had banned all tobacco products in March of 1994. I was clandestinely taking cigarettes from cell grate to cell grate, selling them for the other prisoners. As an ex–prison guard convicted of murdering a grandmother and five children, and burning their bodies in an attempt to cover up the crime, Carter had no friends on either side of the prison bars. To prisoners, he was the scum of the earth and they showed their contempt for him often. To the prison administration, he was just another inmate, no one deserving of any special protection. The wing in which Carter was housed was home to death row's most violent prisoners. Those who were resigned to execution feared nothing. The prison administration had no leverage, except to seal them in a vault called J-21 and J-23.

When Carter's head appeared in the shadowy grate of his cell grate, he immediately asked if I had any cigarettes for sale. I told him that I did. Once his lungs were full of tobacco smoke, I told him who I was and asked him about what Graves told me. I told Carter to tell me the truth because I didn't want to help a guilty man, especially one convicted of such a heinous crime involving children.

In a hushed whisper, Carter admitted that he had committed the murders, and that he had implicated Graves to throw suspicion away from himself. Carter said he would tell the truth, when and if it came down to it—after he was "strapped to the gurney" in the execution chamber. For now, however, he had his own life to think about, and he wasn't doing anything to jeopardize that. I implored Carter to tell the truth now, before it was too late, and Graves was executed. Carter, his few cigarettes in tow, disappeared from the metal grate, ending the conversation. The last time I had looked back through the shadows, for the briefest of moments, I didn't see Robert Carter's face, but that of Edward Scott "Shyster" Jackson, and I thought of the games he must have played with himself, too, to justify the lies he told that sent me to death row. One thing was certain, however; as I looked deeply into the face of Robert Carter, I knew—just as I knew my own innocence—I had witnessed the truth.

PAUL NUGENT AGREED to appeal my conviction and new death sentence. He completed his brief in July 1995 and sent me a copy. A whopping 213 pages, it detailed fifty-five points of error that had been committed by Jones and the prosecution and had resulted in my reconviction. Paul delineated the history of systemic police and prosecutorial chicanery that had spanned eighteen years and three trials and had passed through two generations of the Tyler District Attorney's Office. Though these facts—and the law—seemed to be on my side, I was afraid to hope. I knew my chances of getting this now very conservative court to reverse my conviction a second time—no matter how persuasive the facts and legal arguments to support them—were slim to none.

Having reached a dead end in my quest for legal justice, I went on a relentless search for *internal* truth. Until now I had lived on an appetite of fear: fear of the prosecutors, fear of being executed, fear of dying a violent prison death, and fear of my own courage running out. That path had landed me at the bottom of a black hole from which I only had one place to look—up. I familiarized myself with the Koran, Buddhism, and Catholicism. One day, a volunteer chaplain assigned to death row gave me a book entitled *Evidence That Demands a Verdict*, by Josh McDowell. McDowell had set out to prove the doctrine of Christianity was false. Instead, his intensive investigation led him to write a book of apologetics—evidence *for* the Christian faith. The setting down of facts culled from noted historians—most of whom were atheists—transformed me. In the end, they all seemed to arrive at the same place and agreed with the same conclusion: A man named Jesus Christ *did* in fact walk the earth and *did* perform the miracles mentioned in the Bible. He either was a magician, a lunatic, or was in fact who he said he was. My pilgrimage, like Josh McDowell's, led me to the realization that Jesus was more than a carpenter: He was the Son of God. The evidence was there. I trusted my eyes, and believed it with all my heart.

Paul and Jim visited me to boost my spirits. I was in another place with this new conviction. Each time they brought up the case and their optimism, I changed the subject.

"Kerry, you're worrying me. Are you letting go?" Jim said.

"No, Jim—far from it. I am not saying necessarily that my destiny is to die here, in this place, but if it is—and it is God's will—I embrace that," I told him and Paul. I shared a scripture that had resonated well with me from the Gospel of Mark, chapter eight, in which Jesus said to his disciples,

If anyone would come after me, he must deny himself and take up his cross and follow me. For whoever wants to save his life, will lose it, but whoever loses his life for me and the Gospel, will save it. What good is it for a man to gain the world, yet forfeit his soul?

For the first time since August 1977, I sat with a lawyer and an investigator and talked about something other than my legal ordeal. My epiphany replaced fear with a peacefulness that was ineffable. I had finally figured out that if I were ever to have a chance to get out of this horrible place, the power and strength had to come from somewhere else. I no longer had it in me.

Jim was moved, but he, too, had a story.

"Kerry, you weren't the only one devastated by this new conviction. While you went back to death row, I went to a Catholic retreat center in the suburbs of Philadelphia. I was stunned this injustice continued right before my eyes, and that the jury believed these lying witnesses and how the prosecutors continued to cheat. I had never encountered such a gross miscarriage of justice. My faith was rocked. You went back to death row and I began to question the reality of God." I knew Jim cared deeply about the innocent, but I never knew the depths of that commitment. "Do you exist? Are you real? Why did you let this happen? Why, Lord, why? After you were reconvicted, I checked myself into a retreat because of my own struggle with these questions. I knew a member of the local parish and she put me in touch with the head priest who allowed me to come in and stay there for a week. I lived in a dormitory room, I ate at their dining hall, I communicated with no one for five days and I reflected, prayed, read scripture, asked questions, and had my own conversation with God about why He allowed this to happen. Why do bad things happen to good people? The only answer I could come up with in reading the scriptures was Christ's Sermon on the Mount, in which He talks about how it rains on the just and the unjust and how the sun shines on the good and the bad," Jim said.

I decided in that moment I would not shut out Jim McCloskey. If this were to be my last walk in life, we would walk it together.

IT WAS ALL or nothing: If I was going to spend my days serving God instead of man and my case, then I had to clean out my closet first. *Doyle Wayne,* I whispered to myself, *I have to let you go now—all of the pain, heartache, sorrow, and anger—of losing you.* I sat with my back up against my cell wall with a tiny mirror laid against the bars so I could keep an eye on the guards. I went so deep within myself and calmly came out on another side: I forgave A. D. Clark III, Jack Skeen, David Dobbs, Eddie Clark, Doug Collard, and the cast of players who had conspired to falsely convict me, and to kill me. And I forgave Ben Franklin Williams for killing Doyle Wayne. Since the day of my arrest I had fought for every scrap of paper I could get my hands on that had to do with my case. I coveted these documents like they were pages from the Bible. In a way, they had been my Bible, but I took bundle after bundle to the large trash barrel at the front of the cellblock and threw them away. Paul's brief, Centurion's investigative reports, transcripts from the 1978 and 1992 retrials, and a trial journal from 1994—and dumped it all. It wasn't easy: This had been my only life for so long. At one time it represented my only hope to ever be with Doyle Wayne and my mama and daddy. Now they were all gone, and it just didn't mean that much to me anymore. Instead of representing hope, it just reminded me of my pain and frustration with a court system.

IN JANUARY 1995 I got a letter from a Christian lady named Mikaela Raine, who lived in Allen, Texas, a suburb of Dallas. She and her husband, Richard, had read the *Dallas Morning News* coverage of my trials. Mikaela was concerned for my spiritual welfare. Guilt or innocence wasn't an issue for her, but since I had been resentenced to death, whether or not I knew the Lord was. We began exchanging letters. I was terribly alone and longed for a friend I could trust and exchange normal human emotions with. And with the new death sentence and the increasing conservatism of the legal system since Ronald Reagan, I wanted to make sure I got to be with Doyle Wayne, Mama, and Daddy in the afterlife. Because I had no outside financial support, Mikaela, a home-school teacher, sent me small sums of money so I could purchase stamps, envelopes, and writing material. In time, Mikaela sent me my own Bible and she gave me Bible study courses. Instead of toiling on legal strategies, I pored over the scriptures.

Mikaela, her husband, Richard, and their four children offered me more than just brotherly love and companionship: They extended themselves to me as family. I spent my energy reading and writing to Mikaela and her children. Corey, the oldest at about ten; Chandler, eight; Chelsea, six; and Christina, four, visited me, and brought me Cherry Pepsis and jelly beans from the vending machine. They laughed as I dug through the bag searching for the black one that tasted like licorice. Before I knew it, I longed for their letters, especially from the kids, who began their notes with "Dear Uncle Kerry . . ." After being hated for so long, I wanted to be loved, and this family loved me unconditionally. This simple sense of family was tremendously empowering and filled an emptiness I had felt inside since Doyle Wayne and my father had died.

The more time I spent with the Raine children, the more I thought about having my own who would call me "Daddy." I would have given anything for that, though being called uncle by these four beautiful kids was pretty cool, too. I had come to believe I was going to die, and though I knew that having become so close to the Raines would make it harder to face that ending, for now, I just wanted to bathe in the love this family gave me.

I was still wrestling with tremendous amounts of self-loathing at the time. Over the years, no matter who I was or showed myself to be, I could not shake the reputation I had in prison because I

had been raped and "turned out." So one day, despite the humiliation I stopped putting up a struggle when abusive situations occurred. I just surrendered to it. At the same time I had begun
staying up all night because it was the only way to find quiet. I
wrote letters, and I read the Bible. I searched for spiritual truth
ravenously. And it was only after I had let go—I mean, *really let
go*—that a miracle happened.

"COOK, YOU GOT a phone call in the warden's office. Damn, who
you been sucking off?"

I was hard asleep in early November of 1996 when Officer
Thornton—we nicknamed him "Ro-Bo Kop" because of his aggressive behavior and because he was a stickler for regulations—
kicked my cell door. Indeed, it was a rare occurrence when the
warden himself ordered a prisoner to be escorted to the Segrega-
tion Office to use the phone. I splashed cold water that still smelled
like rotten eggs after all these years over my face, dragged a tooth-
brush across my teeth, and knew—just *knew*—this had to be about
the only remaining family tie I had left in the world.

As I walked down the hall I was convinced that my mama
had died—*Why else would I be going to the office to use the phone*, I
thought.

I stepped into the office, and an officer named Wooten handed
the phone to me.

"It's your lawyer," he said, smiling.

"Hello?" I croaked, still foggy from sleep.

"Good morning, Kerry. It's Paul Nugent. Have you heard?"

"Paul? How did you arrange this phone—never mind," I said.
"Heard what? Is it my mama, Paul?"

"Kerry, the Texas Court of Criminal Appeals reversed your
conviction this morning!" Paul said.

I pulled the phone from my ear and looked around. Everyone
in the office was staring at me and smiling. I pressed the receiver

back against my ear. In that moment my hopes quickly skyrocketed, but then fell back down to earth just as hard as they rose: I knew that it would mean nothing if the court had simply reversed my conviction on another punishment phase issue, or on some other technicality.

"What did they reverse it on?" I said into the phone, with my eyes closed, wanting, but dreading the answer.

"They made a rare and extraordinary finding, Kerry. Justice Stephen Mansfield—one of the most conservative law-and-order justices on the court—writing for the majority decision, said that police and prosecutorial misconduct has tainted your entire case from the outset, and that no confidence can be placed in your first two convictions as a direct result of it. Two other justices—Baird and Overstreet—joined the opinion, writing that prosecutors had engaged in 'fraud' and 'fraudulent behavior' to win convictions at any cost. One justice, talking about David Dobbs confronting you at the Smith County Jail and hiding the grand jury page of Robert Hoehn I found him reading from while the 1992 jury was deliberating, the testimony that destroyed their Cook-watching-the-movie theory, wrote that David Dobbs showed reckless disregard for the law." The judges were shocked that this behavior came from members of the bar who were sworn to uphold the law.

My head was spinning. Paul was still summarizing the court opinion for me, but I was in another world.

"Kerry, they found not only that Judge Jones committed serious error when he prohibited us from introducing what Robert Hoehn, James Taylor, and Randy and Rodney Dykes first told authorities in sworn statements and grand jury testimonies under *optional completeness,* but also that the prosecution could no longer use the testimony of Robert Lee Hoehn against you in any retrial because it was fraud and they knew it to be false and fraudulent. And of course Judge Jones committed grievous error when he excluded our expert Robert K. Ressler.

"We've won a major victory. I don't know how the media is going to report this in Tyler, but if they report it accurately, Skeen and Dobbs have got to be running now," Paul said. The decision was by a margin of 5–3, with Justice Sam Houston Clinton recusing himself because he had already made it clear nine years ago in his twenty-two-page dissent that he believed I was wrongly convicted.

"I am going to get you out, Kerry. Just hold on. I am going to get you out—at least on bond for the time being. Did you hear me?" Paul said.

Please, God, let this be real, I whispered to myself. I glided back to my cellblock.

Paul Nugent had literally snatched me from the grave. I knew that the difference between me and the others around me with strong innocence claims was that I had a warrior for an attorney, one whose drive wasn't money or fame, but a strong sense of right and wrong.

TWO DAYS LATER I received the November 6, 1996, opinion by the high court. I consumed it word for word, again and again.

"Prosecutorial and police misconduct has tainted this entire matter from the outset. Little confidence can be placed in the outcome of appellant's first two trials as a result." The court acknowledged the illicit manipulation of Robert Hoehn's trial testimony. "Clearly, any testimony or statements of Hoehn are tainted by the state's prior misconduct, which cannot now be corrected by cross-examination or other means and fundamental fairness and due process forbid their use at any retrial of appellant." I looked up and stared blankly at the dirty yellow wall of my cell. Finally, the prosecutors could no longer rely on Hoehn's incriminating testimony, which they'd twisted years ago to concoct a motive—i.e., I was so frustrated by my inability to have sex with Hoehn and was in a murderous frenzy after we watched *The Sailor Who Fell from Grace with the Sea* that I was driven to kill

Linda Jo Edwards, a woman on whom I had been peeping. The court now acknowledged all this to be in complete contradiction to Hoehn's initial sworn statements and his 1978 grand jury testimony. All the air left my lungs in one tremendous sigh.

I read on:

> The district attorney's office failed to reveal to appellant it possessed evidence appellant and complainant knew each other. Despite having this evidence, the state presented, at appellant's first trial, its theory that appellant and the complainant were total strangers and he had not been to her apartment until the evening of her murder. The state did not provide this highly exculpatory testimony to appellant until years after appellant's first trial.

There were also separate opinions by individual justices that argued for the court to bar the prosecution from prosecuting me again. Justices Charles Baird and Morris Overstreet wrote: "The state's misconduct in this case does not consist of an isolated incident or the doing of a police officer, but consists of the deliberate misconduct by members of the bar, representing the state, over a fourteen-year period—from the initial discovery proceedings in 1977, through the first trial in 1978, and continuing with the concealment of the misconduct until 1992."

I processed the words as I walked through the jungle of legalese.

> The state's theory has been, and the state continues to present evidence that the murder was the type committed by a stranger and not by someone who knew the victim. It was the state's contention that, frustrated by his sexual ambivalence and impotence, appellant saw the victim naked in her bedroom, broke into her apartment through the patio door, sexually assaulted and killed her, and, imitating a scene from a

television movie he had just (allegedly) seen, sexually mutilated the victim's body, cutting and taking part of her lip and vagina as souvenirs. With this theory, the state removed from suspicion the victim's lover, Jim Mayfield, and his daughter, Louella Mayfield, and placed appellant, presumably a stranger, whose fingerprints were on the outside of the victim's patio door, under suspicion. But Robert Hoehn testified before the grand jury that appellant had told him prior to the murder that he had met a girl fitting the victim's description at the apartment swimming pool and that she had invited appellant to her apartment where they had engaged in passionate sexual intercourse. [Actually, we had only "made out."] Hoehn testified that appellant had "passion marks" on his neck, which he claimed he received from the girl fitting the victim's description. Hoehn's statements would have explained appellant's fingerprints on the victim's patio door and were potentially very damaging to the state's theory that a stranger committed this crime.

The weight given Robert Hoehn's courtroom testimony by the juries, the court brought out, could best be captured by the fact that in a total of nine hours of deliberations, the jury repeatedly asked for Hoehn's testimony. Because of the prosecution's theory for the murder, it appeared the suppressed evidence of Hoehn was so highly exculpatory that a different verdict would have resulted from its revelation.

Last:

Therefore, I agree with the majority that having deprived appellant of any opportunity to pursue Hoehn's contradictory and exculpatory statements, the state cannot now use this testimony against him. The point is that the state's willful misconduct has denied appellant the opportunity to investigate and develop his case in the same manner as the state has

developed its evidence against appellant. The state's misconduct in this instance can reasonably be taken to put its case
in such a different light so as to undermine confidence in the
verdict, especially in view of the state's failure to present any
direct evidence of appellant's guilt.

In allowing itself to gain a conviction based on fraud, the
state ignored its own duty to seek the truth and thereby weak-
ened its own ability to obtain a verdict worthy of confidence.

That Doug Collard provided misleading information

is another example of the complacency and illicit manipulation of the evidence which permeated the entire investigation of the murder. Having suppressed evidence unfavorable
to its theory of the case, the state was free to neglect the
weaknesses in its own case and to manipulate the evidence to
support its theory of the offense.

And, as appellant correctly argues, the state's presenta-
tion of a weak case based on less than thorough investigation
increases the risk that the state's misconduct has affected the
verdict; a verdict only weakly supported by the evidence is
more likely to have been influenced by the state's wrongful
manipulation of the evidence than a verdict based on strong
direct evidence of guilt. The record along with the history of
this case support a conclusion that the state's own misconduct has rendered the prosecution incapable of obtaining a
verdict worthy of confidence.

In 1978, appellant was tried and convicted, but as we now
know, this conviction was obtained through fraud and in violation of the law. Appellant's second trial resulted in a mistrial
due to a hung jury. The conviction in this case came after
days of jury deliberation and was gained in large part through
Hoehn's testimony which was clearly a due process violation
since that testimony occurred while the state was yet sup-

pressing Hoehn's exculpatory and contradictory statements in violation of *Brady*. This misconduct amounts to the suppression of exculpatory evidence for as long as necessary to render it useless to appellant, and then bringing him to trial.

The state's misconduct has ripened with the passage of years into a situation where the state cannot demonstrate that a fair trial, free of the taint of its misconduct, will ever be possible. Under these circumstances, appellant's retrial serves no purposes but to subject him to continual mental, emotional and financial hardships. Retrial under these circumstances would violate the most fundamental and compelling notions of fundamental fairness essential to the rule of law embodied in both the Texas Constitution and the United States Constitution. Having irreparably crippled appellant's ability to defend himself, and its own ability to uncover the truth, I do not believe the state should be permitted to abuse its power by again forcing appellant to defend himself against these accusations. Such abuse of state power is precisely what our federal and state constitutional rule of law, in general, and due process and due course of law, in particular, were intended to prohibit.

The high court assumed that only Robert Hoehn's exculpatory evidence was suppressed from the jury. Regarding the prosecutorial sponsored testimonies of Robert Hoehn *and* Randy and Rodney Dykes and James Taylor, they mistakenly wrote that that error was finally cured in the third trial because all of their 1977 sworn statements and grand jury testimonies were made available to the defense and they were free to confront and establish for the first time that the state's witnesses had been testifying to a set of facts the prosecution knew was false. While Paul Nugent finally had all their exculpatory statements and testimonies, both Tunnell and Jones had vehemently prohibited my defense from confronting the witnesses with their prior sworn statements and grand jury testimony. On this matter, the court wrote, "The admission of prior testimony given at a trial during which the state suppressed exculpatory and contradictory grand jury testimony and statements made by the witnesses is offensive to notions of fundamental fairness. It undermines our system of justice with its guarantees that one accused of a crime may confront the state's witnesses with their own contradictory or exculpatory assertions and thereby clarify their statements."

Regarding David Dobbs, the court said, "as late as 1992, the state was still willing to violate the law in the prosecution of this case." And in hiding the missing page of Robert Hoehn's crucial 1977 testimony, then meeting me illegally at the jail on March 1992 to interrogate me on the fingerprint, Dobbs's misconduct "evinces at least a careless disregard to act within the rule of law." Though I was ecstatic about the court's condemnation of the put-up case against me, of course, I was also disappointed that they had *not* gotten a point so central to why I was convicted a second time. In a footnote, Judge Mansfield even wrote:

> We note the acts of misconduct on the part of the Smith County District Attorney's Office and the Tyler Police Department took place nearly twenty years ago and we do not imply any complicity in the said acts on the part of the current District Attorney or current members of the Tyler Police Department.

Smith County prosecutors had argued before the court that no remedy other than the granting of a fourth trial—if the court reached that conclusion—was required because the transgressions of the 1978 trial were remedied when my conviction was reversed the first time and when I was retried in 1992. What the prosecution failed to tell the court—and the majority of the high court failed to note—was that in all three trials I was strictly prohibited by two different judges from informing a jury of any of that misconduct.

The same justices found it odd that, on the one hand, Tunnell had found the 1977 statements and grand jury testimonies of Hoehn, Taylor, and both Dykes brothers highly exculpatory and had said the state should have turned over the materials to my 1978 defense attorneys for cross-examination purposes, but then, on the other hand, had refused to recognize this suppression as prosecutorial misconduct by A. D. Clark—or later even let us use it to show the witnesses were lying to my juries. The two justices wrote, "[it was] curious, since the trial courts (both Tunnell and Jones) should have known that most of the statements were from grand jury testimony and, therefore, were known to the State, and were subject to appellant's pre-trial discovery motions."

District Attorney Jack Skeen had stated that his administration, which began in 1983, had not engaged in any wrongdoing, that all the misconduct was under the administration of A. D. Clark III—his first cousin. The other half of the court disagreed. "Although the most egregious misconduct occurred earlier, as late as 1992, the State showed its continued willingness to violate the law in the prosecution of this case." Instead, Skeen argued publicly that he had righted the wrongs of the previous administration and pronounced that I had been given a fair trial and that justice has been served by the new conviction. Finally, the Texas Court of Criminal Appeals disagreed. And Justices Baird and Overstreet said it best:

> The State's argument is undermined by the retrial record which reveals that when given the opportunity to show that a fair retrial—free of taint from its misconduct—was possible, the State instead demonstrated its dependence on some of the tainted evidence, e.g., Hoehn's testimony.

Paul got part of what he asked for when they agreed to reverse my conviction based on the severity of the systemic misconduct by the prosecutors. However, that was as far as the court would go, as they were reluctant—no matter how well documented the misconduct—to restrict the rights of prosecutors to pursue convictions. And that is what would have occurred had they reversed on Paul's groundbreaking double jeopardy argument. What this failure did, however, was leave the door ajar for Smith County prosecutors to retry me a fourth time, even though a reading of the court's opinion made it clear that even the TCCA felt that would be highly improbable, given their findings. The only thing that really mattered to me was the fact that this horrible conviction was undone, and that maybe—finally—it was over.

I hadn't believed this kind of truth existed in Texas for me. It did, however, and here it was. This ruling was a bomb. It exonerated me; it verified and solidified everything I had screamed from the roof of the world for years. I just stared at the paper, transfixed, in stunned silence. *Was it really over? Was I really going to get to go home finally?* For the first time since August 5, 1977, I slept and dreamt of something other than monstrous police and prosecutors, and the green walls of the Texas execution chamber.

JUST LIKE I thought, Skeen and the local Tyler media, which had always been convinced of my guilt, focused on the footnote in Mansfield's opinion, and *that* was what was floated in the local media—not the incredible story of my exoneration. Skeen publicly argued that the appeals court in Austin had thrown out all of their hard work, and that the misconduct had nothing to do with them and their prosecution of the case.

Smith County immediately filed a motion petitioning for a rehearing to ask the court to reconsider its decision to reverse my conviction. The state also filed a second motion asking for an extension of time so that prosecutors could set down all of the reasons the court was wrong to reverse the conviction, and why the justices should reconsider their decision with the hope of withdrawing the reversal. The seats of three of the five judges who voted to reverse my conviction were going to be vacated come January 1, 1997. The Republican Party had urgently called on its base to vote to take control of the appeals court, and it did, by sweeping the elections. Smith County wanted to take full advantage of this and filed to put off any decision on the motion for rehearing in my case until after the new judges took office.

Paul Nugent saw this for what it really was—an attempt to get a different court to give a result that was more favorable to the Smith County District Attorney's Office. When the court granted its request for an extension of time until January to file its legal arguments, I knew the D.A.'s ploy had worked. I was sweating bullets. The days and weeks turned into Christmas, and then New Year's, and finally, the swearing-in of the new court. Richard, Mikaela, and the kids sent me scriptures to keep me focused and centered. The waiting—the indecision—was the toughest.

But then on March 19, 1997, without comment, the Texas Court of Criminal Appeals *denied* the prosecutors' request to reconsider the November ruling. The 5–3 vote to reverse my conviction stood. I screamed so loud that day guards came from the other end of the building, mistaking my screams for a riot.

ON AUGUST 6, 1997, twenty years and one day after my arrest in Port Arthur, a guard told me to pack my stuff. I was going on bench warrant to Smith County. I had replayed the court's opinion in my mind over and over again in the hot and lonely days since the reversal. When doubts would set in, I would read it again . . . and again. *It's got to be over now. With the exposure by the court's ruling they have to know it's enough and surrender,* I thought. Guards came to my cell one after the other and just peeked. My door swung open.

"Cook, let's go," one of the guards said. They didn't even handcuff me. The only time I had ever seen that done in the history of my stay on death row had been when Clarence Lee Brandley had gone free. As I exited, one, then two, three, four, and before I knew it, a long procession of Texas Department of Correctional guards—who knew what I had endured through the years—were escorting me all the way down the hallway and into the vestibule area of the visitation room.

Smith County sheriff's deputy Travis was waiting with handcuffs and leg irons in hand to take me back to the county jail. Weighted down with chains, we began our walk from the building. Some of the guards followed us all the way through the hurricane-fenced gate to Travis's car. He put me in the backseat, and one by one, we passed the gray uniforms.

"You must be one bad actor, Cook," Travis said, looking at me in his rearview mirror. "It sure took a lot of guards to come and get you just to escort you out! Man, they walked you all the way to the car."

"No, sir. I don't know what that was about, but I am no bad actor," I said back to the face in the mirror. *I'd better just keep my mouth shut.* For the entire three-hour drive to Tyler, the only talking I did was in my head.

AT THE JAIL, I was quickly sealed away in the hated side cell, # 204. A bond hearing was scheduled for November 11, 1997. All I needed was a fair chance. By any accounting, the scales of justice were dramatically tipped in my favor. But then, it had been in my favor after the hung jury in 1992, too, and that hadn't helped. For those three months I constantly had to fight those dark thoughts in the tiny steel tomb with just a metal bunk, an orange jumpsuit, and a light that never went out.

As the hearing got nearer, I could not sleep or eat. My heart continuously raced. The stress was greater than both retrials combined—hope will do that to you.

12

A NOVEMBER TO REMEMBER

The November 11, 1997, hearing before Judge Robert D. Jones was mercifully short. Over the shocked protest of the District Attorney's Office, and for the first time in my long legal odyssey, bond was set—in the amount of $100,000 cash. David Dobbs and Jack Skeen were visibly angry.

Jim McCloskey turned to me at the table, put his hand on my trembling leg, and said, "Kerry, we're going to get you out. Just sit tight and be patient. It won't happen overnight—that's a lot of money—but I *will* get you out, if it's the last thing I do. Your day has finally come."

I remembered all the times Jim had said, "One day, your day will come."

The day before the bond hearing, Aunt Joyce, my daddy's sister, visited me. "Kerry, if the judge sets you a bond, James and I will put up our home as collateral, if we have to, and James said he would put up his John Deere tractor and trailer. That's all we have, but if it will help get you out, I told Jim we would do that. We want you to come home. Enough's enough." I was stunned to be so loved and cared about that they would risk everything they owned for me.

Richard and Mikaela would have given me the shirts off their backs, but with four kids and a single income, those shirts were about all they did have.

It wasn't long after the door of my cell slammed closed that a face appeared in the windowpane of my door. It was Deputy Travis. "Kerry Max, I heard the news. It looks like you may be getting out of here soon. I knew there was something different about you when I came and got you from death row. I said to the sergeant and the lieutenant who followed us out to the car, 'He's really that dangerous—it takes *this many* guards to take him out of his cell?' 'Oh, no—that's not it at all,' the lieutenant said, 'we just wanted to watch him leave because we know he's never coming back.'"

THOUGH I WAS forty-one years old, in many ways, I still felt twenty, as if trapped in a vortex for the past twenty years. The hands of time had moved, the world with it, but I had remained under a pile of lost years. I couldn't imagine what was happening beyond the walls that had held me captive for two decades. After the bond hearing, the thought of leaving that place obsessively occupied my mind. Anytime I heard someone outside my cell I shut my eyes as tightly as I could and sent a prayer up through the metal roof of my cell to God.

Then suddenly, two days later, I heard the distinct clanking of the brass keys. My ears tracked that sound until it stopped outside my door. The gigantic key was inserted and the tumblers turned. The door swung open. The stench of the jail rushed in. Sergeant Sharon Herndon stood in the open doorway.

"You're wanted in Captain Pinkerton's office."

With that she handcuffed me and ordered me to face the back of the wall and kneel down so she could shackle my legs and feet together. I baby-stepped my way to the second-floor jail elevator for the brief descent to the first floor. I stepped cautiously into Pinkerton's office. To the left of the doorway, nestled on a red, soft leather couch sat Jim McCloskey and beside him was Paul Nugent. Behind a large oak desk was Sheriff J. B. Smith. As he got up and moved aside, Sheriff Smith mouthed a few words to a man standing nearby who then moved around the desk to take his seat. This man was wearing a light brown country and western shirt and Wrangler jeans. A smartly dressed woman promptly approached and laid in front of him a thick sheaf of legal-size papers—they looked like bond papers. It was impossible for me to believe it, but if the scene playing out before me was true, then sunlight and freedom weren't far away.

Smith nodded to Sergeant Herndon to remove all of the manacles and leg irons. He instructed her to take me around the corner to be changed out of their orange jail uniform and into street clothes—the secondhand dark chocolate brown pinstriped suit loaned to me for the bond hearing. As I exited Pinkerton's office, I could see the hordes of media through the glass that separated prisoners from their family members.

Thinking something was going to go wrong as it always had for me, I raced out of the orange jail jumpsuit. "I'm ready," I quickly announced. I stepped out into the hallway and met the eyes of Jim and Paul as they stood beaming brightly.

"Are you ready for this?" Jim said.

I smiled, and then I looked at the only true-life heroes I have ever known. "I have been ready for twenty years."

Paul Nugent gently placed his right hand on my shoulder, "Let's go home, then."

We walked up to the wire-meshed glass that was the book-in window. Officer Sherman handed me a slip of paper to sign to receive all my belongings. A small brown paper sack was handed to me, and it constituted my worldly possessions. Finally, Sherman handed me a check for $1.28, the remaining balance in my Inmate Trust Fund. I folded and placed it in my pocket.

We were led to a solid steel door on which NO PRISONERS BEYOND THIS POINT was stenciled in large, bold black letters. Behind us a hidden jail officer pushed a button. Jim pulled open the door to reveal a short hallway with yet another steel door in front of us. Beyond this last remaining electronic door was only the outside lobby of the jail—and then, freedom! The final electronic door hummed as it slid on its tracks and daylight began to appear. We pushed through the doorway.

Well-wishers reached for me but Jim pushed them back. "Let us through here. Get back. Get back. Let the man breathe."

The first person I hugged was my mama. As flashbulbs burst, I buried my head in her shoulder. "I'm home, Mama."

I was led a short distance to where a podium stood, evidently put there so I could be given the opportunity to address the local, state, and national media that had assembled. I stood and leaned into the cluster of microphones.

"When I was convicted in June 1978, I stopped to answer a question from David Barron, of the *Tyler Morning Telegraph*. I said, 'I am an innocent man. I don't care if it takes me ten years or twenty years, one day I'll prove I didn't rape and murder Linda Jo Edwards." I paused. "It took me twenty years to get back to this point."

"What's the first thing you want to eat?" someone yelled out.

"Pizza!" I exclaimed.

A female reporter with KLTV, a local Tyler channel that had always been very pro-prosecution, yelled out, "What about Linda Jo Edwards? Do you ever think about her?"

I was going to reply when Paul stepped in front of the microphones. "After so many years in jail and in prison, I am sure Kerry wants to get out of here. Thank you all for coming," he said, and we all began to move away from the podium.

As the brief interview ended and we began to walk away, from across the street, I spotted David Dobbs seething at the media blitz. All five feet of him rocked back and forth on the balls of his feet. His menacing glare told me that it was not over.

A storm was brewing just on the horizon.

I ARRIVED AT Aunt Joyce's house in Tecula, just outside Jacksonville. My mama didn't want the coming-home party at her house, but Aunt Joyce felt Jim and Paul needed to be thanked before Paul left for the long drive back to Houston and Jim for the airport, so she had it at her house. My mama was jealous Aunt Joyce was involved and said she didn't want to be part of it. We pulled into Aunt Joyce's driveway and entered her house. Pizza boxes were everywhere—local vendors evidently had seen the coverage and had sent complimentary pizzas. Some faces I recognized, others I didn't. There was no one there from my mother's side of the family. The only one of her siblings I really knew and was ever close to was Uncle Jerry. He was like a dad to Doyle Wayne and me, but he had died of a heart attack in the early 1990s.

I was greeting everyone when Jim walked over and tapped me on the shoulder. "The man who gave you the $100,000 cash bond is on the phone. Will you talk to him?" I went into a back bedroom and Jim handed me the phone.

Jay Regan was the generous philanthropist who donated the bond money. Without him, my freedom would not have been possible, and I didn't have the words to describe what I was feeling. I was overcome with emotion. "Mr. Regan, I am lost for words. What do I say to a man who just made the happiest moment of my life possible? If I could be there I would hug you." I fumbled with words. Jim took the phone.

The next phone call came from a California man named David Gellbaum who donated $365,000 to Centurion to help defend me. If Tyler prosecutors were determined to save face and retry me again, without Gellbaum's philanthropy, I couldn't possibly have come close to matching the resources of the prosecution.

Later Jim, Paul, and I got in the car and drove up to my mama's house. She had feuded with Aunt Joyce through the years and it reached a crescendo when my daddy got sick and died. I never understood it.

LATE THAT NIGHT, the full moon caught my graying hair as I sat in an old garden chair facing the farm-to-market road in front of my mama's house. As I gazed heavenward, it seemed as if the world was a mason jar and God had poked holes in the lid and was looking down back at me through them. I was lost in thought, imagining what I would be doing were I still on death row—as I had been for what seemed like my whole life. Beside me a voice I trusted spoke.

"Paul and I have to leave now, Kerry. I will call you from New Jersey when things settle down," Jim said. I turned and saw Jim and Paul standing beside me.

I stood up to hug Jim good-bye, and as I did, he said, "Try not to worry so much. We'll win this time, Kerry. You'll see." Paul smiled, acquiescing, giving me a glance that telegraphed a nervous confidence. These two men had fought valiantly for ten years to make this dream a reality. In that respect it was as much their victory as mine.

"I'd rather die than go back to death row and prison, Paul."

Paul shifted his feet, feeling the weight of that statement. "I know, Kerry. I know."

After they had driven off, I made the short walk to the cemetery next to Mama's house where Doyle Wayne and my daddy were buried at the top of a lonely-looking hill. I searched all over until, finally, I came upon a piece of paper sticking out of the ground with near-faded writing. It was Doyle Wayne's plot. Beside him was my daddy's. This wasn't how it was supposed to be; they deserved more than a faded piece of paper poking up from the cold ground.

"I made it, Doyle Wayne. I made it home," I whispered into the night air.

I talked to Doyle Wayne and my daddy without interruption. The last time I spoke to either of them, a prison guard was telling me it was time to go. It seemed like I never got out all the things I wanted to say. "And Doyle Wayne and Daddy, I'm going to get you a headstone—I don't care how long it takes or what it costs," I said as I knelt down and patted the ground.

I sat in a chair on Mama's front porch until the sun came up. Birds began to chirp and my mama's next-door neighbor's dogs barked. I was so mesmerized by the sights and sounds of my first morning as a free man that I could have been stark naked in the center of Alaska and felt no chill. The early-morning dew clung to the dull, brown November grass. Everywhere I looked, the earth was getting ready for a short Texas winter sleep. The trees had traded their bright green hues for shades of gold, browns, and magentas. Some were bleak and barren, standing with all their branches reaching into the sky as if protesting their growing nudity.

Behind me I heard my mama's screen door creak open.

"Did you sleep at all, Kerry?" she asked as she handed me a steaming cup of coffee. I smiled, and reached for the coffee. "No, Mama, I didn't," I said, shaking my head back and forth. Through the open field I had stared down the road, waiting for a car with flashing red lights coming to take me back to hell. "I don't want to waste a minute sleeping, Mama. I want to savor every second of this because what if it doesn't last—what if they come back and get me? They always find a way to win."

Behind her, a news broadcast informed East Texans that the Smith County D.A.'s Office was engaged in ongoing efforts to have my bond revoked—or at least raised beyond Centurion Ministries' reach. My release was on the radio, the television, and in the newspapers—everywhere. KLTV's evening news featured an interview with a juror from the 1978 trial, with her face blackened in to protect her identity. She stated that shortly after the jury had convicted and sentenced me to death, Sheriff J. B. Smith entered the jury deliberation room to inform them that I had just confessed to the murder, and that I had offered to lead them to where I had allegedly buried the missing stocking stuffed with body parts. The juror went on to express her astonishment at seeing Sheriff Smith outside the jail upon my release speaking so favorably about me to the media, saying how I never posed any problems and was a model prisoner during the time I was incarcerated. She said his remarks confused her. The anchorperson then showed J. B. Smith stating that this juror was mistaken. He swore that at no time did he have anything to do with the Kerry Cook trial or the Cook jury in 1978, and at no time did he ever enter the 241st District jury deliberation room and talk to jurors, as the woman said.

On its lead story, the local affiliate aired an interview with an angry Williamson County juror who in 1999 had voted to reconvict and resentence me to death. She furiously chastised the judge and the legal system for granting bail to a murderer. She went on passionately, saying how hard they worked to convict and send me back to death row, only to have a "liberal" appellant court in Austin reverse the conviction and put me back out on the streets to kill again. The juror said I was a very sick and dangerous person who would rape and kill again. She recalled that the jury was so sure of their decision that they all agreed to donate the proceeds of their jury service money to pay for flowers to send to the grave of Linda Jo Edwards.

The Smith County prosecutor's office fed this kind of thinking by planting stories that I was emotionally unstable and had a history of mental disease. The Smith County media bought this bill of goods and peddled their theme. Now everyone scurried to create stories to fit the persona I had been given long ago. David

Dobbs added to the frenzy by claiming that I was addicted to alcohol, cocaine, heroin, hallucinogenics, and amphetamines. He told the media the bogus story that I had raped Amber Norris. Even my attempts to end my life were used as more proof that I was guilty, dangerous, and violent. It was cleverly concocted and played out with the cooperation of the Tyler media. The gripping fears these stories caused filled my heart with each passing hour— all I could see was the number "204" and the return to my tiny solitary confinement cell.

Amid the circuslike atmosphere created by the local media, perhaps the most frustrating aspect of all was that I was strictly prohibited, under a gag order Judge Jones had placed on me, from addressing any of the issues being disseminated by David Dobbs and the media.

"YOU JUST CAN'T sit round here all day. You need to start looking for a job so you can get your own place. You can't live here with me," Mama declared a few days later.

Mama stormed into the living room, made her announcement, and then turned on her heels and stormed back out. I had been sitting on the sofa holding a picture of Doyle Wayne and got up and followed her.

She was fixing her hair in a large mirror as I entered the open doorway of her room. "Why do you hate me so much, Mama? What did I ever do to bring about this cancerous resentment you have when you look upon my face?"

She spoke into the mirror, never stopping the application of her makeup.

"You think you can just waltz back in after being gone twenty years? You cost your daddy and me everything. We lost our restaurants—everything—because of you. You killed Doyle Wayne and your daddy. Where were you when I had to bury them? You just need to go out and find a job so you can get your own place. I don't want you here. I'll call the police and have them pick you up if you don't find another place to live." Her words stunned me to the very marrow of my bones. I went down on my knees.

"Mama, what are you saying?"

"If you hadn't been living with that queer James Taylor, none of this would have happened. Doyle Wayne would lock himself in his room, get drunk, and play some song called 'Carrie' over and over, all night long. If it hadn't been for you, he wouldn't have been at that club to get killed. You killed him. Live with it. I've had to." Her voice was ice-cold and detached.

"I'm sorry, Mama. I would exchange places with Doyle Wayne if I could, but I can't. I will find somewhere to go," I said as I got up from the floor.

I walked upstairs, and as I wiped the tears from my face, I took a deep breath and called Mikaela Raine in Dallas. I told her what had just happened.

"Kerry, you have to get out of there! Your mother is crazy! The media, the police—that whole situation is so dangerous down there! I know you love your mother, but you have to leave. *Please* let me and Richard come get you," Mikaela said over the phone.

For more than two decades this is the home to which I had fought to return. My mama's words, the prosecution's efforts, and the media circus—it was all too much. Scared, I whispered into the mouthpiece, "Yes. I know, you're right. Please come get me." I called Paul and Jim and told them I was going to have to go to Dallas and live with the Raine family.

Three hours later Mikaela came and got me. I hugged my mama good-bye, and as I walked through her doorway—as if I had never been away for two decades—she casually replied, "You take care now, and be sure and come back and visit. We have to catch up, son."

Richard and Mikaela's children, Corey, Chandler, Chelsea, and Christina, were all up and waiting for me. I walked in to hugs, kisses, and joyous laughter. Richard enveloped me in a bear hug.

"Welcome home, Kerry."

During the holidays, Richard came home one evening with a tan-and-white Jack Russell terrier. He named him Everton. This dog was as introverted and distrustful as any dog could be. He would growl anytime we would try to pet him. He slept out on the couch in the living room each night. Late one night I quietly tiptoed into the kitchen and got out two hot dogs, broke them up into pieces, and like Hansel and Gretel, dropped the bits, leading Everton into my bedroom at the back of the house. It was a slow process and he did bite me a few times, but eventually he slept curled up against my chest.

I JUST WANTED a chance. As complicated and agonizing as death row was for me, and as much as I had dreamed of being free, life on the outside was terrifying. I lacked job skills, social skills, and, most important, life experience to navigate in the free world. I had the wisdom and discernment of a one-hundred-year-old man; it just wasn't very helpful in my new world, nor could it translate into a job. I had survived the most dangerous death row in America for a chance at freedom. This freedom was beautiful in theory, but oftentimes painful and suffocating in reality. It may be hard to understand, but the pressure of freedom and choice was stressful—ordering from a menu, choosing a movie, and deciding where to go and with whom. I had been institutionalized and taught to rely on, defer to, and depend on authority. I was lost without that authority in my everyday life.

Yes, I had made it out, but I was far from actually being free. Mentally and emotionally devastated and paralyzed by my ordeal, I was vulnerable because the charges had not been dismissed. The District Attorney's Office was never going to let go. I had a fourth trial to prepare for, and every day and every night I was haunted by the thought that they could win again and send me back to death row and certain execution.

I probably brought out of prison a Pandora's box of maladies—every symptom the psychiatric profession had observed in those dealing with post-traumatic stress disorder, I had it. That old adage "Whatever doesn't kill you makes you stronger" is false: Just because it doesn't kill you, long-term trauma is a hammer that chisels its signature into your psyche and soul. In the violent theater of prison, I had lived with fear, fear of being stabbed—or killed—around the clock. Without the structure of prison, I needed the structure and the unconditional love of a family. But I didn't have any family; my mother had let go of me long ago. There was nothing or anyone else. Naked freedom didn't seem so luxurious against the backdrop of emptiness.

Mama was right about one thing: I had to get a job immediately. Although my résumé was short, my heart was committed and my determination was long. I wanted independence, including my own apartment. Soon I got my driver's license. Richard gave me an old car and Jim sent me the money so a mechanic could repair it so I could use it to commute back and forth to work, and, just as important, to and from Tyler every week for a mandatory urinalysis.

It was always a frightening experience for me because I did not trust anyone in Tyler, and Dobbs had sought so relentlessly to have my bond denied or raised to an impossible amount that I lived in fear of a corrupted test. I watched what I ate, and I avoided any over-the-counter pharmaceuticals—no matter how bad the tension headaches, or how severe the flu or colds. When going to an eatery, I had to be extra careful to avoid the seeds on top of the buns: I was told that poppy seeds could make the test turn positive because the drug heroin was a derivative of the poppy plant.

Once, a common flu virus morphed into bronchitis and then pneumonia because I was prohibited from taking any medication, no matter how serious the illness, without permission from the sheriff's department, and Judge Jones. I was hospitalized with full-blown pneumonia, telling the doctor he could not give me anything unless he cleared it with the judge: I would be jailed if he treated me with any kind of drugs whatsoever. He did it anyway and called the judge saying I would have died if he hadn't.

WHEN IT CAME to the fight against the death penalty in Texas as a human rights violation, there was one person I heard a lot about—Dr. Rick Halperin, the former chairperson of Amnesty International and a human rights professor at Dallas Southern Methodist University. I contacted him and told him of my pressing need for a job. Dr. Halperin invited me to attend one of the Amnesty meetings held at SMU, and he said that he had a friend named Sandra Pressey who could help me find a job.

I sat at a large conference table with every chair occupied by strangers. Directly across from me, Sandra sat quietly taking notes. A Hokie from Virginia Tech, with degrees in biology and environmental economics, she wore tan stretch pants and weighed about 135. She was beautiful. Rick introduced her to me and told her I needed someone to help me find a job. Sandra was aggressive and asked me pointed questions about the extent of my educational background. Annoyed with my aversion to direct eye contact, she vigorously asked, "Can you show me the courtesy of looking me in the eyes when I speak to you?" Sandra said if I couldn't look her in the eye, how was I going to do it with any prospective employer? I was sensitive, and finally I had to tell her to ease up on the drill-sergeant act.

"Look, I can get you in the door, but you will still need to interview, and there isn't a large job market for someone who comes across as shattered and broken. As endearing as you are, you won't get the time of day in the job market."

Sandra said I needed some basic computer skills. She gave me three tutorial videotapes and asked me to study them, saying she would get back to me in a week, since that was how long it should take me to get through the three tapes. The next day I called her on her cell phone. "I have gone through the tapes," I said.

"No, Kerry, I asked you to call me when you were *done*—not when you were done watching them," Sandra said. "When I said 'done with the tutorial,' I meant when you could get on the computer without help from anyone else, access those programs, and do some of the commands that are on those tapes."

"That's why I am calling you. I did."

FOR A WHILE I worked in Addison doing telemarketing for Lucent Technologies. It was my first interaction in a group setting and my very first job since my release. I innocently looked forward to the camaraderie with my fellow telemarketers.

My second job fit me much better. The United States Constitution and how its laws were applied was the only thing I knew with confidence. That degree came not from a prestigious law school, but the university of death row. I interviewed with a Dallas criminal defense attorney named Donya Witherspoon. After the hour-long interview was over, Mrs. Witherspoon said, "You're bright, you have a good sense of humor. If the look on your face is any indication, you have a burning desire to work, and I think you will work hard and be loyal. When can you start?" I drafted motions, wrote case summaries, served subpoenas, did investigative work, and interviewed clients. I was in my element. One afternoon Sandra took me to lunch. She slid an envelope to my side of the table. In it was one thousand dollars, which she said should be enough to get my own apartment. I promised to pay her back when I could. Sandra waved me off.

"I know you will. For now, the most important thing is that you are happy and reintegrating into your new life." Sandra gave me a queen-size bed with wrought-iron bedposts. Donya Witherspoon gave me an oak table and went out and bought me red plates and other household items. Richard Raine gave me the greatest gift of all—Everton. I found an apartment complex called Beacon Hill Apartments. Donya helped me fill out the application form. I was accepted, and Everton and I spent the weekend moving into our new home.

Through Donya I met a number of people who helped me. One of them was Dallas County commissioner John Wiley Price. One evening, I was coming home from work and was nearly home when a lady ran a red light and broadsided me—the white Ford Mustang was totaled. But Commissioner Price took me to South Dallas to meet a friend of his who owned a Buick/Hyundai car dealership. The three of us went into the owner's private office, and I told him my story and that I had a job, but no work or credit history. Richard Davis sold me a 1998 white Hyundai Elantra, with eleven thousand miles, at factory cost, and somehow—I never knew how—made it possible for me to get it financed. I had never had a new car before. That night, I parked underneath the awning of my apartment and Everton and I slept in it.

IT WAS HARD to keep up with work, Everton, the mandatory trips to Tyler for urinalysis, and my everyday thoughts of what the prosecution was doing in terms of putting me back on death row. I had a pager that was just for Paul Nugent's office, and it only went off when Smith County pretrial services—Cliff Wingfield, the officer assigned to my case—was sending for me. I never knew when that pager was going to go beep, but when it did, I had to drop everything and leave the next morning for Tyler. As for Everton, who was still in that puppy stage, he was as wiry as any Jack Russell terrier could be, and he chewed up everything he could find—including my legal papers.

Meanwhile Sandra had become my most trusted friend and partner. Sandra didn't buy into my innocence solely based on my word. She had had a close relative murdered in Virginia, and she was not against capital punishment. Sandra had researched my story, asked pointed questions, and read all of the *Dallas Morning News* articles and the November 1996 opinion reversing my conviction. Her biggest hurdle was in trying to wrap her mind around the fact that I could be innocent but have served over twenty years on death row, with prosecutors still persecuting me for conviction. She did not come easily to the conclusion that the evidence supported that I had been victimized by unscrupulous police and prosecutors, but when she did, she became ferociously protective and loyal toward me.

One day, after returning from a trip up to see her family in Virginia, Sandra came by my apartment while I was at work. I had put the key underneath the mat for her, hopefully. When I returned, Sandra's sight was a welcoming one—especially for someone who had been alone for so long, was out on $100,000 cash bond, and knew that a county less than two hours down the road had given him every reason to be scared to death. After that day, Sandra moved in and we have lived together ever since as best friends.

THROUGH DONYA WITHERSPOON, I met an attorney friend of hers named Cheryl Wattley, a black woman practicing law in the Dallas area. Cheryl was a former federal prosecutor and had been nominated by President Bill Clinton for a federal judgeship. I would carry over legal documents to Cheryl's office from time to time, and once Donya took me to a barbecue at Cheryl's house. I told Cheryl my story in bits and pieces, and over time, we became friends. In October of 1998, I persuaded Jim to hire Cheryl as a member of my defense team, even though she had yet to ever defend anyone against a murder charge.

Cheryl's job was to prepare me to testify this time around. We couldn't take the chance that Jones and the prosecution would once again—for a fourth time—parade those same lying witnesses to the stand and sponsor their half-truths, all the while tying the defense's hands, preventing us from exposing this "fraud," as the high court had worded it. We knew the hard way that, as horrifying as it was to consider, Jones *again* might ignore the established rule of law known as "optional completeness," which made a witness's previous statements admissible.

The optional completeness ruling, coupled with that which strictly prohibited the defense from apprising the jury of the history of police and prosecutorial misconduct, had sent me back to death row in 1994, and the same ruling would likely do it again if I wasn't prepared to testify. My testifying, while on the one hand a Hail Mary, was, on the other, the only way to stop the judge from letting the prosecution suppress the truth before the jury. I was going to take the stand to scream out the truth. To reconvict me, they would have to bind and chain me from head to toe.

"I promise you, Kerry, I am going to put you in my Ford Expedition; you, Sandra, and I are riding home together," Cheryl said.

HOWEVER, FOR TWO decades Smith County prosecutors had shown that they would stop at nothing to win. Dobbs and Skeen pretended to be crusaders for victims' rights and vowed to put me on trial again, as if the court's historic opinion meant nothing. "We will not rest until he is back on death row and executed," Skeen promised. Such statements fueled my fears and stole my peace of mind.

"Sandra," I said one night as I stared up at the ceiling, "I don't think I will be coming back home once all this gets under way. Promise me you will take care of Everton." Christmas of 1998 had come and gone. It was a trying time—Sandra, Everton, and I lived in Cedar Hill, but we had little money, and I was living every second of my life as if it were my last.

"You're coming back home, Kerry," she said, burying her face into my shoulder crying. She always believed that.

Sleep was impossible to find—and when I did, I had vivid nightmares. A recurring dream had me stretched out on a gurney in the form of a cross, with two harpoon-sized catheters inserted into both arms, carrying deadly chemicals up my veins. I stared frantically at an enormous clock mounted on the wall. My eyes locked on a human form underneath the clock whose head was revolving with a montage of faces, including that of Governor Bush. Just as I started my pleas to stop the execution and tried to scream out the long history of what Smith County had done to put me on this gurney, another face reappeared, and I had to renew the fight all over again, with the seconds ticking down.

The closer I got to the scheduled fourth trial, the more I felt the pressure to have those *what-if* conversations with Sandra. From the moment Sandra and I came together, we walked into the storm side by side. If I was sent back to death row and put to death, I asked Sandra to promise me that she would not let the state bury me in an unmarked grave on Peckerwood Hill.

"I wouldn't let them have you, Kerry!" she would say, frustrated. And then with a burst of anger: "But that is *never* going to happen! It's all just public posturing—they can't and won't retry you." In light of the overwhelming documentation and the TCCA's ruling, Sandra believed the Smith County District Attorney's Office couldn't—even if it wanted to—try the case a fourth time. She thought that all of Dobbs and Skeen's public promises that I would be reconvicted and back on death row were just posturing. "They would never go through with it," she'd argue. "They are just trying to make you scared before they finally have to admit they have no case and have to crawl back into their hole and disappear from our life."

I was grateful to have Sandra there to reassure me. But I also *knew* that Smith County had invested way too much into this campaign and that its prosecutors could *never* afford to let it go. The public reputation of the District Attorney's Office was at stake. Further, Jack Skeen had ambitions to become the district judge in Tyler. The only way to fix his career and satisfy his ambitions was to put me back on death row as soon as possible. Once I was convicted—no matter how—my complaints from death row would be viewed as the disgruntled ramblings of a convicted rapist and murderer. When Sandra angrily vowed I would be coming home to her and Everton—and not in a box—I flashed her a smile, hiding my fear.

13

THE CHOICE

I tried to enjoy every day I had as a free man, taking nothing for granted. But I dreaded the days drawing nearer to Jones and the prosecution. Jim wrote a meticulous budget for the fourth trial equaling $365,000 and mailed it to David Gellbaum. The response, written on the back of the same envelope, consisted of a single word, "okay," and within it, the check. In addition to Paul and Cheryl, Jim hired Houston attorney Steven "Rocket" Rosen. Paul Nugent had recommended him, and Jim thought Rocket's bulldog approach would be a good match for David Dobbs.

Jim was also able to hire eight experts to refute the prosecution's allegations. Our experts would testify as follows. Retired former FBI director of the latent fingerprint division, Mr. Ivan Futrell, would emphatically state that you cannot age a fingerprint, and it is outside of the science to characterize a fingerprint as "fresh." Dr. Richard Leo, professor of criminology at the University of California, in Irvine, and an expert on false confessions, had reviewed all the testimony and statements involving Robert Wickham's "confession story" and was prepared to testify that it was ludicrous and not to be believed. Dr. Paul Michael was a crime-scene expert who flew from Colorado and visited the former crime scene and had read all of the various testimonies. He had concluded that looking into a well-lighted room from the darkened foyer, as Rudolph had done, was the *best* visual environment for identification. In other words, what Paula Rudolph had originally said was what she had seen. Dr. Gary Wells, a leading national expert on eyewitness identification, would effectively challenge Rudolph's evolving testimony that falsely implicated me. Dr. Linda Norton would return and again dispel the missing-body-parts story. Robert Ressler would testify what we already knew and what he memorialized in his affidavit—*sexual ambivalence* was not a motive for murder. Dr. Robert Sadoff, a forensic psychiatrist with thirty years' experience, would echo Ressler's testimony that this was not a "lust murder" but rather a domestic homicide committed by someone intimate with, and in a previous relationship with, Linda Jo Edwards, and who wanted to destroy the very parts of her body so she could never be with anyone else. He also was prepared to say that he had never encountered a criminal situation in which sexual ambivalence was a motivation for murder. Dr. Lloyd White, another forensic pathologist from the medical examiner's office in Corpus Christi, would also debunk the whole missing-body-parts theory. Jim spent the last three months of 1998 setting up these eight forensic expert witnesses and conducting investigations.

But while this preparation was under way, Dobbs had initiated private and confidential plea-bargain negotiations with Paul Nugent. Our team was startled by this extraordinary turn of events. It was in complete contradiction to their public posture. For the past twenty years, the prosecution had labeled me a bloodthirsty sociopathic killer, a walking time bomb who had snuck into an innocent girl's apartment, raped and mutilated her, and then stole her body parts. I was so dangerous, I must die. *Now they were secretly offering to settle the case out of court so they could avoid a fourth trial? Something's going on,* I thought to myself. And Jim agreed. Paul sensed a strategic opportunity. Dobbs had revealed a weakness by initiating plea negotiations. Paul wanted to seize the opportunity and negotiate a plea that would accomplish two goals, each of paramount importance: preserve my innocence and save my life.

Paul thought the fourth trial would be a dangerous roll of the dice. He somberly explained that the experts Jim had lined up could not guarantee victory. Judge Jones might even create an angle to prevent some of the experts from testifying. Paul was also disappointed by the jury-pool demographics in our new trial venue—rural Bastrop County, where our research had shown that next to Wal-Mart, the largest employer was a federal prison. Paul wanted a thoughtful, educated jury who would comprehend our expert testimony. He also warned not to expect another reversal if the jury convicted me again. In other words, a guilty verdict—no matter how illegally obtained—would mean almost certain death. Moreover, Paul didn't trust Skeen and Dobbs in another trial. For over twenty years, he said, the prosecutors had lied and committed fraud to win at all costs. Paul reasoned that if the police and prosecutors had engaged in misconduct for the first three trials, why would they stop for the fourth? Paul continued to have off-the-record discussions with David Dobbs, both on the phone and in person, in an attempt to avoid a new trial. Though Dobbs had originally offered time served in exchange for a guilty plea to a reduced charge of murder (which I instantly rejected), by mid-December Paul felt he could secure a historic "no-contest plea" that included absolutely no admission of guilt and "time served," which meant I would walk out of the courtroom free, never having to serve another day, hour, or second in jail.

Jim, meanwhile, continued to investigate possible leads in the case, and was lining up a host of forensic experts to testify. He said he was frustrated that Paul was not returning his phone calls and that Paul did not seem interested in Centurion's ongoing investigations or the new expert witnesses. Jim felt Paul had lost the faith and was burned out, and just wanted to resolve the case with a plea to prevent an unprecedented fourth trial and the risk of another wrongful conviction. Though he acknowledged that there were no guarantees, he thought we had a good shot to win an acquittal, but in the end, as Jim always told me, it was my life and my decision.

I was frustrated because of the plea negotiations. Each time Paul discussed with me the possibility of negotiating a plea to avoid the risk of trial, I wrestled with the promise of life versus the risk of prison and certain death. I went back and forth in my mind. I didn't want to go back to death row, but I had given this fight the best years of my life, and no matter what, I wasn't going to plead guilty to something I didn't do—even for time served and an immediate promise of freedom. They would have to execute me before that would happen.

My defense team was hopelessly splintered. I was sandwiched between the two schools of thought: Jim's optimism versus Paul's pragmatism.

My entire life hinged on choosing between the opinions of the two people I trusted the most. For me it just wasn't about freedom, it was about what I had sacrificed to get to this stage. With Doyle Wayne and my daddy gone, and my mama ill, I didn't have a lot to live for before I was released. I had half a mind to think that Judge Jones had granted my bond and let me out so I could get a taste of freedom and have something more to lose.

The impasse had to be broken because of the distraction—and jury selection was scheduled to begin in little over a month. My decision was final: I was going to trial. I informed Paul to cease any further communications with the District Attorney's Office because there would be no more plea-bargain discussions—period.

Paul disagreed with my decision to risk trial. He was confident he could keep my innocence intact by getting Dobbs to capitulate to a no-contest plea for time served. But he respected my decision to stand trial and called Jim and offered his resignation on December 15, 1998. Jim begged him to stay on the case, but informed him there would be no plea-bargain in the case: "Kerry wants to go to trial." Although I had made my final decision to go to a fourth trial, Paul and Dobbs continued to have off-the-record plea-bargain discussions throughout Christmas and the New Year. Paul also spoke with Judge Jones. He became even more adamant that I should avoid the risk of trial. Paul was confident he could save my life and preserve my innocence, but I didn't trust Dobbs because I knew he wouldn't put that in writing.

Frustrated, on January 5, 1999, I called Jim. As painful as it was, at my urging, we agreed together that the only solution was to accept Paul's resignation. Jim said he would call and inform Paul that Rocket Rosen would be replacing him. Paul was gracious and offered to help Rocket prepare for trial. He immediately delivered to his office thirty-one boxes, which represented ten years of his life's work on my behalf. Without Paul, who knew my case as well as I, I felt like a Japanese samurai who had just committed seppuku—having chosen death by his own hand rather than death by the enemy.

ROCKET AND CHERYL had very little time to familiarize themselves with my case. Rocket hadn't even had time to read the transcripts from the two previous trials. Because both attorneys were new to my case they were permitted to examine the physical evidence in the case at the Tyler Police Department. Doug Collard, Eddie Clark, David Dobbs, and many others were there clustered in the room. Rocket requested to break the resealed bag containing the blue jeans—the same blue jeans the 1992 jury had shook out and found the missing stocking—and, reaching into one of the pockets, he pulled out yet another piece of undiscovered evidence: Rocket shocked everyone in the room when he pulled out a slip of paper from the pants pocket of Linda Jo Edwards. It was a note. A telephone number of a man she had met at the tennis courts the night she was killed.

Sometime after that Dobbs called Cheryl and tried to explain away the insignificance of the note. He said that man now lived in Colorado, and that his quick investigation showed he was clean and had nothing to do with the murder. The man had met her at the tennis courts the night she was killed and it was nothing. Despite the DA's office innumerable protestations of how thorough and exhaustive their investigation had been, Rocket had found a *new* piece of overlooked evidence.

But that wasn't the end of it—not a week later, Cheryl Wattley received a stunning phone call from David Dobbs.

"Kerry?" I heard Cheryl's voice on the other end of the telephone. The desk calendar by the phone said February 5. She told me exactly what had transpired.

"Cheryl, are you sitting down?" the prosecutor had said, in a voice obviously shaken and in shock. "The Department of Public Safety Lab in Garland found semen on the panties."

"What? Slow down— What?" I was in shock, too.

Cheryl explained what had happened: On February 4, 1999, Doug Collard took the panties Linda Jo Edwards was wearing the night she was murdered to the Department of Public Safety Laboratory in Garland, Texas, to determine how they were removed— either cut off with scissors, or the knife—and to determine if they contained semen. Although the lab technicians were unable to forensically determine how the victim's underwear had been removed, they did find semen. Should further analysis be desired, the DPS Lab requested blood specimens from the victim and any suspects.

In a February 9, 1999, *Tyler Morning Telegraph* story, "Cook Eager to Prove DNA to Clear Name," F. R. "Buck" Files told reporter Jennifer Brown that James Mayfield was eager to submit his blood for DNA analysis. "Mr. Mayfield would be delighted to take a blood test without the necessity of being asked to do so," Files said. David Dobbs told the *Telegraph* that he wanted the results so he could prove *I* left that semen deposit the night Linda was murdered.

"Who knows where this is going to lead us on the road to finding out who really raped and killed Linda Jo Edwards," Cheryl told me he said to her.

I yelled at the top of my lungs. Finally, genetic fingerprints that they couldn't twist and turn into something else! Justice had finally arrived—in the way of scientific DNA evidence.

This was the biggest break my case had ever had.

The prosecution's position was—and always had been—that James Mayfield was like a father figure to Linda Edwards, and that the sexual part of their relationship was long over. Through court documents and sworn depositions, Mayfield, his attorney, and the prosecution had sponsored that theory from 1977, all the way through two retrials. If Mayfield's DNA matched that taken from Edwards's underwear, Mayfield would be placed with Edwards on the night of her murder.

Cheryl emphasized that Mayfield needed to submit a blood sample for analysis. I was eager to get the ball rolling and submit my blood for comparison. I knew the results would finally exonerate me once and for all.

THE FOLLOWING WEEK Judge Jones held a hearing on the semen found at the crime scene. Rocket told Jones that I knew the DNA would not be mine and that I would voluntarily submit a blood sample for comparison. Jones scheduled for James Mayfield and me to go to the Garland lab and submit our blood for DNA analysis on February 11. Lorna Beasley, a scientist with the DPS lab, advised that she had already started the extraction and quantification process. It would be late Wednesday or Thursday before she would be able to tell whether there was enough DNA to test. Jones scheduled a telephone conference for February 11 to further discuss DNA testing.

On February 10, Cheryl called Dobbs to discuss the procedure for me to submit the blood sample. There was still some confusion regarding which lab would be performing the DNA analysis. Under no circumstances did we want a sample of my blood floating around with the Smith County D.A.'s office. We wanted to submit the sample directly to the lab technician and had hired a forensic serologist named Bob Shaler to oversee the lab procedure. Cheryl was advised that Dobbs was in a meeting, so she immediately faxed him a letter stating that once they had decided on the lab that would be doing the testing, arrangements could be made for me to give my blood.

The following morning the conference call between Judge Jones, David Dobbs, and Cheryl Wattley was a nightmare. Cheryl was calling in from Dallas, the judge was in Austin, and Dobbs was in his office in Tyler. Cheryl had no idea that David Dobbs had media members secretly in the room with pen and paper at the ready.

Dobbs began the conference call by alleging that I had refused to submit a blood sample, just days after grandstanding that I would volunteer my blood without court order. Each time Cheryl tried to talk—or explain—it was not a "refusal" and tried to refer to her faxed letter to Dobbs, Jones shut her off. Jones chastised me for dragging my feet after I had made such a big show for the media by saying I wanted to volunteer my blood because I knew the semen wasn't mine.

That Friday morning the newspapers ran the story that I had refused to give a blood sample. Using direct quotes from the telephone conference, the story read that Jones had ordered me to submit my blood, and threatened to put me back in custody to force me to cooperate with the DNA testing—it made me look guilty, like I was afraid the DNA was going to be mine. That was the sneaky underhandedness of David Dobbs, secretly having the media present during the conference call. Worse, Judge Jones had not informed Cheryl that he had allowed the media in his private chambers to listen to the conference call.

Cheryl immediately wrote a motion requesting a hearing before Jones so she could make a record of our charge of misconduct against David Dobbs and Jones. She wrote a second motion requesting the use of an independent laboratory, GeneLex, to retest the DNA to either confirm the state's results or identify errors to be corrected. GeneLex was even open to conducting the retest at the DPS facility so that the evidence could remain in custody. Jones denied both motions. There was more than enough semen for quantification and testing, and Jones ordered the DPS Lab to continue working for a result. Meanwhile, he was not stopping the trial, which meant that the results would come sometime during the proceedings.

THAT SAME AFTERNOON, February 12, 1999, Cheryl and Rocket received a fax from Dobbs and Skeen outlining their "final plea offer." The state's offer was that I plead no contest to the murder of Linda Jo Edwards, sign an attached "stipulation of evidence," and be found guilty of a reduced charge of murder, with rape dismissed as a count of the indictment. Then they would recommend a forty-year prison sentence, with credit for time already served. Alternatively, Skeen and Dobbs would be willing to allow me to plead no contest to a reduced charge of murder under an "open plea" arrangement in which I would be found guilty of murder. This would allow Judge Jones to go lower than forty years, Dobbs said, if Jones deemed it appropriate. The offers were available until February 16, the start of jury selection.

My position had not changed. I would never plead guilty, nor would I *imply* I was guilty by a return to prison. On the evening of February 15, Cheryl and I sat by the computer at the Pecan Inn, our bodies illuminated by the white light of the screen. Together we drafted my last and final response to all their plea-bargaining attempts. I dictated most of what I wanted written:

> Mr. Cook did not murder Linda Jo Edwards. He is innocent. He has proclaimed that innocence from his prison cell for the past twenty-one years. He will not agree to any resolution of this case that requires an admission of guilt and a return to custody. Consequently, Mr. Cook rejects your offer that he plead "no contest" in exchange for a forty-year sentence.

> For purposes of the record, Mr. Nugent never stated that Mr. Cook would be willing to plead "no contest" in return for time served. Mr. Nugent consistently stated that, if Smith County were to make such an offer, he would present that offer to Mr. Cook. Because Smith County has never made such an offer, it has not been presented to Mr. Cook as an option for resolution of this case. Therefore, it cannot be speculated as to his position on such an offer.

Cheryl folded it up and sealed it in the canary-yellow envelope of her stationery. She would hand deliver it to Dobbs before jury selection began the next morning.

I walked up the creaky staircase and entered the room Sandra and I were sharing. I looked down at her as she slept, with no worries except mine. *Tomorrow it began.* It was hot so I opened the old, wooden window frame before climbing into bed. Outside the window a train whistled below as the cool wind blew over me. I will always remember how I scooted closer to Sandra and squeezed her with all the love—and the fear—that was in my heart.

I was still tossing and turning when the sun peeked in over the windowsill, signaling that the final battle was about to begin.

———

AFTER I WAS released on bond, my freedom brought me many new friends, and they all came to trial. Of course Richard and Mikaela Raine came and so did Sandra's mother, Fran, who drove all the way from New Jersey just to be there. I had never had real friends through all of the years of my struggle, other than Kenneth Brock. Now I had to chase away the thoughts of what it would be like to go back to prison and lose these friends—especially Sandra and Everton.

I entered the courtroom a little more nervous, because for the first time, I was without Paul Nugent. Just like in the other two trials, the Edwards family sat directly behind the prosecution's table. Cheryl, Rocket, Jim, and I sat down at our table. Within minutes the courtroom began to fill up, and before long it was packed with prospective jurors. This was the first time I had not been escorted by sheriff's deputies. Dobbs evidently knew the power of this from a prosecutor's standpoint, and he had asked Jones to instruct me to remain seated at all times while the jury panel was in the courtroom. He wanted the prospective jurors to assume I was a dangerous man who was still in custody.

I waited for the entire room to fill up, and then as all eyes turned toward me, I got up to go to the restroom. I walked straight down the middle of the aisle, with jurors on both sides. Dobbs and Skeen looked as white as ghosts.

Jim said to us at the table, as he scanned the countless faces of prospective jurors in the courtroom, that he, incredulously, thought he spotted a man he knew named Dee Ladyman. He was Jim's commanding officer in the navy when Jim was stationed in Japan in 1965. Jim said they nodded in acknowledgment, knowing they couldn't converse.

When I returned, Dobbs walked over to our table with a look of consternation on his face. I could tell that it wasn't the typical nervous jitters on the verge of a capital murder trial. It was something else.

"Cheryl, you never responded. What is your response to our latest offer?" Dobbs said.

She pulled the envelope out of her briefcase and handed it to him. Dobbs took it, and in front of everyone, opened and read it. He folded it up, shoved it into his coat jacket, and walked over.

"We can do the no-contest, no-admission-of-guilt plea, Cheryl," Dobbs said.

I was shocked. "What about the victim's family?" Cheryl said.

"We can take care of that," Dobbs said.

"I don't know, David, this is so sudden. We need to talk to Kerry," Cheryl said.

Just then, Jones glided into the courtroom and took his seat at the bench. Dobbs immediately spoke to Jones. Jones announced the defense had thirty minutes to consider the state's offer.

Cheryl, Sandra, Mikaela, and I climbed in Cheryl's Ford Expedition and made our way to the Pecan Inn. During the short ride, nothing could be heard except the sound of the engine and the transmission engaging. Jim and Rocket pulled in the drive right behind us and we all made our way inside. Everyone looked at me as I paced back and forth.

"What are all of you thinking? Tell me what's going on inside your heads? Jim, you first."

"Kerry, this is so abrupt! I am stunned. Something has gone terribly wrong with their case, but we're not going to have time to find out just what that something is. I'll tell you what I think, however: I think they ran a preliminary test on the semen stain and have at least got a blood type; they know you aren't the donor. I'd give anything right now to know what has caused them to fold their hand like this. They have just completely folded. It's extraordinary. Kerry, I haven't done a single day on death row. I believe we have a shot at winning. But I thought that in 1992 and again in 1994. If they pulled off another conviction, it's not me who has to go back to death row. I will stand by whatever decision you make. This one is all yours, Kerry."

"Rocket?" I said.

"I say we go for it. Go to trial. They're running scared. Something serious has happened. I say we go to trial. We can win—and they know it!" Rocket exclaimed.

"Cheryl?"

"I think we've got a good chance to win, yes, but I know that a bird in the hand is worth two in the bush. I just want to be able to put you in my truck and take you home—alive. This is no admission of guilt whatsoever. I don't think it has ever been done in the history of Texas. Your innocence will be left intact. I think you should take it," Cheryl said gently.

I thought about Paul Nugent and what he would say if he were here. And I heard his last words before leaving the case: "Kerry, in *North Carolina v. Alford,* the United States Supreme Court has recognized that because innocent citizens can and are convicted, it may be an intelligent choice for an innocent person to plead to avoid the risk of a trial."

I shook Paul from my mind.

"Sandra?"

"I don't know, Kerry. There's not enough information here for me to make a life-and-death determination in five minutes. I—"

"May I say something here?" Mikaela interrupted.

"Yes, please do," I said.

"I have information you guys might want to consider. I was milling about in the hallways with the prospective jurors. They didn't know I knew you, Kerry. They were talking as if you were guilty and they were here to correct a technicality and send you back to death row. In their minds, you are guilty," Mikaela almost whispered.

"Oh, that changes everything," Jim said. "Kerry, you can't go in there having to change a mind-set like that. It's suicide."

Rocket then said, "I've wanted to go to trial more than anyone here, I think. But I would be a lousy lawyer—and an even lousier friend—if I told you to go to trial under these circumstances. Take the deal."

"I need a moment to myself," I told the room. I walked to the bathroom and shut the door. Mikaela's words rang like the blare of a locomotive inside my head.

Once I closed the door, I took a deep breath. I flipped on the light switch. The lines in my face and gray hair stared back at me. I was forty-two years old. This fight had consumed my entire life and raped me mentally, physically, and emotionally for more than two decades. I'd lost Doyle Wayne, my daddy, and my mama. I wanted to make a family and have my own Christmases and holidays, instead of having to share someone else's family as an outsider. What I wanted more than anything in the world was a child.

I want to live! I screamed out in my head. *All that remains is the truth, and I would not be surrendering that,* I told myself. *God, tell me what to do—just give me a sign!*

I looked down and on the sink was a small bottle of Aqua Velva from the Pecan Inn. I opened it up and inhaled, taking the scent of my daddy deeply into my lungs. Pictures and memories exploded in my head. I sat the bottle back down, turned the light off, and opened the door. I stepped back into the room. All eyes stared directly at me in silence.

"I want to climb to the mountaintop and tell my story from a warm home instead of a cold, lifeless death-row cell. I will take the deal," I said.

Rocket and Cheryl laid down a sheaf of papers called a "stipulation of evidence" that the prosecution had drafted for my signature. I read it scrupulously because I knew they never did anything in an honest fashion. It didn't take long before I spotted trouble.

"Cheryl, this reads: 'I agree and stipulate that if the state called witnesses, those witnesses would testify sufficiently to prove beyond a reasonable doubt the following facts are true and correct.' And, it says here that these facts will prove I killed Linda Jo Edwards. I will not sign anything that even hints that I committed this murder. I won't sign anything that confuses that issue," I said.

"Kerry, this is standard," Cheryl said. "Your refusal to agree to this stipulation of evidence may be a deal breaker."

"Then so be it—tell them. It's a deal breaker," I said adamantly.

She sat down in front of her computer. "Okay, what do you want it to say, Kerry? 'I agree and stipulate that if the state called witnesses, those witnesses . . .' What? Tell me what you want me to write."

"Any language that infers an admission of guilt has to be deleted or I will not accept the deal. It will have to read something like, 'This is how the state's witnesses might testify, yes, but I do not stipulate, nor agree, that what they would testify to in any fourth trial would be the truth,'" I said resolutely.

"Kerry, you do understand, in all likelihood, this *is* a deal breaker for Smith County? This is a standard form, and they are not going to agree to you rewriting it to fit your plea. I just want you to know this before I type it up and give it to them. Okay?" Cheryl reiterated. Then she finished rewriting the stipulation of evidence, and we headed back to the courthouse.

Soon we all stood before the judge's bench in a half circle. The courtroom was packed once again. Then after having lied about me all the way to the United States Supreme Court in Washington, D.C., portraying me as a modern-day Jack the Ripper, the Smith County D.A.'s Office caved. Jack Skeen and David Dobbs *accepted* my revisions. The no-contest plea was historic—no lawyer could recall a Texas judge, or anywhere for that matter, ever accepting such a plea in a capital murder case and allowing a defendant to maintain his innocence and walk free.

After a twenty-one-year struggle, my case was over in less than ten minutes.

THE NEXT MORNING when it was all over, Jim stayed in Bastrop to close out the Pecan Inn and tie up other loose ends before heading back to New Jersey. He had lunch with Mr. Ladyman, his friend who had been part of the jury pool.

"Dee, what was going on—what were your impressions of the jury pool, how they viewed this case and the defendant?"

"Jim, they were fixing to hang 'im," Ladyman told McCloskey. He explained that the scuttlebutt was that I had gotten off death row on a technicality, and they were just there to iron out the wrinkles and send me back to death row. Ladyman said that after it was all over and all the attorneys had gone, Jones brought the jury pool back in to dismiss them; Jones told the prospective jurors, "The defense took one look at you guys and knew you'd never let him go."

"So, Kerry, *I know* we did the right thing," Jim said.

Moments after I went free, Jack Skeen and David Dobbs told a hungry East Texas media that the Texas Court of Criminal Appeals had gutted their case when it barred their use of Robert Lee Hoehn's testimony in a fourth trial. Without Hoehn, they said, they had no case, and that was the reason they had to let me go.

IT HAD BEEN well over a month since James Mayfield and I had been ordered to submit our blood for DNA analysis. I told reporters that prosecutors knew I was not the donor of the DNA found at the crime scene, and that the reason why this information hadn't been released was that prosecutors were waiting to put that revelation off for as long as possible. Dobbs told the media that he wanted to prove that I was the donor of the semen. When the results came back, he said, "it'll be the final chapter" showing I had committed the rape and murder.

On April 12, 1999, Jim McCloskey filed a request under the

Texas Open Records Act asking for the DNA results. Despite the judge's order, and contrary to how "delighted" James Mayfield would be to submit his blood for DNA analysis, the Department of Public Safety crime lab records showed that James Mayfield didn't submit a sample of his blood until March 18, 1999.

On April 16, 1999, the DNA results were finally released: James Mayfield had produced the semen found at the murder scene. In my mind, *that* was the final chapter in the murder of Linda Jo Edwards.

Prior to the DNA discovery in 1999, the prosecution always maintained that James Mayfield was excluded as a suspect based on his alibi that he was at home asleep with his wife, Elfriede, and daughter, Louella, and because he had no motive to kill Linda Jo Edwards. The police never even corroborated Mayfield's alibi until 1992, when they were forced to on the eve of a second trial. The basis for their "no motive" theory was that according to Mayfield, he was Linda Jo Edwards's married *ex*-lover because he had broken off their affair three weeks prior to the murder. He swore under oath that they had not had sex in three weeks, and that he saw her "as a daughter."

After the DNA results, the prosecution completely changed the "facts" in their case, apparently in hopes the public wouldn't remember what their position had been through the years. Now according to the prosecution, James Mayfield was Linda Jo Edwards's lover, so it was okay that it was his semen. The state didn't address that this new DNA finding refuted their Gomez profile, and matched Mayfield to Ressler's findings, as a domestic homicide and not a "lust murder," nor did they ever address that Mayfield had lied under oath for over two decades in order to make himself appear as emotionally removed from the situation as possible, and thereby having no motive to kill her.

Faced with James Mayfield's genetic fingerprints at the crime scene, Jack Skeen and David Dobbs went into immediate damage control, arguing that the DNA results meant nothing. Basically,

Linda Jo Edwards had been wearing those dirty panties from her and Mayfield's last sexual encounter several weeks before her murder. And if that wasn't the reason his DNA was there, then the semen in the underwear had survived a laundry washing.

The state didn't address its own time line supported by Paula Rudolph, which clearly showed that Linda showered and changed clothes that evening prior to Paula's leaving the apartment that night to go have drinks at a hotel with an old friend. Mayfield could have only deposited the semen after Paula left—and during the time I was with Robert Hoehn.

DNA experts refuted the prosecutors' spin. Even in the face of scientific evidence, they were never going to admit they had made a mistake.

LIVING LIFE

In January 2000, Jay Regan came to hear me speak with Johnnie Cochran at the Harvard Club in New York to raise awareness and money for Centurion Ministries. Afterward, he asked, "If you could have anything in the world, what would you want most?"

"A college education," I replied.

Regan promised he would pay for any college that I wanted to enroll in.

Regan's first gift had allowed me to walk free on bond, and now he offered to educate me so that I could do something with that freedom. I enrolled in Brookhaven College in Dallas and was allowed to transfer credits from the correspondence courses I had taken on death row.

My favorite class was Texas Government, in which Professor Barbara Morchower taught how the legislature operated and how bills were drafted and reached the floor of the legislature for a vote. Once Professor Morchower took the class to the Dallas courtroom of State District Judge John Creuzot. For the first time, I got to be a spectator in the courtroom and watch someone else's trial. After he completed the last arraignment, Judge Creuzot came around to where we were sitting.

After speaking with Professor Morchower, he turned to me. "How are you doing, Mr. Cook?" he said, shocking me, my professor, and the rest of the class.

"I'm well, Your Honor."

"You could teach a class on jurisprudence. Strangely enough, Kerry, believe it or not, I was thinking about you just the other day," the judge said. "I think about you and your case more than you know. Recently I received a motion to destroy some evidence in an old case. The state was short on space in the evidence room. Your case is the reason I denied the state's motion to destroy the DNA. I suggested they build a larger evidence room, if they were that short on space." My professor and all of my fellow students looked on in amazement.

I INTERVIEWED FOR a general manager position for a U-Haul storage and moving facility in Plano, Texas. I got the job. While I went to classes in the morning, Sandra managed the store. In the afternoons, I relieved her. My responsibilities were to open and close, deposit the cash at the end of the day, and do the payroll for the three employees who worked for me.

One night after stopping off at a convenience store on the way home, Sandra said, "Kerry, I have a surprise for you." She knew of my love for music and how it had always played an integral role with me. "I was at the checkout counter and they had these '80s hits. Look," she said as she pointed to track seven, "it's that song by Europe, 'Carrie,' that you've been looking for. The one your brother played and thought of you."

I had never heard this song that Doyle Wayne had been listening to obsessively in the two weeks between the time they confirmed my conviction and he was murdered. I slipped it into the stereo and forwarded to track seven as we pulled onto the highway. Line after line it rattled my soul and catapulted me into the memories of Doyle Wayne. I barely made it into our parking lot. Sandra jumped out, ran to me, and smothered me as I opened my door and spilled out onto the pavement, as Doyle Wayne talked to me from the grave through the stereo speakers of my truck.

Later, Sandra helped me into our apartment and bed. We lay there staring into the darkness, with Everton curled up against my chest. From the first day I met Sandra, every day had been about trying to survive. We shared an unbreakable bond, forged from steel because of the life-and-death struggle we experienced leading up to my final freedom. That night, Sandra and I talked about having a baby.

A few weeks later Sandra said to me, "Hello, Daddy."

IN SEPTEMBER, I was in the middle of an algebra exam when my teacher interrupted. "A friend of yours just called. She said it is an emergency—you have to get to the hospital. It's Sandra and the baby."

Sandra had been diagnosed with severe hyperemesis (excessive vomiting), brought on by a rare disorder that caused her to be allergic to the pregnancy hormones. That day Sandra had gone in for a routine checkup with Dr. Nora Jaffee, her obstetrician, and to have some blood work done, and she was admitted to Plano Presbyterian Hospital. She had gone toxic. In an attempt to save her—and our son—they were inducing labor.

My professor explained that she was sorry but she would have to fail me on the test if I left during the exam. I understood that and said I was sorry, too, but Sandra and our baby needed me more than the math did.

As I entered her hospital room, Sandra was crying. She was scared. I gently took her hand and promised her it was going to be okay. We would get through this, and at the end of the day, we were going to be parents of the most incredible baby boy. My cell phone rang and I stepped outside to answer it.

When I walked back into her room, Sandra was crying even harder than when I had left her five minutes before: Dr. Jaffee had just called the room and informed her of the results of Sandra's blood work. It was bad: The doctor wasn't waiting another moment and was on her way up to the room to start a Pitocin IV drip, to induce labor.

"It's time! It's time! We're going to be parents!" I said to Sandra, as she smiled weakly back at me. We knew from a prior sonogram we were having a boy, but we'd yet to decide on a name. We had searched the Web, bookstores, and everywhere else, and asked other people, trying to find just the right name that would capture all that he meant to me, to us. He was a miracle baby, and we both knew it. *Maybe something after my brother, my daddy?* I was thinking to myself.

Sandra's room was filled with all our friends. Dr. Jaffee ordered them all out of the room; it was time to bring our baby into our world. "Okay, Sandy, *push*," Dr. Jaffee commanded.

Sandra did, and Dr. Jaffee and the attending nurses were shocked at how fast it was happening. This was a baby who was in a rush to be free. In fact, after just two short pushes, Dr. Jaffee had to tell Sandra to slow down. In just three pushes, our baby was peeking out at the world with a head full of hair. Then Dr. Jaffee was holding him, and I cut the umbilical cord.

Please, God. Let him be okay, please let him be okay. This is the only justice to ever come for me in this world. I— That's it! "Justice!" I said aloud. "That will be his name—Kerry Justice Cook!"

The nurse cleaned him as he wriggled and cried and then she handed him to me.

"Kerry Justice, stop, it's Daddy," I cooed. As soon as I spoke his name, he immediately went quiet. The room filled with medical personnel who looked on with genuine surprise.

"I guess he likes his new name. And he knows his daddy's voice," Dr. Jaffee said.

During Sandra's pregnancy, I sang children's songs and told him nursery rhymes, placing my mouth close to Sandra's stomach. Sometimes he would kick to let me know he heard me. I walked carefully to the side of Sandra's bed. Sandra stared into the little bundle as I eased him down, gently laying him in her arms.

"Say hello to Justice, Mama," I said, with tears streaming down my face.

"Finally, a little Justice in Texas," Sandra said, smiling.

MY TRAVELS

> There is a great difference between knowing
> and understanding: you can know a lot about
> something and not really understand it.
>
> —CHARLES F. KETTERING

Bottled up within me was a wealth of empirical knowledge about how our American justice system worked in practice, not just in theory. When the court system lifted the gag order, it also lifted the lid that had kept my story sealed from public knowledge. What happened to me in a Texas courtroom, underneath an American flag, was a story I wanted to share with the world in the hope that that education could bring about reforms. I had given everything a human being could give or sacrifice, other than his or her life, to live to tell this story. Now I was finally free to tell it.

My very first speaking engagement was before the Texas government class of Professor Michael Lobel, at Brookhaven College, in March of 1999.

> I am *not* here today as proof that our legal system worked, as some would argue; my presence today is the evidence of how it failed, horribly so. Had it not been for Jim McCloskey and Centurion Ministries, David Hanners and the *Dallas Morning News,* my story would have been buried with me, as just another statistic, much like the 985 men and women that have been put to death since the United States Supreme Court's 1976 landmark *Gregg v. Georgia* decision reinstating the use of capital punishment in America.

The future belonged to the kids, and I wanted to be part of their education. One girl whose father was a former chief of police was so moved she walked up to me afterward.

"Before your story, I believed in the death penalty wholeheartedly. After hearing you speak and tell your story, I could never again believe in a legal system capable of making such a terrible mistake," she said.

"It's people like you who give people like me the courage to go back into that house of horrors and confront those evil spirits, giving me the courage to tell my story," I replied.

FROM THE RURAL South to Ivy League colleges, I traveled up and down the East Coast, even stopping at Yale University as guest of honor at the Master's Tea. I lectured on "understanding American law, and how it affects the innocent convicted." From Columbia University to Princeton and the Harvard Club, I have labored to educate the lawyers, prosecutors, judges, and politicians of tomorrow.

I have dotted the globe with my story, from New York to Paris, London to Germany, and Geneva to Rome. I was invited to a private lunch with Lord Russell-Johnston, president of the Council of Europe, in Strasbourg, France. I attended a worldwide press conference as a guest of the secretary general of the Council of Europe, Walter Schwimmer. Later that evening Bianca Jagger and I held hands as we led well over five thousand French citizens down the streets of France in silent protest against the death penalty.

One of my most fulfilling accomplishments was when I addressed the seventy-seventh Texas Legislature. Representative Harold Dutton had sponsored a bill calling for a moratorium on the death penalty because of stories like mine, and he asked me to testify so I could put a human face on capital punishment in America. I worked all night long at my computer and drafted what was to be my statement. Before a crammed committee hearing, I told Texas lawmakers that our legal system was fraught with error and that there were gaping holes through which the wrongly convicted poor were sentenced to their deaths. Lawmakers listened with genuine interest for the entire length of my testimony. Silence echoed throughout the capitol's breezeways as I closed out with these words: "For years you haven't believed in me. I am here today because I still believe in you." Representative Harold Dutton's bill ultimately failed, though it did get out of committee. But I consider it a success in that it has furthered the public debate on capital punishment in Texas.

Though my story is used as a textbook example of how wrongful conviction occurs and is recognized as perhaps the worst documented example of police and prosecutorial misconduct, I am ineligible for compensation from the State of Texas because I have not officially been pardoned. To get a pardon in Texas, you need the convicting trial court, the district attorney, and the sheriff of the county to all agree you were wrongly convicted and were innocent. That recommendation—and it has to be unanimous—goes to the Board of Pardons and Paroles, which then has to recommend it to the governor. This has never happened in a death penalty case.

———

IN THE SUMMER of 2000 a young couple named Jessica Blank and Erik Jensen showed up on the doorstep of our apartment. They had heard an innocent man speak via telephone at Columbia University from the Chicago prison system, and together, they felt it was time to do something about the issue. New York theater owner Allan Buchman loaned them some money and they took off across the country to interview those who had been wrongly convicted and put on death row.

In October of 2000, Blank and Jensen's play *The Exonerated,* featuring the words of six American stories of injustice, opened to a sold-out audience at Allan Buchman's 45 Bleecker Street Theater in Manhattan. Actor David Morris brought my story to life before a live audience, with Sarah Gilbert playing the role of Sandra. Later, a host of celebrities would lend their voices to our stories: Richard Dreyfuss, Aidan Quinn, Peter Gallagher, Robin Williams, Brian Dennehy, Gabriel Byrne, Fran Drescher, Kristin Davis, Mia Farrow, only to name a few. Eventually, *The Exonerated* opened in sold-out venues all across America and would go to London, England, and Dublin, Ireland—and it picked up just about every award a play can attract along the way. It won Court TV's Scales of Justice Award, and Court TV president and CEO Henry Schleiff wrote, "*The Exonerated* exposes the potentially devastating anguish inflicted by the death penalty and is a catalyst for the reevaluation of capital punishment laws."

For a while, Sandra, K.J., and I lived in lower Manhattan, thanks to a friend who loaned us the upper floor of her town house in the West Village. I would walk the short distance down to the Bleecker Street Theater, and at the end of the play, a cast member would introduce me to the audience. I would give a brief speech and thank theatergoers for caring enough about what happened to us to come and hear our stories. Although we didn't get any money from the box office or ticket sales of the play, Allan

Buchman and the actors informed the audiences of our lack of compensation and took up a collection each night. Sandra, K.J., and I lived off those donations. When it was time to leave Gail Furman's house, we were faced with returning to Texas. Allan Buchman used my share of the donation money to help us secure a rental house in upstate New York. It was one of the happiest times of my life.

In the fall of 2005, I was asked to go by private Learjet with a cast of Mia Farrow, Montel Williams, Aidan Quinn, Larry Block, and Jim Bracchitta, for a private performance before the American Bar Association, in Houston, Texas. Afterward, former Harris County prosecutor Rusty Hardin apologized on behalf of the State of Texas.

Finally, I was asked to perform my own role with the rest of a rotating cast. I performed along with Mia Farrow, Montel Williams, and Billy Dee Williams at Guild Hall in East Hampton, Long Island, and the critics wrote glowing reviews. My close friends Chad Lowe and Hilary Swank sat in the audience and watched me perform. I met New York Senator Hillary Clinton while in East Hampton. My story was of such interest to her she wanted to know if Erik and Jessica could bring the play to the Kennedy Center in Washington, D.C., in the hope of getting members of Congress to attend. She wanted the very people who created the laws to see firsthand the injustice of our legal court system. It is a fantastic idea, and I hope someday this will happen.

In upstate New York, we lived just up the road from friends Aidan Quinn and his wife, Elizabeth. One evening over dinner at their house, Elizabeth said she wanted her sister, Lorraine Bracco, to see the play and meet me. Unfortunately, Lorraine had a demanding schedule with *The Sopranos* and couldn't get to the New York City show, but when her daughter Margeaux said I would be playing my own role at Guild Hall, Lorraine bought a block of tickets and I finally got to meet her. Soon after, Lorraine approached Court TV president Henry Schleiff—who was a huge fan of *The Sopranos*—and persuaded him to meet with director Bob Balaban about making *The Exonerated* into a movie. On January 27, 2005, the movie version of *The Exonerated* aired on Court TV, starring Aidan Quinn as myself.

Perhaps the greatest accomplishment for *The Exonerated* was when the play went to Chicago, Illinois, and an all-star cast of Danny Glover, Richard Dreyfuss, and Brian Dennehy told our stories to Republican Governor George Ryan in late 2003. Ryan first focused the spotlight on the possibility of innocent people being executed in his state in 2000, when he declared a moratorium on all executions. He was scheduled to leave office in January and was faced with a tough decision—whether to commute some of the death sentences in Illinois to life imprisonment. At the end of the performance, Governor Ryan was visibly shaken. I was given a brief audience to talk with him, and I knew I had to make my words count.

"Governor Ryan, my story was played by actor Richard Dreyfuss. I was on death row nearly twenty-two years, and I needed every moment of that to prove I was not guilty of the crime prosecutors and police had sent me to death row to die for. Since capital punishment was resumed in 1976, 117 men and women have gone free from America's death rows. How many innocent people have we left behind? This is the only penalty in which the state gets to bury its mistakes."

Over my shoulder, Richard Dreyfuss said, "Governor, history is your only constituency."

In one of his last acts before leaving office on January 13, 2004, Governor Ryan addressed a standing-room-only crowd of media and students at Northwestern University and made history with the following words: "Our capital system is haunted by the demon of error: error in determining guilt and error in determining who among the guilty deserves to die. What effect was race having? What effect was poverty having? Because of all these reasons, today I am commuting the sentences of all 167 death-row inmates."

On January 10, 1999, staff writers Ken Armstrong and Maurice Possley of the *Chicago Tribune* published an award-winning investigative exposé on the state of the death penalty in America with particular focus on Illinois, illustrating that for eleven people executed, Illinois had freed thirteen completely innocent persons from death row. My story, even though from Texas, was featured under the category "The Verdict: Dishonor."

I went to death row as a high school dropout. My legal education was forged from a caldron of suffering, and through this, came a depth of human insight and understanding. It is something I could have never discovered without death row. I took this experience and vowed to apply it to fighting for those who were silenced by their death-row cells and their poverty. I learned many things, but what I learned most is that it's not necessarily the color of a person's skin that determines who gets the death penalty and who doesn't; it's the color of money. It's wealth that determines who gets Saks Fifth Avenue justice and who suffers Wal-Mart justice. Being associated with the play was a platform to use my story to speak for those who couldn't. It became a worldwide microphone, and I believe it has stirred the national debate on a subject so forgotten in the vicissitudes of everyday American life. After all, in the absence of light, darkness prevails.

ON JUNE 22, 2000, I sat in an NBC studio as a guest on *Live with Geraldo Rivera*, taking part in a national debate on the death penalty while Texas death-row prisoner Gary Graham lay strapped to a gurney in the death chamber at the Walls Unit. All types of arguments were used to support his execution, with the most prevalent being Judeo-Christianity—"an eye for an eye and a tooth for a tooth' (Exodus 21.24)—from a pit bull of a man who represented one of the southern states as their attorney general.

"If we are to throw Christianity into the national arena as the reason to support capital punishment, why not turn the page and read the rest of what God had to say? In Numbers 35:30 it reads: 'Anyone who kills a person is to be put to death as a murderer only on the testimony of witnesses. No one is to be put to death on the testimony of only one witness.' Gary Graham is being put to death today based on the single vacillating trial testimony of one witness," I said.

In San Antonio, Texas, Bexar County officials, though fighting tooth and nail to avoid acknowledgment of a tragedy as brought to light by Lise Olsen and the *Houston Chronicle,* may have executed an innocent man when they put Ruben Cantu to death on August 24, 1993. Texas stands to duplicate that irrevocable mistake in putting other innocent people to death with cases such as those of Anthony Graves, Delma Banks, and perhaps others unknown to all of us. You didn't know about *me* for the longest time.

Texas's death row has coughed up only a few of its innocent through the years. Randall Dale Adams had his conviction reversed in the summer of 1980, and he was fully exonerated in 1989. He was featured in a 1988 Errol Morris documentary, *The Thin Blue Line.* David Harris, on death row for another murder, admitted he shot and killed the police officer in the crime for which Randall spent four years on death row. Muneer Deeb's conviction was reversed, and a jury later acquitted him on January 16, 1996. Frederico Macias's conviction was reversed due to the egregiously ineffective assistance of his counsel. Clarence Lee Brandley's case was reversed and he was ordered set free. Ricardo Guerra's conviction was reversed due to egregious prosecutorial misconduct—Harris County prosecutors hid the exculpatory evidence evincing his innocence. He was released and immediately deported back to Mexico. John Skelton's conviction was reversed, and he was later acquitted October 9, 1990. And finally, on October 6, 2004, after Earnest Willis had spent seventeen years on death row, prosecutors admitted that he had faced death all those years because of a mistake.

I had a ringside seat to 141 executions while a member of death row. I believe James Beathard was put to death innocent, possibly Gary Graham. The fact that there is any doubt at all underscores problems in a legal system that promises proof of guilt beyond reasonable doubt. In my long journey as "Cook, execution number 600," I witnessed many things that have forever changed my perception of justice for the poor.

From 1995 until his departure in 2000, it took Governor George W. Bush and his attorney general, Alberto Gonzales, only five years to sign off on 152 executions. It's hard to see "compassionate conservatism" when you're Terry Washington, black, thirty-three, and with the established mental capacity of a seven-year-old. He was put to death on May 6, 1997, despite pleas to Governor Bush that no jury had had the benefit of his overwhelming history of mental retardation. It's even easier to kill the mentally handicapped; they can't speak very well, and they can't be heard over the tsunami of American politics.

Take the case of Walter Bell—considered the dean of death row because of his twenty-eight-year tenure—the year before the United States Supreme Court had outlawed the execution of the mentally retarded. At the punishment phase of his trial, Jefferson County prosecutors argued that because Bell was so retarded, he could not ever be free in society and therefore he had to be executed as a future danger. After Bell's conviction and death sentence—and after the Supreme Court outlawed the execution of the mentally retarded—prosecutors argued that they didn't really mean it when they argued before the jury that Bell was retarded. Incredibly, an assistant district attorney actually told a reporter for the *Austin American Statesman* that murder was a sign of normal or greater intelligence, as mentally retarded individuals are unable to kill. These issues are not endemic to just Texas, but are pandemic, wherever there is a death penalty law and a politician to exploit it. Our nation's prison system has replaced HUD to become the new urban housing projects for minorities and the poor.

Texas may have NASA and the space shuttle program, but when it comes to justice, we are still in the Stone Age. Despite the fact that a bill to protect the mentally retarded in Texas from being executed was passed in the Texas Legislature—an incredible feat in itself—Republican Governor Rick Perry vetoed it and prevented it from becoming law in 2001, claiming that Texas wasn't executing the mentally retarded so there was no need for such protection.

On December 6, 2005, North Carolina put to death Kenneth Boyd, making him the one thousandth person executed in America since the U.S. Supreme Court allowed executions to resume in the 1976 *Gregg v. Georgia* decision. Since that time 122 people have been freed from America's death rows. These are not stories in which the heroes are members within the judicial system, discovering the mistakes and then correcting them. Our saviors are Centurion Ministries, Barry Scheck's Innocence Project, and sometimes just a gumshoe reporter like former *Dallas Morning News* reporter David Hanners.

In 2001, Springfield, Massachusetts, federal judge Michael Ponsor wrote in the *Boston Globe,* that after presiding over the first death penalty case in Massachusetts in several decades:

> The experience left me with one unavoidable conclusion: that a legal regime relying on the death penalty will inevitably execute innocent people—not too often, one hopes, but undoubtedly sometimes. Mistakes will be made because it is simply not possible to do something this difficult perfectly, all the time. Any honest proponent of capital punishment must face this fact.

It took me twenty-one years to prove that the basis of my arrest, trials, and persecution were the result of gross prosecutorial malfeasance. I needed every second of those twenty-one years to prove I was railroaded and innocent. I advocate life without parole as an alternative to the death penalty because, as William Shakespeare once wrote, "Time is the justice that examines all offenders."

———

I BOUGHT BOTTLES of Aqua Velva and Jōvan Musk cologne. I keep them in my bathroom in upstate New York, where I wrote this book. In those two bottles are the memories of my daddy and Doyle Wayne. Sometimes, before even the morning wakes up, I uncap one or the other—or both—just to have my daddy and brother with me again.

I finished my book under a blue October sky in the meadow down from our house in upstate New York, while Kerry Justice sang, danced, and chased imaginary villains. My best friend, Sandra, was collecting multicolored autumn leaves from the trees while Kerry Justice swung a stick for Everton to chase.

Me? I'm still chasing justice, just Justice of another kind—my five-year-old son.

And Jim McCloskey was right: In the end, the whole world does know I was innocent.

I wrote this book in between chicken tenders, oven pizzas, multiple repeats of *Shrek*, running from room to room, in a lighted closet, a bathroom, at Chuck E. Cheeses, in the garage, on a plane, a train, and in an automobile, as my wonderful five-and-a-half-year-old son popped in and out, with a smile that swallows up my past—"Are we there? Are we there yet, Dad?"

"Yes, K.J., we're there. We're finally there."

My name is Kerry Max Cook. This is my story. I wrote every word of it.

EPILOGUE

My life has been a long and winding road with many characters decorating the hills and valleys along the way. My story would only be partially complete if I did not include what happened to all those who formed the montage of my life.

THE LATE FORMER 241st state district judge Glenn S. Phillips died in Tyler after serving on the bench for twenty-three years.

Governor Mark White appointed Joe Tunnell to the 241st judgeship in 1985. He retired on June 2, 1993, at age seventy-five. During his retirement ceremony, speaker F. R. "Buck" Files Jr. said, "He had a bond with us who came to the courthouse to see that justice was done." Judge Joe Tunnell died on June 9, 1998.

District Judge Robert D. Jones is still hearing cases and traveling around the 254 counties of Texas.

Former appointed Smith County district attorney Amrie (A. D.) Clark III is employed by the Texas Attorney General's Office as a staff attorney.

Former 1978 assistant district attorney Tom Dunn became the Honorable Judge Thomas A. Dunn in 1996, presiding over Smith County Court at Law Number One.

The Criminal Justice Section of the State Bar of Texas honored Jack Skeen in September 1997, naming him "Prosecutor of the Year." On October 28, 2003, Governor Rick Perry appointed Skeen to the position of state district judge over the 241st Judicial District Court of Smith County. Skeen served four terms as district attorney, making him one of the longest-serving district attorneys in Smith County history.

David Dobbs divorced his wife, and on August 8, 1998, married former assistant district attorney Deborah Tittle. Dobbs retired from the Smith County District Attorney's Office on July 31, 2002. He and Tittle are in private practice together in Tyler.

On June 11, 2000, investigative reporter Evan Moore, and the *Houston Chronicle*, published an article entitled " 'Win at All Cost' Is Smith County's Rule, Critics Claim," which brought about serious public scrutiny and accountability for the subversive unethical conduct used to persecute and convict; my story was one of the examples cited. The story was so convincing, the evidence so strong, Jack Skeen, David Dobbs, and current Smith County district attorney Alicia Cashell filed a civil defamation suit, claiming the story was damaging, false, and malicious.

On March 11, 2005, by a vote of 9–0, the Texas Supreme Court dismissed Skeen, Dobbs, and Cashell's suit on the grounds that Moore's reporting contained no malice. Further, though they did not rule on the truth or falsity of the article's claims, the court made a point of acknowledging that "Moore had many sources corroborating the criticisms of the Smith County D.A.'s office."

Captain Douglas Collard retired after thirty-one years with the Tyler Police Department in March of 1999. According to Collard in his farewell comments to the Tyler media, "I'm not disappointed, but the only thing I regret is that he (Kerry Max Cook) didn't plead guilty and actually say he did it."

Detective Eddie Clark is still Sergeant Eddie Clark, though he is no longer a detective, but a patrolman. He heads the Crime Stoppers Program in Smith County and is back on the streets of Tyler.

F. R. "Buck" Files continues to represent criminal defendants while maintaining a cozy relationship with the Smith County prosecutors' office.

Edward Scott "Shyster" Jackson remains in the Missouri State Penitentiary serving life without parole for murder.

David Franklin Hunter, prisoner number 368174, and Susan divorced. David Hunter is listed as "Departed and unavailable" in the Texas Department of Corrections registry, having been sent out of state to another prison system for his own protection because of his planned false testimony in my case.

Sheriff J. B. Smith recently won reelection. He's been the unbeatable sheriff of Smith County for nearly thirty years.

Danny Stallings, the former Cherokee County sheriff who accompanied Eddie Clark the night I was arrested even though he was the sheriff of a different county, wrote a letter to the *Jacksonville Daily Progress* after I went free. I thought parts of it were worth sharing here:

It is no mystery that innocent people plea-bargain and accept conviction. The power of Government is a reality that criminal defendants and their attorneys accept every day. The Government has at its disposal police investigative power, prosecutors, and often a jury, which is predisposed towards the prosecution. In short the deck is stacked in favor of the prosecution. In the Cook trials and reversals, we have been shown that information was withheld, questionable testimony was used, circumstantial evidence was in question, and the prosecutorial integrity compromised. If we allow lies and insufficient evidence to convict the guilty, will we not allow the same to convict the innocent?

In a letter dated April 11, 1994, the American Psychiatric Association expelled Dr. James Grigson from its ranks due to his consistent practice of testifying to a defendant's future dangerousness without actually examining the defendant. He died in June of 2004.

On April 10, 1988, the *Dallas Morning News* published a front-page article entitled "Views on Inmate Disputed," exposing Jerry Landrum's 1978 perjury before the jury. Landrum, using his Tyler attorney, Duane Stephens, sued the newspaper for libel. In 1992, all of Landrum's claims were thrown out of court. Landrum died in a Tyler hospital in November 1999 of an undisclosed illness.

James Mayfield was never charged with the rape and murder of Linda Jo Edwards. In an NBC Special Report called "Deadly Justice," Geraldo Rivera sat outside Mayfield's Houston home all night seeking a comment on the discovery of his semen at the murder scene. None came.

THE MAN WHO murdered my brother, Ben Franklin Williams, pled guilty to the reduced charge of voluntary manslaughter, with a deadly weapon and was given a sixteen-year prison term. He served four and was released on parole October 6, 1992.

Richard Raine added three more children to his family, giving them seven. Richard was diagnosed with leukemia, and after winning numerous battles, Richard Stacey Raine lost the war and died on September 13, 2005, in a Dallas hospital. Other than Sandra, Richard was my closest friend, and the closest relationship to another brother God could have given me.

On August 26, 2005, K.J., Sandra, and I were temporarily staying with my mama at her home in the country in Tecula, Texas. She had been diagnosed with leukemia, a lung disease, and heart disease, and I was using the upstairs loft, working on my book, while cooking and caring for her. One morning I woke up to Sandra's screams and a wall of thick smoke. Everton and I were trapped upstairs. I fumbled my way in my underwear to a nearby window, kicked it open, and climbed out onto the roof. Through the smoke and flames, I could see the faces of Sandra and K.J., screaming up at me from down below to jump. I was knocked unconscious upon hitting the ground. Sandra and a longtime next-door neighbor named Letha Raye helped my mama out of the burning house and onto the lawn to await help. My mama was care-flighted to the Burn Unit at Parkland Hospital in Dallas, with burns on 11 percent of her body. After a two-month fierce struggle to live, on October 4, 2005, my mama died. Everton died in the fire.

I fulfilled the promises I made to Doyle Wayne and my daddy the morning after I got out. In February of 2004, I purchased the headstones for my brother and father, and my mama was buried next to them.

Night after night, before going to bed, by the soft yellow nightlight, Mama and I talked before I retired upstairs to bed, and she told me how much she loved me, how grateful she was that I came home to take care of her. I can still hear her laughter as we watched the motion picture *The Wedding Crashers*. My mama howled so hard and so loud, I thought they were going to ask us to leave the theater.

AS OF THIS writing, Anthony Graves is still incarcerated on Texas death row. Concluding that former Burleson County district attorney Charles Sebesta intentionally withheld evidence from Graves's defense team at his trial—including Robert Carter's statement that he committed the crimes by himself—a three-judge panel of the Fifth Circuit Court of Appeals reversed Graves's conviction and directed the state to retry or release him. The state has until June 5 to submit its appeal. U.S. District Judge Samuel Kent of Galveston ruled that the state must retry Graves by September 12, 2006. I believe he will finally be exonerated and set free by a jury, if he is retried.

Jerry Joe Byrd suffered a massive heart attack on the eve of his execution. Medical officials saved him long enough so that he could still be alive to execute.

Randy Greer and Raymond Riles are still on death row.

The *Houston Chronicle* once characterized James Demouchette, who carved "Good Pussy" into me, as the most feared and dangerous man on death row. While behind bars, he raped, stabbed, burned, and murdered. "Doom," as we called him, was so mean he stabbed one of the most fearless guards to ever work the Ellis Unit death row—Major "Big Jelly" Steele. James "Doom" Demouchette was put to death on September 22, 1992.

All others I was on death row with mentioned in this book were put to death by the State of Texas during the 141 executions I lived to witness.

SCOTT HOWE IS a constitutional law professor at Chapman University Law School in Anaheim, California, where he lives with his wife, Jetty, his teenage daughter, Jordan, and his older son, Mario.

David Hanners works for the *Saint Paul Pioneer Press* in Minnesota. In addition to his writing, he is raising his son, Ian, now sixteen, and he has a folk band. They've released two CDs.

Steven "Rocket" Rosen is still battling state and federal prosecutors. He and his wife, Robin, live in Sugarland, Texas, with their four daughters.

Chris Flood established his own law firm. Chris, his wife, Rene, and their four children live in Houston. Chris continues to be frequently chastised by state and federal judges for his zealous representation of his clients.

John Ament is still practicing law in Jacksonville, Texas, and Larue Dixon is still a judge in the neighboring county of Cherokee.

Paul Nugent continues to fight for justice in state and federal courts throughout Texas and the United States. Paul has now earned more than one hundred not-guilty verdicts. I am forever grateful that Paul worked tirelessly on my behalf for nearly a decade, not for money, but because he was offended by how justice had failed me. Paul and I are close friends and I enjoy my visits to Houston when I stay in the Nugent home with Paul, his wife, Mary, and their six wonderful children, Francis, Patrick, Nick, Jack, Anna, and Dorothy.

Cheryl Wattley lives and still practices law in Dallas, Texas. She is reunited with Centurion Ministries and is currently working again with Jim McCloskey to free another wrongly convicted prisoner out of Dallas County named Ben Spencer.

Jim McCloskey went on to free fourteen more innocent lives, including A. B. Butler out of Smith County, Tyler, Texas, for a rape he did not commit. This brings the grand total to thirty-seven lives saved. He still lives in Princeton, New Jersey, and is still single. "No woman will have me," he says. He and his right arm, should-have-been-his-wife Kate Germond, continue to plead for money from the private sector so that they can afford the cost of investigating and then returning the innocent back into the society from which they were stolen.

THE PROSECUTION'S PARTING SHOT

Shortly after Court TV aired *The Exonerated* in January 2005 and in an apparent effort to give David Dobbs and the former prosecution and police equal airtime, an episode of *Body of Evidence: From the Case Files of Dayle Hinnman* aired on the network. My case was the topic. Crime-show host and psychological "profiler" Dayle Hinnman presented false and misleading evidence—obviously supplied by Smith County sources—that, in most instances, had been thrown out by the highest court in Texas as fraudulent or outright false. Based on this "evidence," Ms. Hinnman profiled me guilty for the rape and murder of Linda Jo Edwards. Watching this painful national television program while my five-and-a-half-year-old son slept in the next room made me feel like I was back on death row, battling all of those lies that nearly got me executed. The simple fact is, as perhaps you yourself now know, the truth in this case was never as important as the careers of those who were in a position to suppress it.

ACKNOWLEDGMENTS

To my editors at William Morrow, executive editor Henry Ferris and assistant editor Peter Hubbard, and to publicist Samantha Hagerbaumer: Thank you all for your incredible support throughout this lonely and arduous journey. A special acknowledgment to Peter, who worked closely with me over many drafts and was there for me throughout the entire voyage of this memoir.

Author and Rice University creative writing instructor, Marsha Recknagle, who I first met at Saint Pete's Dancing Marlin in Houston, Texas. You gave me the confidence that I could write a book, hugged me, and waved me good-bye sometime later as I headed to New York in search of a dream.

Moses & Singer entertainment attorney Liz Corradino, who helped me once I got there even though I had no money.

Paul Nugent and paralegals Elena Padilla and Blanca Lujan— the nuts and bolts of Foreman DeGeurin and Nugent. John S.

Ament, Judge Larue Dixon, Scott W. Howe, Cheryl B. Wattley, Stephen "Rocket" Rosen, and Chris Flood.

James "Jim" C. McCloskey, office manager Lisa Kurtz, and all the volunteers who make up Centurion Ministries, past and present. An asterisk to Kate Germond, who's been such an incredible friend and confidante to me.

David Hanners and the *Dallas Morning News*. Without your original probe into the facts and circumstances that led to my arrest and subsequent conviction, I would have been reduced to the obituary section of an East Texas newspaper. Gail Ablow, ABC's Dan Harris, Chris Bury and Ted Koppel; Geraldo Rivera; legendary former anchorman Peter Jennings, and *Frontline* producer Ofra Bikel. You brought me into America's living room and turned on the light in a Texas courtroom that had operated in darkness. Samantha Swindler, former editor of the *Jacksonville Daily Progress*, for finally allowing the truth of my story to be told in my hometown newspaper, when no one else in East Texas would, so my father, brother, and now my mother could be buried in peace.

Dr. Rick Halperin, elected chairperson for Amnesty International, USA, and also human rights professor at Southern Methodist University. Former executive director Jim Marcus and current director, Andrea Keilen, of the Texas Defenders Service. Special appreciation and respect to TDS staff attorney and friend, Melissa Hamilton. Dave Atwood, former president of the Texas Coalition to Abolish the Death Penalty, and the countless volunteers, grassroots organizations, and other overworked and unseen advocates for reform scattered throughout the continent, who tirelessly lobby for justice for the poor in the knowledge that the poor can only afford their grief. You know who you are.

Barry Scheck, Peter Neufeld, and The Innocence Project; Bryan Stevenson, Equal Justice Initiative, Montgomery, Alabama; and Stephen Bright, founder, Southern Center for Human Rights,

Atlanta, Georgia. Thank you for your unheralded efforts on behalf of the convicted poor.

Donya Witherspoon, who gave me my first job out of death row, and to Lora Lee McMillan, whose recommendation to Chuck Farch gave me my second and only job thus far in America. Dallas County City Commissioner John Wiley Price and Richard Davis, who helped me get my first car.

Actor and friend Cary Elwes, who after the August 26, 2005, house fire that ultimately ended my mother's life and destroyed most of my belongings—including 400 pages of my book—gave me the money to purchase another laptop so that I could rewrite the lost pages, and feed and clothe my son. I also want to thank those generous people who sent clothes, money, and prayers.

Chad Lowe, Aidan Quinn, Robin Williams, Gabriel Byrne, Richard Dreyfuss, David Morse, Easi Morales, Andrew McCarthy, Tim Robbins, Cary Elwes, Eric Roberts, Fisher Stevens—to name just a few of the cast who have portrayed my story in *The Exonerated*—thank you for bringing my story to life before live audiences around the globe. Special affection for Mia Farrow, Lorraine Bracco and Hilary Swank for their friendship. Hugs and respect to the incredibly talented and caring nightly cast of not-ready-for-prime-time actors and actresses who became my friends while I performed with them and during the long run of *The Exonerated:* Bruce Kronenberg, David Brown, Jr., Amelia Campbell, April Yvette Thompson, Phillip Levy, Larry Block, Curtis McClarin, Charles Brown, William "Bill" Marshall, Jim Brachitta, Ed Blunt, and Katherine Leask. And Montel Williams, who showed me such enormous care and concern when I stepped into the lights at Guild Hall in Long Island, New York, for my first performance.

Manhattan dentist Dr. Anthony Classi, who fixed my teeth for free. Child psychologist Dr. Gail Furman for giving me a roof over my head so I could walk back and forth and address audiences each and every night after *The Exonerated*. Julie Ratner, who gave me guidance and direction. And my demented, crazy, zany friend, Roger Ratner, who lives in Geneva, Switzerland, and would call just to make sure I was all right, returning me to a state of laughter as I privately wiped tears from my face on the other end of the phone, having just written painful portions of my story. Dr. Ryche Marshall and Dr. Phyllis Cohen, two therapists who gave me the benefit of their time free, unraveling the yards and yards of gauze and bandage that had mummified me.

Former Court TV president and CEO Henry Schleiff, who courageously had the vision and concern to adapt *The Exonerated* into an original movie for television on the Court TV network. Later, the theater owners, directors, and students, who fought to have the play brought to their schools and theaters so people could see the real face of justice for the poor behind the media headlines.

Carol and Nina Fineman, publicists for *The Exonerated*, Nina Pratt, Culture Project Theater owner Allan Buchman, and director Bob Balaban. Thank you all for making *The Exonerated* the success it has been. And of course, playwrights/actors Erik Jensen and Jessica Blank for caring about injustice so much that they they wrote the play so they could weigh in and do something about it.

World karate champion, Jonathan Winstrel, the best father to his two children and best friend anyone could ever ask for. I love you like a brother.

Philanthropist George Soros and the bright minds that comprise the Open Society Institute, who shine a flashlight down the darkened alleyways of an often forgotten society of inhabitants.

Sandra Pressey, who helped me wade through more than half a million pages of legal transcripts and other related minutiae during the researching and writing of this book. Like the struggle to overcome death row, so the reliving of the story in slow motion did not occur without exorbitant costs, most significant, the loss of our marriage. Thank you for being my best friend. Without Sandra, I could not have completed this book.

For Earnest Michael Cook, who had to grow up without a father. Michael and Barbara raised two beautiful children. Rickey, eighteen, who is serving his country in the military, and Megan Cook, twenty-one. Carrying the legacy of our DNA, we have the knowledge within us that life isn't always fair, but it's incumbent upon us—and only us—to persevere against the vicissitudes of life, to triumph, and to secure our contentment. I love you all, not as the last vestiges of family, but because, like me, you four have walked through the raging fires of life, persevered, and stand as living memorials of this.

God for parting the political Red Sea in Texas and holding back those hell-bent on killing me so I could safely reach shore. All I ever needed to be acquitted of all charges was a fair and impartial trial. The more factually innocent I became, the less even money could have attained that.

And former prison guard Lorie Hopper, who built my website and kept it running against her own financial woes as a single parent raising two children, all so that people could find me.

My father's sister, Joyce McElyea, who after death row had taken everything else—including my sanity—withstood the tsunami of an East Texas media and community that had embraced a lie. You loved and stood by me unconditionally.

Kerry Justice Cook, my six-year-old son, for without him, there wasn't enough left inside to tell the story.

To my parents who gave me the DNA to overcome it all.

Finally, to all the men and women who suffer, helplessly and hopelessly, lost somewhere in an American prison. In the end, it was you who inspired me the most and drove me relentlessly to tell this story, in the hope that you could be found. I will never abandon the fight on your behalf.

Way go ken san.